"*When the Pine Needles Fall* is a remarkable and revelatory account of the 1990 siege of Kanehsatà:ke and Kahnawà:ke, when provincial, municipal, and national armed forces targeted these Mohawk communities. It is also one of the best first-hand accounts of Indigenous activism that I have ever read, relayed in moving and extraordinary form. An essential addition to contemporary First Nations history and the growing field of Indigenous Studies."

NED BLACKHAWK, Western Shoshone, author of
The Rediscovery of America: Native Peoples
and the Unmaking of U.S. History

"As a treatise on women and culture-based governance from a remarkable Haudenosaunee leader, *When the Pine Needles Fall* offers me hope and renewed energy. Through her life work, Ellen Gabriel demonstrates how to persevere, remain optimistic, and continue with creative and activist endeavours. The book effectively situates the 'crisis' within its centuries-long context, marking a tipping point for Canada while highlighting ongoing challenges. It also examines how mainstream narratives are constructed around Indigenous struggles, providing a comprehensive profile of Gabriel's diverse contributions to Indigenous resistance and resurgence."

KIM ANDERSON, author of *Life Stages and Native Women: Memory, Teachings, and Story Medicine*

"Katsi'tsakwas Ellen Gabriel's personal account of the 1990 siege of Kanehsatà:ke and Kahnawà:ke is a crucial contribution to our understanding of these dramatic events and of the political context of the time. Her lifetime dedication to the defence of Indigenous peoples and women's rights is truly exemplary and constitutes an inspiration for generations to come."

BERNARD DUHAIME, professor, Faculty of Political Science and Law, Université du Québec à Montréal

"In *When the Pine Needles Fall*, celebrated activist Katsi'tsakwas Ellen Gabriel gifts us with an expansive account of the 1990 siege of Kanehsatà:ke and Kahnawà:ke. This alone provides a captivating analysis of this seminal moment and its legacy within larger movements for Indigenous sovereignty on Turtle Island. But Gabriel, an artist, also paints the negative space, braiding her relationship to the land, Kanien'kehá:ka teachings, and the language with her tireless work against settler colonialism, extractive capitalism, and patriarchy. This essential book is an inspiring conversation reminding us that decolonization is world-building rooted in an ethics of relationality and care."

NAZILA BETTACHE, MD, MPH; assistant professor
of medicine, Université de Montréal; social justice
organizer and co-editor of *Reflections on Illness*

"I honour my sister whose words speak the truth. One of the most powerful quotes by Katsi'tsakwas is: 'I'm a Kanien'kehá:ka woman who cares deeply about our land and I want a better future for the generations to come.' Everything she speaks about in this book is directly connected to these words."

BEVERLEY JACOBS, CM, LLB, LLM, PhD; Kanien'kehá:ka,
Bear Clan, Six Nations Grand River Territory; associate
professor, Faculty of Law, University of Windsor

KATSI'TSAKWAS ELLEN GABRIEL

with Sean Carleton

WHEN THE PINE NEEDLES FALL

Indigenous Acts of Resistance

Between the Lines
Tkaronto (Toronto)

This book is dedicated to my late brother,
Archie Billy Gabriel, whose kindness, warmth, and
talent has left us with the gift of song that will live
on in my heart forever.

KATSI'TSAKWAS ELLEN GABRIEL

When the Pine Needles Fall: Indigenous Acts of Resistance
© 2024 Katsi'tsakwas Ellen Gabriel

First published in 2024 by
Between the Lines
401 Richmond Street West, Studio 281
Toronto, Ontario · M5V 3A8 · Canada
1-800-718-7201 · www.btlbooks.com

Pages 183–185 from Lee Maracle, *Bobbi Lee: Indian Rebel* (Toronto, Women's Press, 2017) reprinted by permission of Canadian Scholars/Women's Press.

Library and Archives Canada Cataloguing in Publication
Title: When the pine needles fall : Indigenous acts of resistance / Katsi'tsakwas
    Ellen Gabriel ; with Sean Carleton.
Names: Gabriel, Katsi'tsakwas Ellen, author. | Carleton, Sean, author.
Description: Includes index.
Identifiers: Canadiana (print) 20240380959 | Canadiana (ebook) 20240381505 |
    ISBN 9781771136501 (softcover) | ISBN 9781771136518 (EPUB)
Subjects: LCSH: Gabriel, Katsi'tsakwas Ellen. | LCSH: Indigenous peoples—
    Canada—Politics and government. | LCSH: Indigenous peoples—Canada—
    Government relations. | LCSH: Government, Resistance to—Canada—
    History. | LCSH: Indigenous peoples—Canada—Social conditions. |
    CSH: First Nations women activists—Biography. | CSH: First Nations
    activists—Biography. | CSH: Kanyen'kehà:ka women—Biography. | CSH:
    Kanyen'kehà:ka—Biography. | LCGFT: Autobiographies.
Classification: LCC E99.M8 G33 2024 | DDC 971.004/9755420092—dc23

Cover and text design by DEEVE
Printed in Canada

We acknowledge for their financial support of our publishing activities: the Government of Canada; the Canada Council for the Arts; and the Government of Ontario through the Ontario Arts Council, the Ontario Book Publishers Tax Credit program, and Ontario Creates.

CONTENTS

FOREWORD

If ever there was a book that needed to be written, it is this one. There have been many news articles, op-eds, and books about the so-called Oka Crisis, or Canada's violent siege of Kanehsatà:ke and Kahnawà:ke (Mohawk communities and territories) in the summer of 1990; but this is the first book from the perspective of the Kanien'kehá:ka (Mohawk) spokesperson, Katsi'tsakwas Ellen Gabriel.

Despite the trauma inflicted on Onkwehón:we (Indigenous) people by the Canadian Armed Forces, the Royal Canadian Mounted Police, and the *Sûreté du Québec* (SQ), before, during, and after the siege in 1990, Ellen never waivered. She stood her ground, using Kaianera'kó:wa (The Great Law of Peace)[1] and the teachings she received from the Longhouse, to guide her words and actions, as she explains in great detail in this book. Through her actions, she reminded Canada that we, as Kanien'kehá:ka, Mi'gmaq, and Wet'suwet'en, are still here, still resisting genocide, and we'll never stop protecting our Sovereign Nations, or the lands, waters, and all living things in our territories. Katsi'tsakwas Ellen Gabriel was, and continues to be, an inspiring symbol of Indigenous resistance and a role model for Land Defenders.

I remember the first time I heard of Ellen. In the summer of 1990, she was in the media as the spokesperson for the Onkwehón:we people impacted by developers, politicians, and law enforcement over the protection of their sacred lands, known as the Pines—a place, as Ellen explains, the Mohawks consider a sacred place of protection. Her voice was always calm, but firm. I had just turned twenty and was working in a bar while going to university. The TV was on, and I was listening to the reporters describe the tense situation. Many of the patrons of this bar came from an army base not far away. Day after day, I was mortified to hear the racist, misogynist, and violent words and slurs hurled by these soldiers at the TV. As a Mi'gmaq woman, I grew up surrounded by racism, but the hateful statements being made by these soldiers were even more frightening. As the only person who worked at the bar, and the only Indigenous woman around, I didn't feel safe.

I was still learning about the world when the events unravelled in the summer of 1990, but what I saw and heard from these soldiers struck me in a way that helped me understand Indigenous-settler relations in a way I never could have learned from my university textbooks. The more I watched Ellen on TV, the more I grew to respect her strength in the face of armed police and soldiers. The media images felt like some kind of Western movie, where the cowboys ride in to kill the Indians; except this time, they were armed Canadian soldiers riding in on army vehicles to confront the Mohawks. But why? The Mohawks were not posing a threat to the government or presenting a danger to society. They were simply protecting their sacred Pines from destruction for a golf course. I was struck by what was happening as the Canadian Armed Forces have always promoted their mission as "to protect Canadians." I came away from the events of that summer with two things I knew for sure: the police and military don't consider Indigenous people worthy of protection, and I must follow and support Ellen's work to protect her people and the land. Ellen became a role model for me and many others.

I'm a Mi'gmaq citizen, registered "Indian" under the Indian Act (1985) and band member of Ugpi'ganjig (Eel River Bar First Nation), but I wasn't always so, due to sex discrimination in the Act. So, part of my life was centred on advocating for the rights of First Nations women and children while raising two young boys by myself. After bartending, I went on to study Native Studies and law and when I completed my doctoral studies, I went on to become a professor. During this time, I sought out Ellen's work and her writings, as well as those of other Indigenous Land Defenders, Water Protectors, and human rights advocates. At the same time, I continued my work at the community level with Indigenous grassroots groups and organizations that covered many social issues for First Nations people who lived on and off reserve— everything from housing and education to treaty and land rights. I knew that someday, if I could combine all the knowledge I received from my activist siblings, First Nation leaders, Elders, and grassroots community groups, together with Ellen's work, I could help make a difference in the struggle.

Today, I'm a lawyer, professor, and activist, still doing my best to follow Ellen's lead. While I've always been part of the Mi'gmaq Nation, it was the work of First Nation women advocates like Ellen, together with Mary Two-Axe Earley (Kahnawà:ke), Yvonne Bedard (Six Nations of the Grand River), Jeanette Corbiere Lavell (Wikwemikong), Sandra Lovelace Nicholas (Tobique First Nation), Sharon McIvor (Lower Nicola Indian Band), Lynn Gehl (Pikwàkanagàn First Nation) and many other women, that my children and I were finally registered as "Indians" so we could officially belong to our community. So when I finally got to meet Ellen at a parliamentary committee we were both presenting at, she confirmed everything I knew about her. She was a strong woman with a soft voice, whose energy radiated love and commitment for her people. I was so honoured to meet her and to have the chance to thank her for everything she has done, when Ellen reminded me that it is through our collective work—not just hers—that real change happens. We are all connected. I learned a great deal about humility that day.

Now, I follow Ellen's calls to action and use her opinions as guideposts when I'm unsure about how a specific law or policy will impact Indigenous Peoples generally, or Indigenous women, specifically. Yet, there's so much more to Ellen than people can see. It's her work behind-the-scenes—providing mentorship, guidance, and support to all the other Indigenous women activists out there trying to make substantive changes on the ground—that's so special.

Seeing her in action, and never giving up, despite all the barriers, gives me hope that we will be successful in our resistance. Indigenous resistance isn't about challenging a few laws or policies, it is about challenging ongoing genocide which results in mass violations of our basic human rights. I learned this from Ellen. She works night and day to empower others to lead our resurgence as Land Defenders, Water Protectors, climate change activists, and human rights advocates. She also reminds us that we must put an equal amount of energy into the cultural revitalization of our traditional languages, customs, and practices. Her commitment to her language and the energy she puts into her artwork was a wake-up call for me to also focus on cultural revitalization. So, imagine how honoured I was when she asked me to write the foreword to her book.

When the Pine Needles Fall is written by Ellen with support from historian Sean Carleton in a conversational style—the book's title being a reference to when the Mohawks defended the Pines in 1990 during the summer, when the trees usually start to lose their needles. The way they present this book, as a series of conversations between them, makes the reader feel as though they are sitting around the kitchen table, listening to them, and learning from the stories and lived experiences of a true warrior—someone who embodies love for the land. Ellen makes it clear in the book that she isn't the "troublemaker" she has been negatively stereotyped as by government propaganda. To the contrary, her commitment to her people and the land demonstrates a powerful woman with a warrior spirit of love and peace based on Kaianera'kó:wa. Even in the face of guns and army personnel, Ellen's goal was always a peaceful resolution to protect their sacred lands from being turned into a golf course. The same cannot be said for municipal, provincial, or federal governments during the so-called Oka Crisis. Ellen's warrior spirit has inspired countless Indigenous activists.

Throughout each chapter, or conversation, we get a deeply personal account of the events during the 1990 Resistance at Kanehsatà:ke and Kahnawà:ke, an account that was purposely shielded from Canadians in most media reports. The conversational style of the book is the next best thing to actually listening to Ellen tell the story herself—a story of strength, love, and commitment in the face of state violence, oppression, and genocide. Readers will also come away with a better understanding of the connection between the events in 1990 and the current struggles faced by other First Nations across the country, like the Mi'gmaq or Wet'suwet'en Nations. She skillfully weaves her experiences and the lessons learned while protecting the lands into a story about her own growth as a Kanien'kehá:ka woman. I can hear her voice as I read this book and know that it will be one of the most important books ever written—a true gift to all of us.

The other part of this conversation is Sean Carleton, a settler scholar who studies the history and political economy of colonialism, capitalism, and education in Canada. But he is truly more than this. Sean is an ally in every sense of the word; someone who actively seeks out ways to support Indigenous Peoples, from a place of knowledge, respect, and reciprocity. As a professor of History and Indigenous Studies at the University of Manitoba, he has studied, researched, and written many critical op-eds and magazine and peer-reviewed journal articles on different aspects on Indigenous-settler relations. Sean is an informed ally, one who doesn't shy away from calling out state oppression, while at the same time, doing his part to lift Indigenous voices like Ellen's, and following their lead.

Readers will appreciate the unique way in which Sean engages in this series of conversations with Ellen. He doesn't centre himself or his experiences, but instead poses questions to Ellen in an open way that allows her to take the reader in whatever direction is necessary to understand the issues at hand. He sets many of his questions within the context of writings from other Indigenous Peoples, and in so doing serves to centre Indigenous Knowledges, experiences, perspectives, and critiques of the current relationship with Canada. This is a refreshing shift from the old-school centring of police, government, and corporate interests and their usual public relations spin on our lived reality. The many quotes and references from Audra Simpson (Mohawk), Arthur Manuel (Secwépemc), Jeannette Armstrong (Syilx), Leanne Betasamosake Simpson (Nishnaabeg), Nick Estes (Lower Brule Sioux Tribe), Glen Sean Coulthard (Dene), myself (Mi'gmaq), and many others, helps readers understand the interconnectedness of Indigenous struggles and their role in achieving social justice—including land issues that have never been resolved.

One of the most important contributions of this book is that we get to know Ellen beyond her role as spokesperson during the 1990 Resistance. We get to know her as a political leader and thinker through her work as President of Quebec Native Women—an organization advocating for the rights of Indigenous women in Quebec—and as a human rights defender who has travelled the world to work in solidarity with other Indigenous Peoples and at the United Nations. We see Ellen as an Indigenous expert who has made numerous presentations to Parliament and Senate on laws impacting Indigenous Peoples, especially Indigenous women. Readers will come to appreciate her many contributions on the political front, but what is less known is her contribution to preserving Onkwehón:we languages, as well as her work as an artist—something we also learn about in this special book.

While the hashtag #LandBack is a relatively recent one, the quest to reclaim and protect Indigenous lands predates the creation of Canada. *When the Pine Needles Fall* captures the essence of Indigenous resistance and the Land Back movement and helps us understand Canada's genocidal past and present. We also learn what is at stake if we don't take concrete steps to work in solidarity with Onkwehón:we Peoples to return our lands for proper care and protection. All of life on earth depends on what humans do in the coming years to halt the destruction of our precious ecosystems. While this book may not have been intended to be a traditional history book, it may well be one of the most important history books of our time. Truth can only be shared when all voices are included, and Ellen's voice is critical to understanding both historical and current conflicts related to land and the risk to personal safety and freedoms experienced by Land Defenders today.

When the Pine Needles Fall is a rare literary gem that will help educate current and future generations about the violent, oppressive relationship between settler governments and Indigenous Nations, and the many social justice issues that remain unresolved. From residential schools to murdered and missing Indigenous women and girls and the incarceration of Indigenous people, it's all about the land. It always has been. The reader will walk away with new insights that will inspire them to action.

Niawenkó:wa,

Wel'alin,

Thank you, Ellen, for all you have done to inspire Indigenous activists and allies coming behind you.

PAMELA PALMATER

PREFACE

I first met Ellen on a cold and snowy night in Nogojiwanong (Peterborough, Ontario) in 2015. Historian John Milloy, then the Director of the Frost Centre for Canadian Studies and Indigenous Studies at Trent University, had invited Ellen to give a public lecture at Trent's downtown college. Before the talk, John asked a number of graduate students, myself included, to join Ellen for dinner. As a settler scholar studying the history of colonialism, capitalism, and Indigenous resistance, I was excited to meet and learn from Ellen.

We ate at one of the best spots in the city that night, a Tibetan restaurant with delicious food. I got to sit next to Ellen. I remember being starstruck and a bit intimidated, but we hit it off and had a great conversation about history, art, and activism—some of our shared interests—as we waited for everyone else to arrive. Over the course of the meal, she then regaled the table with stories from her three decades of activism in the Indigenous resistance movement.

Her talk that night was titled "Colonial Pipelines and Propaganda: Impacts of Development on Indigenous Peoples' Human Rights," and Ellen pulled no punches. Drawing on her experience as the Mohawk spokesperson during the Kanehsatà:ke and Kahnawà:ke Resistance in 1990—commonly referred to by Canadians as the "Oka Crisis," though Ellen prefers to call it the Mohawk Crisis or Kanehsatà:ke Siege—she delivered a stinging critique of white supremacy, heteropatriarchy, settler capitalism, and the environmental destruction that risks the lives of Indigenous Peoples and jeopardizes the survival of the planet. The packed crowd appreciated the opportunity to be in dialogue with such a knowledgeable and inspiring speaker. At the end of the night, I thanked Ellen for her talk, and we promised to stay in touch. We started to correspond over email, and I profiled some of her writing in an activist magazine.

When I finished my PhD and got my first university teaching job, I was asked to design a course that examined a conflict in its historical context. I immediately thought of Ellen's talk and the lessons she shared about Indigenous resistance from the siege of Kanehsatà:ke and Kahnawà:ke in 1990. As a settler historian and Indigenous Studies scholar, part of my responsibility is to find ways to amplify Indigenous voices and perspectives about the past that can, like Ellen's talk, offer insight into how to improve the present and future. I decided to model the course around understanding the Mohawk Resistance of 1990 and its legacy.

As a textbook for the class, I assigned Leanne Betasamosake Simpson and Kiera L. Ladner's *This Is an Honour Song*, a collection of essays, poems, and art marking the twentieth anniversary of the Kanehsatà:ke and Kahnawà:ke Resistance. The book features key contributions from a range of brilliant Indigenous thinkers, writers, and activists, from Simpson and Ladner to Wanda Nanibush, Clayton Thomas-Müller, and Melina Laboucan-Massimo. The book's epilogue is written by Ellen.

In reflecting on what has changed since 1990, Ellen writes:

The Mohawk peoples have been waiting for over 300 years for a peace that never seems to come. A peace blocked by arrogant, racist governments and their forced assimilation policies concealing their coveting of our lands and resources through their legislation. And so . . . what has changed? It is evident that very little has changed and that there's a continuation to defraud not just the Mohawk peoples of

Kanehsatà:ke of our lands and access to those resources,
but all Indigenous Peoples living in Canada.[1]

Ellen's words resonated with my students, and they saw her
as an inspiring role model.

I also invited Ellen to join the class to share her knowledge and speak about her experiences as a Land Defender.
One of the things she helped me and my students understand was that the root issue from 1990—land theft—was
never resolved. In fact, colonial land fraud and profiteering is
ongoing, and Kanehsatà:ke has actually lost more land in the
thirty years since the conflict. Most people don't realize that.

Aside from teaching the course and raising awareness
about the ongoing land fraud in Kanehsatà:ke for my students, Ellen and I started to discuss how I could use my position as an academic, as a settler historian and Indigenous
Studies scholar, to further amplify her voice and calls for
justice. Ellen explained that she had wanted to write a book
about her experiences, but things always got in the way. I
didn't feel comfortable being a ghostwriter and adopting her
voice to co-write the book, especially since Ellen speaks so
powerfully and eloquently. So, we decided on the idea of
talking on the phone and recording, transcribing, and publishing our conversations in book form as a way of sharing
our knowledge—and her experiences specifically—with a
wider audience.

In addition to enacting relationality and reciprocity (all
of the book royalties go to Ellen), the project was also a
way for me to "stand with" Ellen, in the words of Sisseton
Wahpeton Oyate scholar Kim Tallbear, to witness, converse,
and be transformed as an ethical practice and Indigenous
methodology.[2] My objective was not to "extract" Indigenous
knowledge for academic purposes, as has often been the case
with "research" on Indigenous Peoples in colonial settings.[3]
Instead, as Leanne Betasamosake Simpson has explained, the

goal was to divest my power and authority as an academic to create space for Ellen's brilliance.[4] My role in the project was to hold space and amplify Ellen's voice, while also co-creating together through conversation.

We started our formal collaboration in 2019, with hopes of finishing the project for the thirtieth anniversary of the siege of Kanehsatà:ke and Kahnawà:ke in July 2020.

But then the COVID-19 pandemic happened.

Ellen and I continued to talk on the phone during the early days of the pandemic before switching to Zoom. Our conversations became more personal. We talked about our lives, and we shared our fears about the current state of the world as well as our hopes and dreams for the future. Talking with Ellen during the hardest parts of the pandemic was a bright spot for me, something to look forward to during a difficult time. Our conversations helped put things into perspective.

In moments of crisis and change, a critical understanding of the past can help people dream of a better present and future, and so we talked a lot about history, too. As Ellen helped me understand, Indigenous Peoples have been living in a post-apocalyptic world for more than five hundred years, and her brilliance and resilience is truly an inspiration—as you will see for yourself in the coming pages. This book is a snapshot of our ongoing dialogue about Ellen's life and the interconnected nature of history, Indigenous resistance, and the decolonial future. Our conversations highlight that the land is an important teacher and that committing to respect, reciprocity, and gratitude for the world around us is a key part of building a better future.

When the Pine Needles Fall's conversational format is borrowed from similar books of communion. Most recently, Robyn Maynard and Leanne Betasamosake Simpson's *Rehearsals for Living* is comprised of intimate letters exchanged by the authors during the pandemic, meditating on the connections between Black and Indigenous struggles for liberation. Through their letters, readers are exposed to the keen insights of two brilliant thinkers/doers dreaming of a better future at what felt like the end of the world. *When the Pine Needles Fall* is similar, but different.

This book is more modelled after Staughton Lynd and Andrej Grubacic's *Wobblies and Zapatistas*.[5] Lynd is a prolific historian and committed working-class activist with decades of experience. Grubacic is a younger historian and sociologist committed to supporting Zapatista-inspired direct-action movements. In the book, Grubacic's role is mostly to ask questions and facilitate the sharing of knowledge by Lynd for a new generation. The two discussants come from different backgrounds, but they share a common commitment to radical social transformation. Whereas *Rehearsals for Living* is a communion between peers, *Wobblies and Zapatistas* is an intergenerational exchange between friends designed to preserve and share Lynd's radical insights. *When the Pine Needles Fall* follows the structure and purpose of *Wobblies and Zapatistas* but picks up on some of the themes of *Rehearsals for Living*—the importance of history, Indigenous resistance, decolonization, anti-capitalist organizing, abolition and liberation struggles, and climate justice—but roots them in Ellen's lived experience.

My hope is that this book will help people understand Ellen's many important contributions and plant seeds that will nourish new generations as they work to build a better world.

SEAN CARLETON

OHÉN:TON KARIHWATÉHKWEN
(The Words That Come Before All Else)

My life as a Kanien'kehá:ka Land Defender has been one of travel and adventure, meeting interesting people, and trying as best I can to remain true to the teachings of my Elders. A life dedicated to defending the land and Indigenous Peoples' human rights is filled with many lessons.

I'm often asked why I keep advocating on the same issues that we fought for in 1990 and speaking out against ongoing colonial land theft. It's because the struggle continues and we're all responsible to try to leave something behind for the children, youth, and future generations. Just as the generations before us did for us.

It hasn't been easy, but when life's challenges arise, one needs to ground oneself. For some it's walking in the woods, spending time with family, activities that bring you happiness. Grounding yourself is a daily routine. It's a practice based on seeing the world as it is: a flawed society, but one in which there are so many people with talents and gifts to offer. We have a beautiful Mother Earth who, with every season, gives us gifts and new things to marvel at.

For the Rotinonshón:ni (the Haudenosaunee), the protocol of grounding oneself in gratitude for these gifts begins each day with Ohén:ton Karihwatéhkwen (The Words That Come Before All Else). It's not a prayer, but more a giving of thanks, an acknowledgement and a reminder that we're a part of the natural world, not separate from it. We belong to Mother Earth, and we have a duty to share her gifts in harmony with our four-legged relations, the plants and medicines, the birds, the fish, and the sacred pine trees and many others who nurture us and give us life. The natural world teaches us how to preserve and protect the land we live on for present and future generations. The words we say before all else, then, are about gratitude and reciprocity and our connection with all of our relations, honouring those life cycles and forces and reminding ourselves that all of our decisions affect them as well.

Before any meetings—be they discussions, ceremonies, socials, or festivals—we recite Ohén:ton Karihwatéhkwen, which takes time, to honour all of our relations, to give thanks and express gratitude for our special gifts, and to be mindful of the kind of legacy we'll leave behind. These words remind us that the decisions we make during deliberation of an issue must include all our relations as they too are affected by our decisions. These words convey a different way of thinking and connecting to the world around us.

This is required under our Protocol, under our Constitution, Kaianera'kó:wa. Otherwise, the decisions we make during our meetings are not considered a consensus, if they don't take into consideration all of our non-human relations. In other words, consensus amongst all the Clans wouldn't be official unless the words of Ohén:ton Karihwatéhkwen begin our meetings. It's a way of giving thanks to the land and natural world for all the gifts they provide us. We must start by recognizing all of our relations and pledging our commitment to respect, reciprocity, and gratitude. For these reasons, I want to begin this book with that acknowledgment.

As an artist and activist, as well as a Longhouse person, the land and the natural life forces are part of my strength, and I find solace in my walks upon Mother Earth. I grew up in a Christian household. A result of colonial oppression and the brutality of the Seminary of St. Sulpice's efforts to erase the Kanien'kehá:ka from Kanehsatà:ke for three hundred years. Christianity and the rule of the Sulpician missionaries were accepted as the norm by many in my community.

For five hundred years, genocide has been committed against Indigenous Peoples through racist and violent government policies, and the destruction of Indigenous identity and way of life has been justified and legitimized by Christian colonizers through their harmful religious ideology. Colonization and Christianity are interconnected. And it must be said that I have no problem with those who are Christian, it's the manipulation of a religious ideology which has formed the base for the genocide committed by so many European monarchs and states. It's a fact, and hence, it's important to say that the institutions colluded with the governments to inflict genocide upon Indigenous Peoples of Turtle Island.

In the early 1700s, when the Sulpicians travelled in the dead of winter with Christian Mohawks, Nippissings, and Algonquins to our lands, they knew they would be greeted by the Kanien'kehá:ka who were already living there and who would help them survive. As missionaries, their goal was to convert the "savages" who lived in Kanehsatà:ke and gain access to our lands. This is when the real trouble began. Violent dispossession and land theft by the Sulpicians who, through oppression and the help of the British, warped the written history of Kanehsatà:ke. This incorrect narrative (or propaganda) about our community's history of the Kanien'kehá:ka presence on our Homelands is still being used by lawyers and governments to deny Kanehsata'kehró:non (people from the community of Kanehsatà:ke) our inherent rights to our Homelands three centuries later. This is the heart of our struggle.

Still, many Kanehsata'kehró:non practised their ceremonies in secret, to keep our traditions alive and so they wouldn't be harassed by the bullies hired by the Sulpicians. There were certain groups, amongst the Christian Indigenous delegation the Sulpicians brought with them, who would spy on the Kanien'kehá:ka People in our community and inform the Sulpicians if ceremonies or meetings were being held. These efforts to erase our traditional ways—which were later adopted and implemented in the Residential and Day School systems—were brutally intense but, in the end, not entirely successful. We're still here. We're still committed to protecting our Homelands. We will never give up.

However, the land issue that rose to public attention in 1990 during the Kanehsatà:ke and Kahnawà:ke Siege stems from colonization and actions by the Government of Canada in collusion with the Sulpicians to defraud us of our Homelands. This warped narrative denies the fact that there was any evidence of land theft by the Sulpicians, the French, and English—as if the great white man knows better than those who have existed for centuries upon the Homelands of the Rotinonhshón:ni—and so the land issue remains unresolved today.

So why continue the fight, the struggle to defend our rights? Simply put, because colonial land theft continues and unless we're vigilant, we risk losing more of our Homelands. This is why I continue to be engaged in the Indigenous resistance movement. Its momentum and increasing support are owed to those previous Indigenous generations who fought so hard for us to have what we have today.

When I was reinstated into the Longhouse in the late 1980s, I was named, and asked in a ceremony if I agreed to uphold Kaianera'kó:wa for the rest of my life. I was presented with wampum shells, and as I held them I agreed to follow this way of life; to protect and uphold the laws of Kaianera'kó:wa, to live for the land and for all of our relations, human and non-human alike. It's an oath I take very seriously and have done my best to honour throughout my life.

The daily lives of Indigenous people are affected by the threats of colonialism, capitalism, and the dysfunctional process of bureaucracy and rule of law whose justice is founded on genocidal ideologies. For some Indigenous people, the only way to have peace is to keep your head down and not be engaged in the struggle. But sitting on my hands and ignoring my human rights to self-determination would violate the oath I took and would be, in a sense, silent agreement to the destruction of our way of life. Mother Earth needs protection, as do the people and all our relations. We're told in the Longhouse that what we do today impacts seven generations from now. All of us have roles to play in protecting the land, all of our relations, and fighting for the rights of Rotikonhsatá:tie (the faces not yet born).

Fighting to protect our inherent rights to our Homelands, our identity, our cultures and languages isn't only for survival, but a way of life. Defending the land is about protecting the preciousness of life for the future. It's also about learning our history, deepening our understanding of our Onkwehón:we languages, exploring our environment, and listening to Mother Earth and all our relations. Non-Indigenous people have a role to play, too. Listening to nature's language and learning lessons from the land is part of how we can all survive the climate crisis.

As our land base continues to shrink to make way for more condos, golf courses, mines, pipelines, and other forms of capitalist development, so do the habitats of animals—and that includes those developments that threaten and contaminate our aquifers that impact the fish and our drinking waters. It never ends. That is, unless we do something about it. But it's important to understand that all of our actions and decisions are interconnected.

I treasure my parents' teachings and I'm grateful for them giving me my language; they both spoke Kanien'kéha at home but, as we got older, they allowed us to speak English at home, thinking it would help us do better at school. But I was surrounded by the richness of my language on a daily basis as all my relatives spoke it to each other. My connection to the language is one of the most precious parts of my identity as an Onkwehón:we person. In all the work I do, I think of these gifts. I think of my relatives and previous generations who resisted and would never have thought of themselves as "Land Defenders." They were just Onkwehón:we who were trying to survive colonization and protect their lands and community.

I think of my family and my ancestors a lot in the work I'm doing. I stand on their shoulders, building from all the blood and tears they experienced trying to protect and preserve our Homelands for the generations following. Their sacrifices made it possible for my generation to protect our Homelands, to have a language, pride in our identity, and to love Mother Earth. It's for past, present, and future generations to come that I continue this work.

For all the Onkwehón:we who continue to resist, and to our allies who stand beside us, Niawenkó:wa—a big thank you. We could not have come this far without this unity. It's the most important part of our relationship. Solidarity makes us stronger. Developing new ways to work together to protect the land and the waters will only benefit us all, Mother Earth and all our relations. We must learn and renew our relationships and think seriously about how we want to live together. In remembering Ohén:ton Karihwatéhkwen we must understand that we're all connected, past, present, and future. I hope this book can help people understand this lesson and inspire them to carry on the fight for a better future.

Skén:nen, wishing you peace,
KATSI'TSAKWAS ELLEN GABRIEL

1

THE LAND
IS OUR TEACHER

SEAN: Many people will recognize you as the Kanien'kehá:ka spokesperson from the summer of 1990 during the Mohawk Crisis, the siege of Kanehsatà:ke and Kahnawà:ke by the *Sureté du Quebec* (or SQ, the provincial police) and the Canadian Army. The images of you from that summer are iconic, instantly recognizable by many who remember that conflict. But what was your life like before that summer?

In *A Short History of the Blockade*, Leanne Betasamosake Simpson states that being on her Michi Saagiig Nishnaabeg Homelands taught her about life as being "continual, reciprocal, and reflective."[1] How did you learn about your relationship to the land, as an Indigenous person, as a Kanien'kehá:ka from Kanehsatà:ke, and what made you want to put your body on the land and your life on the line to defend your Homeland?

ELLEN: Well, that's an easy answer: the land is everything to me as a Kanien'kehá:ka person, as an Indigenous person. The land is a teacher. Land is life-giving and life-sustaining, and it's a privilege to be able to use some of my life's energy to help protect the earth and ensure it can support the next seven generations. That means everything to me, that is an important part of my life's purpose.

Growing up on a farm I learned how to love the land, Mother Earth, and appreciate all she has to provide us. I was out on the land daily, learning what is safe to touch and what we should stay away from. As children we're fearless and love to explore. Laughing and playing on the land, I was always outside enjoying nature. My siblings and I worked on the ranch feeding horses, cleaning stalls, bailing hay, and doing other chores outside. There were no video games when I was growing up, and TV was kind of a special treat at that time. My mother Annie was a skilled gardener and could do anything she set her mind to. During summer vacation, she would send us outside to weed and tend to the garden, as she had learned to do growing up with seven siblings. There was a special connection for me right from the beginning. I would say it's innate, and inherited somewhat from both sides of my family and Kanien'kehá:ka ancestors.

Land is everything for us as Indigenous Peoples. After my mother passed away, my aunties on my mother's side became like our second mothers and kept us grounded in our identity. In fact in Kanien'kehá:ka culture, aunties are called "Ista" which means mother, followed by their names. So aunties are important in the raising of children and strengthening the family unit. I'm grateful for having them in my life as they also shaped who I am today.

When I learned that Québécois developers were planning to cut down the Pines—a most sacred part of our community and an integral part of our identity here in Kanehsatà:ke—that motivated me to pay greater attention to what was going on around me. I began to realize I had to join the Onkwehón:we (Indigenous) Peoples' movement to protect the land, to stand up for the land, if I wanted to continue enjoying it and make sure future generations can too.

I started going to the Longhouse where I learned the songs, dances, ceremonies, and participated in the political discussions. Kanonhsésne (or the Longhouse under the

Haudenosaunee) is a form of governance that existed before European Contact. In the 1980s, when I was in my twenties, I wanted to learn more about our history and our ways as Kanien'kehá:ka. Being a part of the Longhouse, and connecting with traditional people, became something I identified with and could feel an affiliation or belonging to.

The Longhouse was a very educational place for me and others. It was also where I learned more about how to protect our lands and was taught about what had been done for hundreds of years at that point. I learned more about our history, and about the Pines in particular, as a kind of last vestige of our common lands in the community, a symbol of our freedom. So, it was an easy decision to become part of the movement to protect the Pines and our land from more colonial development.

In terms of relationships to land, I can't speak for anybody else except myself and my perspective, of course. The Pines remain a very magical and spiritual part of the environment that I live in and grew up in. That connection to land is just something that you feel inside. And to know that it's being threatened because someone just wants to extend a golf course was frustrating—that's what was proposed in the late 1980s and early 1990s, you know? What was even more insulting is that the developers were going to dig up our family members, our ancestors in our cemetery, to do it! That was just too much. It was an affront to us as Kanien'kehá:ka. Our community of Kanehsatà:ke has been fighting these kinds of incursions on our lands for three hundred years now. That fight for our survival is in our blood. The land is really important. If you don't have land, you don't have anything. And that's something I was taught early on by my parents and other community members.

My parents were both Kanien'kehá:ka and they spoke Kanien'kéha (the Mohawk language) and so it's my first language. We spoke Kanien'kéha at home and I was surrounded by first language speakers growing up. I also experienced racism at a very young age, which made me fearful because as a child, racism is scary especially if it's adults who are carrying it out. I became angry when I learned why it was happening and that certainly shaped my view of the wider world.

I understand the determination of Indigenous Peoples to protect all parts of our identity, and why we may be perceived as fierce. That fierceness to protect ourselves and land is misinterpreted, conveniently mind you, by government and society as being violent. It's become a stereotype used to influence the public to oppose our human rights. But we're strong and determined, like the many generations before us, and so the will to protect ourselves and our Homelands is something we have inherited. We know who we are and why protecting our land is so important to us, it's for our survival's sake.

SEAN: Thanks for sharing, Ellen. I'm reminded of Secwépemc leader Arthur Manuel, who talks a lot about how colonialism

Kanehsatà:ke Lacrosse team, with (my father) Archie second row, left.

and anti-Indigenous racism shaped his perspective. In *The Reconciliation Manifesto*, Manuel and Syilx author and Grand Chief Ronald Derrickson call racism a "wounding weapon" that settlers "wield against us." They say,

> For Indigenous peoples, racism is the invisible force that fills the jails and too often the graves with our people in a way that also ensures a minimum resistance at the community level. Racism is one of the essential tools of colonialism and without understanding the workings and effects of racism, you cannot fully understand Canadian colonialism.[2]

In terms of the racism you mentioned growing up, were you experiencing this at school?

ELLEN: Yes, at school. My paternal grandmother, Gladys Jacobs, was sent to the Shingwauk Indian Residential School in Sault Ste. Marie in Ontario, which was run by the Anglican

Ellen's parents Annie Montour and Archie Gabriel Sr.

Ellen, seven years old.

Church between 1873 and 1970.[3] My parents attended the Indian Day School in Kanehsatà:ke, as did I. Methodists opened the school in the 1880s and it was actually the last Indian Day School to close in 2000.[4] The goal of Day Schools was the same as the Indian Residential Schools: "to beat the Indian out of the child."

My parents' generation were punished if they spoke their Kanien'kéha language and experienced cultural shaming just like in the Indian Residential School system. My parents came from a generation of hard-working people who lived with oppression, racist-rooted poverty, and started working to help out their families when they were very young. As oppressed people, the common experience instills a strong sense of community; a shared realization that united we can help each other from the evil Sulpicians and Canada.

I did my first two years at the Indian Day School in the community. Then I was bused to a predominantly white public elementary and high school about seventeen kilometres away.[5] At the start of each day we were told to sing "God Save the Queen" and "O Canada," and I still remember all the words today.

Racism, especially from some of the teachers and students, was subtle in school. Even though I was a good student, I was called a "stupid squaw" by one of my teachers—a derogatory slur for Indigenous women. I was one of three students that scored perfect on a science exam, but I was still called a "stupid squaw." I'll never forget that as long as I live. It's scary because as oppressed people, we were taught not to be seen, not to be heard, not to be noticed. Keep your head down, you know? That's part of the intergenerational cultural shaming that comes from colonization for many Indigenous people, not just from residential schooling, but just the education system in general. I never felt comfortable in school and did not like school at all.

SEAN: As a historian of schooling and colonialism, I understand what you're saying. Public schools are also settler colonial institutions. In *Slash,* Syilx author and activist Jeannette Armstrong talks about the racism and bullying many Indigenous people experienced in public schools in the 1960s and 1970s.[6] Was the racism you experienced mostly from teachers? What about your white classmates?

ELLEN: It was a mix. I once got into a fight with a white girl who called me a "stupid squaw" when I was about twelve. I won. Afterwards, my mother sat me down and told me that it wasn't right what the girl said, but to not fight. She said, don't act like they expect you to, you're not a savage. She understood why I fought back but told me to never do that again. I was surprised by her warm support, as I expected some sort of punishment and none came. Only a suspension from school. My mother understood why I did it, why I fought that racist girl, but she wanted me to turn the other cheek. She wanted me to rise above it, not get dragged down by the racism.

My mother was very understanding because she herself had experienced a lot of racism with French people in the town of Oka—which is part of our original community of Kanehsatà:ke. Racism was all around us, and my mother and father shared with me some of the racist taunts they experienced with certain Québécois people in the village. My mother told us about being called "savages" and how she and her sisters would have to hold back her late sister, Martha, from fighting.

Learning this allowed me to understand her experience and let me know I wasn't alone. It wasn't just happening to me, you know? That helped. I started to learn that we were viewed and treated differently. We knew that we had to be careful. If we stuck up for ourselves, it was always used against us. I learned that quickly when I got suspended for fighting that girl.

SEAN: You were suspended? That seems unfair. What about your racist classmate?

ELLEN: She wasn't suspended. Just me. Yeah, it was just accepted back then because the teachers were also calling us racist and derogatory names. As children, it's very intimidating to be called racist names by adults, so I stayed quiet.

If we fought back or disagreed in some way, we were the ones to blame. We were always seen as the troublemakers. And so you learn early on, as an Onkwehón:we, you're treated differently. Your identity is viewed as different, deviant. As children or youth, we, like those who attended Indian Residential Schools, internalized that cultural shaming rooted in colonial racism. We had to battle those internal struggles, to resist what some of our teachers and classmates were saying about us, and all the injustice we faced daily. It was exhausting.

I never liked school. But, when you're a kid, you accept your lot in life. As a collective of Kanien'kehá:ka children, we all knew we were experiencing similar things, with racism and such. And, you know, even from within my community. If you did well in school, you were seen as different. You were ostracized or teased for being studious. So, there were those two sides that were challenging for me. Nowadays, some parents put their kids in private school and encourage them to do well. But back then, you know, you were seen as an oddity if you did well in school, if you excelled in the "white man's" school.

Even though I did well academically, I never liked school. To this very day, I don't really like school. We, as Indigenous Peoples, are the most researched people on the planet. We're still enmeshed within academic standards while academia picks the brains of Indigenous Elders and people, then claim what they have learned as their intellectual knowledge. There are good academics, and there are those who still see us as a stepping stone to their careers. But today education is important to make change. We just have to remain true to our Indigenous selves and use our own Indigenous laws, protocols, and customs in every aspect of our work and life. But I'm happy that there are now so many brilliant Indigenous academics who can place our stories into context and understand our fight to resist colonialism.

We must remind ourselves of our goal, and ask ourselves how much of our identity we want to include in our work. As for non-Indigenous academics, I have to ask if they're sincere in what motivates them, and about what they're doing to help our struggle, you know? Some don't take the time to get to know us and build a relationship, like you're doing. That doesn't help things. I mean, I love learning and education, but colonial "schooling" is still a tool of our oppression, and I know a lot of your own historical research looks at this, so I know you understand. But people need to realize that there is a lot of racism and discrimination against Indigenous people in public schools. The curriculum hasn't evolved to include enough teaching about Canada's colonial history and the genocidal acts that have been committed, like the Indian Residential School system.

SEAN: Yes, I agree. In terms of thinking about learning and education outside the colonial "classroom," many Indigenous writers have talked about the influence that movements and events had—like the American Indian Movement, the reoccupation of Alcatraz (1969–1971), and the Trail of Broken Treaties (1972)—on the Indigenous resistance movement in so-called Canada.[7] Stó:lō author Lee Maracle talks about her involvement in socialist organizing and the Native Alliance for Red Power, an Indigenous women's organization formed in 1967 in Vancouver, that had a consciousness-raising news-letter meant to spread awareness and inspire action.

Cherokee author and scholar Thomas King talks about reading books like *Custer Died for Your Sins*, by Lakota author and activist Vine Deloria Jr., and being inspired by Red Power activists in the 1960s and 1970s. And, in her novel *Slash*, Jeannette Armstrong acknowledges the international nature of Red Power organizing across colonially-imposed borders in the 1970s, and she also speaks to the importance of tracing political influences. She says, "As I begin to write this story, I think back. I search my background. . . . I must examine how I changed and what caused the changes. I must understand it and, understanding it, I may understand what changes our people went through during those times and what we are coming up against."[8]

So, with that in mind, I'm curious about your early political influences and inspirations. Aside from your negative experiences with racism at school, and the teachings you received in the Longhouse, where did you learn about political activism?

ELLEN: There were many sources of education and inspiration for me, actually. I started to learn about Indigenous Peoples' history under oppression and the occupation of our Homelands in the 1970s through a newspaper in Ahkwesásne (a Kanien'kehá:ka community near Cornwall) called *Akwesasne Notes*. But it was through the stories of my parents and Elders, stories of Kanehsatà:ke and about the strength of resistance (even for such a small community) that I learned about the three hundred years of struggle and organizing within our community to protect our land.

Kanehsatà:ke's history is detailed in the book *At the Woods' Edge*, by Kanien'kehá:ka authors Brenda Katlatont Gabriel-Doxtater and Arlette Kawanatatie Van den Hende. This book tells the story of our community and people, which

I encourage everyone to read. I also encourage reading *This Is an Honour Song*, a collection edited by Leanne Simpson and Nehiyaw scholar Kiera L. Ladner, and similarly influential books by non-Indigenous academics such Isabelle St-Amand's *Stories of Oka*.[9]

The more I learned about our struggle, the more determined I became to stop and be part of the movement to address the centuries of land theft and ongoing colonization in our community, first by the French and then by the British and Canada. As a youth, I felt like I didn't fit in, but I could relate to those who were trying to protect the land and help save endangered species; those with a love for the land that is respectful and encompasses the rights of Mother Earth, all our relations, and the humans responsible for taking care of the land. That learning motivated me to get involved and learn from our traditional teachings heard in the Longhouse. There, I felt connected to the past and present in a tangible way. I began learning about what it really means to be Kanien'kehá:ka from Kanehsatà:ke and what my responsibilities are to my community, my Clan, my Nation, and the faces not yet born.

I was also learning about other Indigenous struggles across Turtle Island by hearing about the work of the American Indian Movement (AIM) that started in Minneapolis in the 1960s and 1970s. As a young person living during the times of the AIM, it was all so impressive. There was also the anti-nuclear movement that I paid attention to. I mean, when I was growing up there was the Vietnam War and the peace movement on television all the time, and I remember being horrified by how destructive war is. I made an effort to become more educated and interested in how to fight against imperialism, at home and abroad, and in figuring out what we can do to bring about more peace and justice in the world. So, there were a lot of everyday teachings that accumulated over time and motivated me to get more involved.

In terms of all the organizing going on in Indian Country, as we call it, *Akwesasne Notes* was amazing when I think back on it. That was a great source of information to learn about what was happening, and there was a lot of learning by word-of-mouth as well. We heard stories from older youth about the people who were involved in the AIM, and we heard about the bravery of Mi'gmaq activist Anna Mae Aquash.[10]

I grew up with Cowboy and Indian movies, and in those stories we always lost. So, in learning about the AIM, and the different actions that were happening, it was kind of like we were rooting for ourselves finally. But there was also a lot of propaganda at the time, surrounding what was going on at Wounded Knee. It was a scary time, to be honest, and had a deep impact on me. While we had all experienced racism in various forms, at the time of Wounded Knee we had not heard of any form of extreme violence like that. That was all new to us. Still, there was always talk of injustice and struggle, and a growing consciousness among Indigenous people at the time.

We weren't immune to attacks in our community either. There were incidences of assault on community members by Québécois people. A Mohawk man was killed in a hit and run, and after the incident we heard rumours about the killer bragging, "I got Indian blood on my car. Now there's one less Indian to worry about." Those racist attitudes were prevalent because we're living with the French on our lands who believe they're oppressed (by the English)—unable to see themselves as an oppressor.

Most people don't realize that our community isn't contiguous, it's more like a checkerboard, with French settlers scattered throughout—a direct result of our lands illegally being sold by the Sulpician priests dating back to the 1700s. It's an unusual division of land, most reserves aren't like that, and it creates a lot of tension for us because their rights trump ours. It's challenging, annoying, because on top of that, we're

located in a colonial province where language is an issue, so
we face layers of racism.

During my last few years in high school, I became more
aware of the history of Indigenous Peoples. The AIM began a
contemporary resistance movement that started to alert and
wake our people up, but it wasn't just the AIM that woke up
society. The 60s and 70s were revolutionary times in every
aspect. I learned about the Black Panthers and the plight of
Black people in America. I knew about Martin Luther King
and Malcolm X, and that the Black Panthers supported
Indigenous people at Alcatraz during the reoccupation, and
so I started to see connections between Black and Indigenous
liberation struggles.

Aside from *Akwesasne Notes*, and these inspiring movements, I learned a lot from other interested Mohawk youth
who either had older siblings or knew others involved in the
AIM or supported the resistance movement. So that information filtered down to us. Although I didn't like school, as I
said, I did meet and connect with other Mohawk youth and
my horizon was expanded, I guess you could say. The bus
to and from school, in particular, was a kind of safe space
for us to talk about our issues and share information. You
could hear people talking about things on the bus. So, you
could say I learned about the wider world through the "moccasin telegraph," as they called it. I wasn't a student activist
or anything, but I had a lot of good people around me. I
tried to soak it all in as I was growing up, I was curious and
wanted to learn.

In the late 1980s, I began my search into my history
and identity. My upbringing was rooted in strong ancestral
values, and my siblings and I were richly supported by my
parents, my aunties, and my grandmother. They were kind
and gentle, giving us lots of love. Speaking Kanien'kéha at
home, I already had the language. But the history and culture
were another issue, something that was missing, not unlike

many other Indigenous youth. I had an older cousin who was going to the Longhouse. I grew up going to church (not the Longhouse), so I became inspired, overcame my anxiety, and decided to go too—I was always interested in what I was missing out on. In the Longhouse, there were kind Elders who shared their knowledge with me, so I had good teachings and opportunities to learn which stuck with me during the Siege.

For example, when the first blockade went up to protect the Pines and prevent the golf course extension in March 1990, before things got really intense, the atmosphere was defiant but there was a sense of community—a sense that we were all in this together. Because I had started attending the Longhouse and learning more about our ways—that's where you really have those kinds of discussions about the environment, our laws, and ceremonies—I was able to stay grounded. I felt very at ease and at home there, in the Longhouse. The world started to make sense to me there, and I started to put things together. So that was a big influence for me.

In the late 1980s, while I was still in university, I was trying to fight a little bit of the patriarchy and the lack of understanding about Canada's colonial history and its impacts, that were embedded in the institution. I was also trying to address the misconceptions people had about Indigenous people. But in the Longhouse, people made me feel welcome. There was an older generation of people who knew oppression first-hand, and that sparked my interest in getting involved in our struggle, in taking action. I learned about the ways of the Longhouse and the different teachings and laws that are upheld under Kaianera'kó:wa.

We didn't believe in going to Canada's court to fight for our land because it meant we were going to our oppressor to fight land dispossession. And so, it didn't make sense to go to court. As Rotinonhseshá:ka (The People of the Longhouse) said, we don't recognize the authority of the injunctions that the courts were issuing, on behalf of the Municipality of Oka, to continue the golf course expansion. We don't recognize Canada's jurisdiction here, in Kanehsatà:ke. That is seen by some as a radical position, but it's based on our teachings and experience and the fact that we never surrendered our Homelands to any colonial entity.

Our connection to the land and our own laws are stronger than any kind of loyalty to Canada. The events of 1990 confirmed my teachings and strengthened my desire to fight for the land and for the future. All of my experiences up to that point prepared me, in a way, for what was to come.

SEAN: You mentioned university. What role did that education play in your development?

ELLEN: Well, when I graduated from high school, I went to CEGEP since that is the procedure in Quebec, so I didn't go into university straight away. I went into nursing after high school. When I was a youth the choices for women were either to become a secretary or a nurse. So that's basically the path I followed. Society was very patriarchal in the 1970s and remains so today. My parents wanted me to be able to provide for myself and get a good education, to be independent. Nursing was an honourable profession, but art has always been my passion. I didn't become a nurse but the education I received in the program was valuable in my daily life.

In 1986 I enrolled in the Fine Arts program at Concordia University in Montreal. While I was studious, I'm a visual learner and my way of learning was frustrating because if I couldn't visualize something, I didn't understand it. And so, art was my way out of that frustration. I was always drawing, and my parents encouraged me from a young age. They always brought home sketchbooks and materials to nurture my love of art. My parents were very supportive in that way, they were very nurturing.

SEAN: You graduated from Concordia in the spring of 1990, so I'm guessing you must have been a student at the time of the *École Polytechnique* tragedy, the antifeminist mass shooting.[11] You talked about the patriarchal nature of society and your frustrations there. Do you remember that violent event where fourteen female students (Geneviève Bergeron, Hélène Colgan, Nathalie Croteau, Barbara Daigneault, Anne-Marie Edward, Maud Haviernick, Maryse Laganière, Maryse Leclair, Anne-Marie Lemay, Sonia Pelletier, Michèle Richard, Annie St-Arneault, Annie Turcotte, and Barbara Klucznik-Widajewicz) were murdered?

ELLEN: Yes. I actually had classes that evening, December 6, 1989, and I kind of knew there was something strange going on. You could feel it in the air. I was in the Fine Arts building, and I heard someone mention the attack. It was terrifying, we didn't know the full story right away. When I found out what happened afterwards, that a man deliberately targeted female students, it was shocking. I think it was a pretty scary time for everybody, especially for women. *École Polytechnique* is only a fifteen-minute drive from where I was studying. Montreal is only an hour or so from Kanehsatà:ke. I couldn't believe someone could do such a heinous act—just shoot and kill women in a school because he didn't like women. I still try to attend the vigils, to gather with other women and protest violence and misogyny and be with the families and survivors. It's an issue that affects all communities.

The mass shooting also showed me the misogyny in society and reminded me how force and violence is often used to intimidate people into submission, to silence their voice. This is what happened with the genocidal acts of Canada's colonial history. So, I can relate to those who are intimidated by acts of violence and threats to their lives and the lives of their families.

Even though I was shy and am deep down an introvert, I was determined to use my voice to defend my community. But I never could have imagined that I would be thrust into the public spotlight and become the Mohawk spokesperson during the summer of 1990. I guess all of that education, whether in school or my life experiences, helped prepare me. My experiences and the teachings I received up to that point helped me to become a voice for my community. I was determined to demand justice for our community and for Indigenous Peoples and knowing what my parents and previous generations went through also motivated me.

Because I was exposed to three languages growing up, I was able to speak a bit of French and was one of several people on the frontlines of the barricades who could. That's one of the reasons I was selected as the spokesperson. We needed someone who was trilingual there to be our community's voice to the outside world; someone who knew about the Longhouse, our land struggle, and the racism we face. We were alternating people for a while, taking turns speaking to the media, but I was also a woman and we needed a woman's voice because under our laws, Kaianera'kó:wa, title to the land belongs to the women.

Women are the title holders, and it's our responsibility to protect the land. That's another teaching I learned in the Longhouse. That's how I became the spokesperson that summer, although I'm still surprised that things got to the point where the police and army occupied our community and Kahnawà:ke. All we were doing was peacefully blocking a secondary dirt road to inform people about our land struggle and the reason why we opposed the golf course expansion, we never blocked a major highway until we were attacked by the SQ.

2
PROTECTING THE PINES

SEAN: When people think of the Mohawk Crisis, they often recall the dramatic images of the police siege of Kanehsatà:ke on the morning of July 11, 1990, and the death of Marcel Lemay, a Corporal with the SQ.

ELLEN: Yes, but that clouds the issue and serves to hide the root issue: our land. It's terrible that Marcel Lemay died to protect the self-serving interests of Oka and their investors.

SEAN: As a historian, I'm always interested in the relationship between context and change over time and examining who controls the historical narrative. In *The Wretched of the Earth,* Frantz Fanon talks about this. He argues that decolonization is a "historical process" and requires a struggle because,

> the colonist makes history and he knows it. And because he refers constantly to the history of his metropolis, he plainly indicates that here he is the extension of the metropolis. The history he writes is therefore not the history of the country he is despoiling, but the history of his own nation's looting, raping, and starving to death. The immobility to which the colonized subject is condemned can be challenged only if he decides to put an end to the history of colonization and

the history of despoilation in order to bring to life the history of the nation, the history of decolonization.[1]

In thinking about history as a tool of decolonization, I think it's really important for people to understand the longer history of the Kanehsatà:ke land struggle, prior to July 11, 1990.

At your suggestion, I recently re-read *At the Woods' Edge* to learn more about the history of struggle leading up to that morning in July, going back three hundred years.[2] The events of 1990 are just the tip of the iceberg, really, when it comes to the fight against colonial land theft in Kanehsatà:ke. Can you explain more about Kanehsatà:ke's history and the Mohawk struggle against land fraud?

ELLEN: Yes, our community has been protecting its land base since the early 1700s when the Seminary of St. Sulpice were given a land grant from King Louis XIV (a teenager at the time), who gave them ownership rights but with the condition that they had to Christianize the "Indians." As soon as the people of Kanehsatà:ke created an agreement with them, the Sulpicians twisted the words and claimed that they were in charge of the land instead of the other way around. Initially it was the Kanien'kehá:ka who told them that they needed to be consulted before any tree or land was to be used.

Instead, these rich blue bloods from France hired a security force to oppress the people, to stop us from resisting what was going on, and to start selling land without community knowledge or consent. It was theft. Plain and simple. The Sulpicians were businessmen disguised as priests, and they helped create the town of "Oka" in the middle of Kanehsatà:ke by stealing and selling our lands. It's a story of British and Canadian oppression—colonialism at its most depraved. We're still dealing with the ripple effects of the deplorable acts by the Sulpicians.

SEAN: And there was always organized resistance, by the community, to the theft, this form of colonial land dispossession?

ELLEN: Of course. And there always will be. I hope we don't have to fight for another three hundred years or more to get justice, but we'll fight as long as we have to. We're going to win. There is no other choice for us but to fight and win our land back.

SEAN: In *At the Woods' Edge*, the authors explain that despite many attempts to stop the land theft, successive French, British, and Canadian governments (federal, provincial, and municipal) have all allowed it to continue. Multiple court rulings in the early 1900s sided with the Sulpicians, which allowed for more development, including the eventual creation of the Oka Golf Club in 1959 on the disputed land that is connected to what happens in 1990.

ELLEN: Colonial courts protect the interests of the Crown. It's a legitimized form of land dispossession that continues to this day.

SEAN: And the Municipality of Oka allowed the golf course to be built in part of the sacred Pines without consent. Then, in the 1970s, the Mohawk Council of Kanesatake filed an official land claim with Canada, but it was rejected. This set the course for the future of more land theft by the private owners of the Oka Golf Club to work out a deal with the Municipality of Oka to expand the club into an eighteen-hole course with an additional condominium development. The golf course parking lot would be expanded by removing the Kanehsatà:ke cemetery in the Pines. The Mayor of Oka, Jean Ouellette, agreed to halt the project in July 1989 for more negotiations, but he lifted the moratorium in March 1990, ultimately giving the golf course expansion the green light—and clearing the path for conflict. Do I understand this correctly?

ELLEN: Yes, well, there was a lot of big money behind the push for development. There always is. That golf course had private membership. There were connections, with judges and people in government and business who were heavily invested, in various ways, in the project. We were the only ones standing in the way. The politicians and businessmen underestimated our resolve and commitment to protecting our land and community. It was wrong to assume that we're so divided that they could come in no problem, that the division would be a benefit to developers. The government always likes to use the excuse: "Who do we talk to?"

SEAN: It was at that point, on March 9, that the community members working alongside The People of the Longhouse decided to erect a small barricade on a dirt road that led to the disputed land. Can you tell me more about how this action started and what it was intended to achieve?

ELLEN: Again, there is no dispute. The land is ours. But, yes, that is the longer history of struggle behind our action that most people don't fully understand. The police's siege and the army's invasion that summer diverted attention away from what our action was all about. It all started with our centuries-long land struggle and that dirt road barricade in March 1990. When Oka lifted the moratorium, the community decided it was time to act—as a continuation of our longer struggle.

The Pines, or "the Commons" as it's sometimes called, is very special to us historically. It's a sacred place because, in the history of Kanehsatà:ke, it isn't just a place to admire its beauty, but was a place of refuge during my grandparents' time, away from the security forces of the Seminary of

St. Sulpice. It remains the oldest existing community of the Kanien'kehá:ka Nation, and it's mentioned in the ancient rite of condolence of Chiefs and Clan Mothers because it was the first to accept Kaianera'kó:wa. So, it existed before European Contact. It's a place of protection for our community, and the stories of our people are deeply rooted there.

The Sulpicians were bullies and would forcibly enter people's homes to intimidate Kanehsata'kehró:non—to try to force us off the land so that they could sell it to make more money. During these attacks, men were forced to hide in order to escape the brutality, often leaving the women behind because it was thought that they wouldn't be harmed. That assumption was wrong. The women were harassed late in the evening, by the priests and their bullies. To have protection they would leave their homes and sleep in the Pines at night. So, the Pines are a place of refuge.

It's so peaceful there, energizing to the spirit. The Pines have a real significance for our community as far as the history and stories of our people. We don't just see them as trees, to be cut down and sold for profit. Instead, they are sacred, and considered our grandfathers who protected multiple generations from acts of violence. It's not only a special place of beauty but one of protection for our people.

When the moratorium on development was lifted, people decided that because the Pines are so precious, they needed our protection. It was as simple as that, really. The original goal of taking action was to try to monitor the Pines, protect them, and make sure people didn't start cutting down the trees or desecrating our cemetery. Oka obtained an injunction in April that ordered us to remove our barricade, but we didn't recognize the legitimacy of that order, and we invited other Mohawks from other communities because we saw it as a Nation issue, not solely a community issue. And so, we asked for help from the Iroquois Confederacy, inviting others to join us in protecting our Homelands and community.

Oka, and its private investors, didn't like us standing up for ourselves. The SQ's surveillance of us and their actions were reminiscent of the Sulpicians' bullies from previous generations. They seemed to view us as an annoyance rather than rights holders. They refused to recognize our sovereignty or our rights to our Homelands. We refused to recognize their authority and their claims to our unceded territory.

SEAN: Your explanation has me thinking of Mohawk scholar Audra Simpson who calls this kind of response "refusal," which strikes at the heart of colonial hegemony and calls state authority and its legitimacy into question.[3] So that's how things started, on this dirt road with a conflict over the barricade and an injunction?

ELLEN: Basically. You have to understand, this was a continuation of our centuries-long land struggle that boiled over to the present day, because we wouldn't dismantle the barricade on our community's secondary dirt road. Back then, the road wasn't even plowed during the winter months. In 1990 spring came early, with nice warm weather, which made it easier for us to meet, organize, and teach people about the Pines and our struggle. The weather enhanced our mood and strengthened our resolve to be at the barricades for as long as it took to protect the Pines.

When the injunction was granted to the Municipality of Oka, allowing the expansion to go ahead, that motivated us to be more determined than ever. It brought us together and clarified our purpose. We said we didn't recognize the jurisdiction of the colonial state and the injunction, and so the barricades stayed up.

On May 1 there was a raid planned by the SQ to try to dismantle our barricades, but it was called off. Tensions were already mounting, for sure. Representatives from the provincial and federal governments came and tried to convince us to take down our barricade, but we refused. Some people were scared off after the SQ's aborted raid, and rightly so; it caused a lot of people to leave the frontlines at that point. People were worried that another, bigger raid was imminent, and that the police would be back to enforce the injunction and we would all be jailed. That's what we expected would happen: we'd be arrested and go to jail. It was a peaceful form of protest; never did we imagine that we would be shot at by a SWAT team.

Early in the morning of July 11, at 5:15 a.m., the SQ made their move. It was just a small group of us left, mostly women, and some people from other Kanien'kehá:ka communities who had come the day before for a meeting with us. So there was a presence there, that morning, of Kanien'kehá:ka people. Within about forty minutes the whole community arrived to either watch us get arrested or to support and the tension was mounting with every passing minute. In previous months leading up to July 11, we had invited Kanien'kehá:ka from Kahnawà:ke and Ahkwesásne to come to a meeting and help us strategize since there were so few people defending the barricades at that time—especially after May 1.

We knew something big was going to happen, but we didn't expect the SQ to shoot at us. We also knew why we were taking action and we were determined to stand up for our community and the Pines, just as our ancestors had done before us. It was the least we could do to honour those before us who fought for our Homelands, it was necessary to take a stand.

SEAN: In *A Short History of the Blockade*, Leanne Betasamosake Simpson notes that

> blockades are rich sites of Indigenous life, of a radical resurgence. In the spaces behind the barricades, you'll find parents with children. You'll find Elders. You'll encounter

ceremony, sacred fires, and language learning. Art making. Singing. Drumming. Storytelling. . . . Living as a creative act. Self-determination, consent, kindness, and freedom practiced daily in all our relations. . . . Living with the purpose of generating continual life.[4]

With these thoughts about the radical potential of blockades, as a strategy of resistance and resurgence, can you tell me more about the initial barricade on the dirt road. What purpose was it serving in the struggle? Were you preventing everyone from getting to the Pines? Were you handing out leaflets or talking about the history of the community?

ELLEN: Our initial focus was on educating the public, especially the people in Oka, and protecting the Pines. We had a lot of important discussions that spring. Just talking with people, sharing information about our history and the importance of the Pines. Community residents were allowed to come and go, we had left enough space for their cars to go through. We also had a lot of community support at the beginning. People would bring us coffee and donuts and chat with us. They encouraged our work. Elders would come and talk with us. So even though they would go home after a while, their support meant a lot to us.

The barricades were erected to prevent municipality workers from entering the Pines to cut down the trees. Some of the Québécois would come up and ask questions and asked to be let through. But we refused and informed them that it wasn't personal—the blockade was a tactic to strengthen our position to protect the Pines. Many non-Mohawks agreed with us. There were lots of discussions and we were learning new things, that spring and summer, about our history, the level of resistance over centuries, and our issues. It was really heartening, and it was a powerful educational moment for a lot of people in the community, too.

I can only speak for myself, but I learned a lot from the discussions from people from other communities like Kahnawà:ke and Ahkwesásne talking about Kaianera'shera'kó:wa (The Great Shining Peace) and our history. It was, for me, a very enriching time and experience, building on my earlier work with the Longhouse. It was a continuation of my education regarding our own Traditional Laws, in a way that connected me to my ancestors who fought for our lands before me. That gave me strength and the resolve to stay at the barricades.

SEAN: Sioux historian Nick Estes, in his book *Our History Is the Future*, talks about this very kind of intergenerational connectivity. He says that for many Indigenous Nations, "There is no separation between past and present, meaning that an alternative future is also determined by our understanding of our past." Moreover, "Indigenous resistance draws from a long history, projecting itself backward and forward in time."[5]

ELLEN: Exactly. For example, as part of our education I learned more about Joseph Swan, his Kanien'kehá:ka name was Onahsakén:rat, who was organizing the community around our land issue in the 1850s against the Seminary of St. Sulpice.[6] He was a contemporary of Louis Riel, and they even went to the same seminary school in Montreal. After finishing at school, they both went home and tried to help their people because they learned how to read and write the colonizer's way and learned the full extent of the lies and deception that was going on to control the people and steal our land. They were hungry for justice. Joseph Swan started reading historical documents and realized how the Sulpicians were being dishonest, stealing our land and selling it to settler farmers to make money. Onahsakén:rat started to tell people about what was happening, and he tried to organize the people to protect our lands.

For this, he was criminalized by the Sulpicians. They confiscated his land, caused his wife to miscarry, and brutally harassed him for his resistance against their corruption and oppression—while they continued to steal and sell our lands through the use of force and intimidation. That's the heart of the issue: centuries of colonial land theft in our community. And so, we started to understand how this multigenerational struggle began and why it hasn't been resolved.

It was, and remains to this day, a land struggle. It's about protecting our Homelands for future generations and leaving a legacy for them. Our actions helped unify many people across the country, and it inspired Indigenous people from other communities to come and support us too. Many of us had never considered ourselves "warriors." And it was really the media who called us that even though we insisted that we're citizens of the Kanien'kehá:ka Nation. We were keenly aware of the trouble in Ahkwesásne in 1989, just before our barricades went up in March, and our goal was to unite our Nation, to say that we all face the same struggles against land dispossession.

The idea of a Mohawk Warriors' Society began with Louis Hall who created the Warrior flag now called the Unity flag. But in 1990 there was a lot of negative connotations around that word which seemed to be part of a smear campaign against us to distract from the land issues and discredit our action. This is part of the strategy, by settler governments and their representatives, to criminalize Indigenous Land Defenders—it's something out of the colonial playbook. Even today, we're still considered public enemy number one.

But this misconception, equating the term "warriors" with "thugs" or "criminals," has been part of the propaganda machine mobilized by colonial governments. In fact, there was an RCMP report in 2015 that identified Mohawk "warriors" as being the number three threat to public security. So, you see, that rhetoric is being used even today. The government's response to us, even prior to July 11, was really connected to these stereotypical notions and centuries-old propaganda that frame Iroquois, or Mohawk, people as the most "war-like." We're always viewed as being more "savage" and ruth-less, bloodthirsty even. You still see this in history textbooks and educational curriculum. It's frustrating.

We have this beautiful governance system that combines our spiritual cosmology and political worldview together. It's the same structure of governance and political framework that inspired the United States and their political system, the inspiration for today's democracy. Many people are oblivious to this fact, they just treat us like our sole motivation is to be troublemakers.

The only exception to the government's indifference we faced was the late John Ciaccia, who was Quebec's Minister of Indian Affairs. Although he made mistakes too, I believe he was sincerely trying to help everyone avoid further conflict in the lead-up to July 11 and afterwards. He was the only person in government—provincial or federal—who held out his hand to us, trying to bring about a peaceful resolution. Mr. Ciaccia really tried to resolve things peacefully, but he was betrayed by his own government—which is something, I know from our discussions after the Mohawk Crisis, that hurt him deeply.

With a letter dated July 9, 1990, Ciaccia warned against a police intervention. He saw that history had denied the Mohawks of Kanehsatà:ke any justice. He acknowledged that "sometimes the law is an ass," and he said: "[the Mohawk] people have seen their lands disappear without having been consulted or compensated, and that, in my opinion, is unfair and unjust, especially over a golf course."[7] This letter was important for our struggle, it meant someone in government understood the issue. Although he was obligated to follow the "rule of law" for Quebec, it was still an important warn-ing that remained ignored and unheeded.

What hindered him was the Quebec government's and the SQ's agenda to criminalize the Kanien'kehá:ka. He was given a narrow mandate and, like Alex Paterson, the Quebec government's negotiator, the real concern was about the inconvenienced motorists on the south shore of Montreal. So, the dismantling of the Mercier Bridge barricade was the only issue they were willing to discuss, not the ongoing land theft in Kanehsatà:ke nor a peaceful resolution. Just the continuation of the criminalization of Kanien'kehá:ka people and our allies.

SEAN: Was there any non-Indigenous solidarity, like people from Oka who stood with you, in the days before the July 11 Siege?

ELLEN: Yes, there was actually. There was an environmental group that was created by some people in Oka, people who supported us. They did a study on the trees to show how old and important they were—some of them were over two hundred years old at the time. And I know that many of the people from Oka who supported us were harassed and threatened over the course of the summer by those who were racist or misunderstood the issue. They were also harassed by police, which makes me sad. It was a tense climate with so much uncertainty and mistrust, and all of us suffered from the colonial dysfunction on all sides. There was a very heavy police presence, even before July 11.

After May 1, the police stepped up their intimidation, which I think led to an increase in fear and caused some people to stay away even though they were supportive. The SQ increased their car checks as well, more planes and police helicopters were flying over watching us. People forget that the tension rising in both communities was fuelled by fear mongers comprised of the Mayor of Oka, Jean Ouellette, and their investors. July 11 was the result of centuries of abuse.

It personified the way we have been treated for hundreds of years, so we knew that the barricade would spark attention to our struggle. Although we were waiting for something to happen, we did not expect what was to come. Again, we just thought we'd eventually be arrested.

After much discussion and many meetings, we agreed on a plan. Because the women are the title holders to the land, we decided that the women were going to go to the front to meet the police. We thought people would be arrested, and that meant we needed others to stay behind to help get them out of jail, bail them out, that kind of stuff. That was our strategy. And there was even a training session, by some group in Montreal, on how to get arrested and how to engage in peaceful civil disobedience without having your arms dislocated when police drag you away, which was helpful.

This was meant to be peaceful, there was nothing other than getting arrested on our minds, there was no violence that was going to come from our side. And this is why the women were the ones that were supposed to go to the front, to speak to police and possibly get arrested. As title holders of the land, and leaders in that respect, the women agreed to go to the front when police arrived and that's exactly what we did.

SEAN: The waiting must have been stressful, especially with the increased police presence.

ELLEN: No, not in the typical sense. We were united for a good cause: the protection of the land and our sovereignty. We knew what we were doing and why, so that was helpful, and we had support from the men. That helps too. As oppressed Peoples, and considering our history of resistance, we're always going to defend our land. Always. That's why the history part is so important to contextualize our situation. This wasn't just about a golf course or condo development but addressing the long-standing historical land issues!

After so many generations of being pushed around, we felt like we were the generation that wasn't going to take it anymore. Not that previous generations didn't. It was just another chapter in our history of trying to protect the Pines and we were willing to put our bodies on the land and our lives on the line to do it. I don't think we thought about fear, really. Perhaps some did, because they never came back after May 1. But those that remained weren't ruled by their fear, at least not at first. In fact, we became more defiant, more resolved.

SEAN: Were there earlier attempts to negotiate, between when the injunction was levied in the spring and the events of July 11?

ELLEN: Well, we actually had three injunctions against us. But the first two named the Mohawk Council of Kanesatake so we said those don't apply to us. The last one which came in June was more general and against the community to remove the barricades, and this was the basis of the SQ raid, but it expired on July 8 or 9.

There were two negotiators who came to our barricade to talk. Pierre Coulombe represented the province and came to the barricade on May 1, but he was stopped by the women at the front barricade who challenged his credentials. I don't think he expected that, and it took him by surprise. He wanted to speak to the men and we just laughed. Colonial leaders have always ignored Indigenous women. In short, these negotiations did not get very far because both levels of government did not offer anything and there was no good faith or will to negotiate honestly. They did not respect our rights to the land. They just wanted the barricades to come down.

There were also some meetings at the Longhouse with the federal negotiator, Yves Désilets, but he was really arrogant. He often had back-door meetings with the Mohawk Council of Kanesatake, undermining the people at the barricade. I think there were one or two meetings in the Longhouse, but these talks were a stall tactic to make it look like they were trying to negotiate, all the while the SQ was organizing and preparing to take more forceful action against us. This is how colonial governments work, and have always worked, against our people. They try to divide and conquer. They advance their agenda by manipulating the band council, who they control with financial agreements, the moderates who are more palatable to the government's agenda. Then they try to paint the Longhouse people as "radicals," a tried-and-true colonial tactic intended to cause doubt, shift blame, and produce shame amongst our own people so we lose our focus.

Building on historical stereotypes of the "savage Indian," the government tries to convince the public that we're dangerous. But that's not true. We're simply defending our sovereignty, our inherent right, the right to self-determination. We're protecting our land so that present and future generations may enjoy it. I guess that would be considered "radical" in a colonial and capitalist society.

The dirt road barricade was supposed to bring more awareness to our struggle, to help people really understand our history, our culture, and why the land is so important to our identity, but all that was lost in the chaos that ensued on July 11 and afterwards, directed by the media and government propaganda. The Siege and its aftermath, including the invasion by the Canadian Army, altered the course of that summer dramatically.

3

THE SIEGE OF KANEHSATÀ:KE AND KAHNAWÀ:KE

SEAN: In continuing our discussion about the events of 1990, what do you remember about the morning of July 11 and the 78 days you spent behind the Mohawk barricades during the Mohawk Crisis?

ELLEN: You know, sometimes it feels like you're just put in the right place at the right time, or the right place at the wrong time. Those of us who were still at the barricades, after the SQ raid was called off in early May, knew that a larger action was being planned behind-the-scenes. We could sense it coming, although, like I mentioned, we just thought we'd be arrested. In early July, tension increased, as did the police presence. We knew that the Municipality of Oka was determined to go ahead with the golf course expansion and development in the Pines, so we maintained our position and remained at the barricade.

On the morning of July 11, I woke up as usual at 4:50 a.m. An Elder woke us up for the tobacco burning ceremony we always started our day with, to guide us and help us remember why we were taking this stand for the land and our community. There were only a handful of us left at the barricade by this point, but we had a meeting the night before with Mohawks from other communities who had slept over.

During our morning tobacco ceremony, at 5:15 a.m., the SWAT team arrived. Things felt different, ominous even. We knew then that *this* was the moment; the raid was happening. All of a sudden, a chipmunk came down the tree and started chirping at us, almost as if to warn us about what was going to happen. The four other women who were standing with me at the sacred fire looked at each other and agreed it was time we go to the front, just as we had agreed in the community meeting.

As we approached the front barricade, the police yelled at us, saying they wanted to speak to our leader. We looked at one another, and thought, *we* are the leaders. There were five of us at first, and we were later joined by nine other women. We were fourteen in total. The paramilitary force, comprised of the SQ, the Montreal urban police, and members of the Canadian Army were there as well, didn't know what to do with us. We told them that "the women are the leaders!"

SEAN: The SQ was supported by other police?

ELLEN: Yes, people said that the RCMP were there too, with a special tactical unit. It was a paramilitary force under the SQ. It was a large operation, and it became even bigger in the days that followed.

There was a lot of racist sentiment at the time. A racist group called *Les citoyens d'Oka* (the citizens of Oka) demanded that the police flex their muscle and go in with guns blazing and tear down our barricades to clear the way for the golf course to be built. They said we were defying the rule of law—suggesting that should justify a crackdown on us. But when the police arrived to "do their job," we stood defiant yet peaceful. We told them they did not have jurisdiction or authority over our lands. They didn't care. They had their orders. The captain told us "the time for politics is over, we're here to do a job."

The SWAT team started shooting tear gas at us, and each time the wind picked up it threw the smoke back at them. When the women stepped back from the front to discuss what to do, the police shot tear gas and concussion grenades at us. This happened three times. We would retreat and then reapproach the front. The police came with an agenda, and at the end, it was to kill us. Some had their faces painted, some were shaking as they were aiming their guns at the women. We later learned that the SQ used three different kinds of tear gas on us that morning. It all seemed so surreal.

I had family living behind the SQ lines in the village of Oka, as it's called today. After three hundred years of steadily chipping away our lands, first by the Seminary of St. Sulpice, Kanehsatà:ke remains a checkerboard without a contiguous land base. My family, my aunties, and my sister, some other Mohawks that live in the village, were there behind the SQ's barricade, and we were told that the SQ had body bags ready on July 11. And so, our families were very scared for us, and I feared for them. They were afraid that Oka, Quebec, and Canada were going to make an example out of the Mohawks of Kanehsatà:ke to not resist the centuries-old land dispossession.

At about 8:30 a.m., the police opened fire with their guns. I was standing with a group of women at the time. We could actually hear the bullets whizzing by our heads, hitting the sand and hitting the trees and branches. At the time I didn't think of being afraid, but being shot at, having bullets fly by my head, that got my adrenaline going. I was thinking, are they really shooting at us? I couldn't believe it. We just ran for cover. So, just like our ancestors had done, some of us sought shelter and protection in the Pines. And we stayed there until we saw the payloader driven by a community member who told us the cops had left. Then we knew it was safe to move.

I remember talking to one officer who was saying that he was just there to do a job. I told him, "so are we." Our job was to protect our land and we weren't going to leave. I could tell he was frustrated by that. He didn't understand. I think they thought if they opened fire on us, we would just give up. They underestimated our resolve, our determination to defend the land. They were ignorant of our history. As oppressed people, we knew that there was so much at stake.

The rest of the day was a blur. At the end of the day, I learned that in the chaos a police officer—Corporal Marcel Lemay—had been shot and killed. In the confusion, it was unclear who shot him. Journalists were saying that he was shot by friendly fire, but the SQ were intent on controlling the narrative and said he was shot by a Mohawk—to justify the violence they had initiated. It was a total mess.

The SQ officers believed they were just doing a "job," but they got paid to shoot at us that day. Racist propaganda paved the way for the escalation. It could have been peacefully negotiated, but there were so many people who were invested and who would profit from the golf course expansion. We were defending our community, our Homelands. And yet we were framed as the bad guys, even though the SQ initiated the violence.

SEAN: What else do you remember about that day, July 11?

ELLEN: After the SWAT team raid, we learned that Kahnawà:ke had blocked the Mercier Bridge in solidarity during the early morning. Someone radioed them that we were under attack, so as soon as they heard about the raid, they blocked it. It was then we got a sense that things were getting bigger.

The men here were in connection with Kahnawà:ke through CB radios and that's how we communicated that summer. The rest of the community also took action, hemming in the SQ SWAT who occupied all of Highway 344. On the other end, going west on 344, the community had set fire to some tires as a protective deterrent. The SQ were afraid from the beginning, and when things became serious, they ran away. That's why we believe they left their vehicles and their payloader behind. In a sense, they gifted them to us, I guess you could say. We used those vehicles to reinforce the new barricades needed for the highway since the whole community was now under threat. By the end of the day, that secondary dirt road barricade was moved to become a highway barricade. We had no choice but to protect the community in response to the police's attack, firing their weapons at us. It was an unjustified use of force and intimidation, and as a result, people were really angry about the police shooting at us.

In the midst of everything, I was told to go to the front to answer questions from the media. We didn't have cell phones back then, so I had to go to somebody's house to do media work at first, to talk to reporters on the phone. At the time, I had just graduated from Concordia University and had moved to Kanàtakon (the village of Oka is referred to by this name) where my new apartment was actually right behind the SQ barricade. I couldn't go home all summer and only had the clothes on my back, so I stayed in the Pines.

We didn't have time to stop and think about what had just happened. We were all running on adrenaline and wondering if anyone was hurt. I was thinking of my family, hoping they were okay, and wondering if they knew I was okay too. It was a difficult time. It was like we were on "automatic mode" and doing what was necessary to survive.

I was chosen as a spokesperson because I'm trilingual, I speak Mohawk, French, and English. Even if I didn't speak French perfectly, I tried my best and having those languages was an asset. So, my role was to deal with media, but it was amongst so much chaos and uncertainty. We couldn't really monitor what kind of narrative was unfolding out there because we didn't have a TV behind the barricades to watch how the media told our story. Radio was a different situation, and others would tell us what was being said. But honestly, there was too many other things to focus on, so I didn't grasp all the news coverage of what was happening.

People would tell me what was being said by both French and English media. And there were the newspapers, so I had to piece things together from what people had heard and saw on TV. That helped me understand the impacts of what happened on July 11, and as things were evolving, it seemed like this was going to be a long haul.

The first day was hectic, I was busy trying to meet and talk with people all day. They would ask, "what are we going to do? What's going to happen?" I think the following day some people from Kahnawà:ke arrived as well as people from Ahkwesásne. And because the roads in the area were blocked by the SQ, people were coming by boat—Kanehsatà:ke is on the Ottawa River so that was an advantage for receiving food as well. But it also made us vulnerable in other ways. There were some brave people, like Gilles who was from Montreal, who entered by foot through the woods to bring us bags of food, on July 11. I have the deepest respect and gratitude for this man and others who braved the SQ checkpoints and harassment to bring us food, or to support us.

During the first night, I slept in the Pines on a confiscated golf cart because there was no where else to go. Because we were in the woods there were lots of bugs, and I had to cover my head with my hood to protect against the mosquitoes. I think I may have slept thirty minutes that night before we were woken by gunshots coming from the SQ side. They were trying to provoke another shootout. But the desire to survive was great and we were angry that the SQ would shoot at us. We also knew that we were right in what we did because this is our land, the land of our ancestors who fought for us, so we were the next generation to continue this struggle. We were learning and adapting almost every minute. It was an exhausting day, and we couldn't rest. But we realized pretty quickly that we were in it for the long haul.

SEAN: What was day-to-day life like behind the barricades, for those 78 days during the resistance? What stands out in your memory?

ELLEN: You know, the media mostly focused on the men in camo gear and ski masks holding guns, because they weren't permitted to go past the main road barricades and they weren't allowed into the community. So they focused on the guns and on criminalizing the community instead of paying attention to the real culprits: the federal, provincial, and municipal governments and the original land thieves, the Seminary of St. Sulpice.

Unfortunately, the media's portrayal of the Mohawk Crisis, along with their lack of knowledge of Canada's colonial laws and history, gave people a really skewed idea of what was happening on a day-to-day basis. But you have to remember, the SQ also accused the Mohawks of killing Corporal Marcel Lemay, without any evidence, rather than admit any guilt of their own. So they were arresting every single Kanien'kehá:ka man and torturing many of the men they had in their custody. Fear and intimidation were how they felt they could control the situation.

That's the reason why it was necessary for the men's faces to remain covered, to protect the families of the men who weren't from Kanehsatà:ke and those who weren't from the community. Things have to be put into context at this point. We have to remember what had happened in Kanién:ke (in New York State) and the issue of casinos in Ahkwesásne in 1989–90: There seemed to be a civil war amongst the Kanien'kehá:ka communities then, between people who were called "Antis vs. Warriors." It wasn't an easy period in our history, and the media, government, and our own people exploited that fact. We couldn't trust anyone and so masks were part of the security for the men on the frontlines, so the masks are totally justified. We remained vulnerable to that aspect of reality, the inability to trust. We're thankful to the men who protected us, and I know that they risked their lives for the people. They are heroes for their strength to be on the frontlines.

In our local meetings before the raid, we asked other Kanien'kehá:ka citizens to help us, and to view the Kanehsatà:ke barricade as a Nation issue, not just a community issue. However, there was a division between some local community members who disagreed with the act of erecting a barricade, and they did their best to discourage the people at the barricade through harassment.

The media manipulated the optics. Instead of focusing on why our action was necessary, they framed it as a criminal issue, about "breaking the rule of law" (colonial law). Many journalists ignored the root causes of our land dispossession and consequently distracted from the colonial paternalism of the Canadian government who did not act in good faith before or after the raid of July 11, 1990.

It was the first kind of contemporary "Indigenous resistance" to get mass attention in Canadian society, aside from incidents like the raid that happened at the Restigouche Reserve by the Quebec Provincial Police in 1981. All of these acts of resistance are connected, and the root causes remain the same: racist doctrines of superiority, like the Doctrine of Discovery; and systemic racism causing Indigenous Peoples' land dispossession. Tensions had been building up on reserves for quite a few decades, and I think people can be pushed only so far.

But 1990 was explosive and sensational during a time when major media outlets were evolving with new technology as they began using satellite dishes for in situ reporting.

Sensationalizing the images of masked men with weapons, the media ignored the reality of why Mohawk men were forced to pick up weapons to protect the land and her peoples in the first place. Many journalists had this dismissive attitude, like they couldn't believe "the audacity" of the Mohawks for defending their lives and their land. Most of the journalists were not informed about Canada's colonial history. European journalists, on the other hand, did their research and asked pertinent questions about the Siege. But not knowing Canada's history and attack upon Indigenous Peoples, this is part of the residual racism of Canada's colonizing attitude towards Indigenous Peoples generally, that we should just accept colonization quietly. As if we should be happy for the crumbs the colonizers left us. People need to understand that while Indigenous Nations survived Canada's genocidal efforts, the fight to protect our sovereignty remains because colonialism is ongoing.

The media also chose to focus on images of warriors for their nightly newscasts, inciting fear and hatred in a society that hasn't told the truth about the genocidal acts against Indigenous Peoples. And so, it was easy to justify the use of force by government authorities and to demand that "normalcy" would return to relieve inconvenienced motorists. The Premier of Quebec at the time, the late Robert Bourassa, kept saying things like "everyone must follow the rule of law," referring to the image of a masked warrior with a gun. This functioned like propaganda, further framing us Mohawks as the threat instead of acknowledging the role of colonizers and their police and military forces. Colonial governments have a history of exploiting existing fears and racist attitudes to justify their use of force, and eventually to bring in the military to crack down on Indigenous resistance efforts and protect the colonial status quo.

That focus on the men, then, was deceiving because the women were really the leaders of the movement. Many of the men understood our Traditional Laws and supported the women's role in protecting the land. The women helped the men stay calm during the times when the SQ and army were taunting them, especially at night. The men listened to the women, and it was an amazing thing to witness a kind of revival of a traditional form of governance.

Under Kaianera'kó:wa, women are title holders to the land, in charge of protecting the land, and the men understood that. The "macho man" narrative that the media tried to foster was an imposed narrative, it was in essence trying to justify the use of force against Indigenous people who have resisted colonial law and authority for many generations. But the gender imbalance, a perspective promoted by the media, also overshadowed the important role that women played in defending the land, in our resistance. It was a very strong role, it's important that people understand that.

Our day-to-day was mostly just meetings on negotiating the dismantling of the barricades, with the focus on safety for all Kanien'kehá:ka people, especially for those who wanted to return home to their communities like Ahkwesásne and Kahnawà:ke. Back then I was getting three hours of sleep per night. I was being bombarded with questions from the community about when and how things were going to end. There was a lot to consider and deal with on a daily basis. Aside from trying to survive the day, we were dealing with fear within the community as well. There were non-community members coming into the community, partying with community members who had no clue how dangerous things were. And there were some Mohawks trashing the homes of Québécois people who evacuated—we were so dejected and demoralized that this was happening. It took away the righteousness of what we were doing.

It was a steep learning curve not just for me but for everyone. We learned on the fly, we did the best we could to support each other and try to make sure that no one got hurt. But there's only so much that could be done given all the challenges of a community under siege by government authorities.

I did media interviews and scrums (press conferences) in the evening or early in the morning, but the rest of the day involved meetings to find a way to resolve this siege peacefully. At the police barricades every single Mohawk man who tried to leave the community for necessities, like groceries, was arrested and many were beaten by police as a misguided retribution for Corporal Marcel Lemay's death.

There was a lot of tension and fear in the community because of that, and I was the spokesperson, so anytime something happened I would try to reach out to the SQ liaison. I was also in contact with John Ciaccia, Quebec's Minister of Indian Affairs. We had to let the outside world know that the SQ was provoking us, especially at night. They were trying to create an incident with a violent outcome, and we had to be vigilant that everyone remained calm.

They were arresting Mohawk people, especially the men, for no reason at all. They were beating and torturing our people and no one in government could control the SQ. Minister Ciaccia was aware early on that the SQ were uncontrollable, that they had taken the law into their own hands and didn't care what the government told them to do. They were acting outside of the rule of law, but they didn't care. They were focused on getting revenge for something the Mohawk People weren't responsible for. They wanted to make an example out of someone and targeting Kanien'kehá:ka men was their strategy. It was a scary thing to realize that the police were out of control and that any moment they could start another attack on us. There's a macho, racist culture within most police forces, and it's unnerving when you're vulnerable, outgunned, and have enormous odds against you. That made things worse. The SQ had a score to settle even though there was no evidence to support their claim.

They were denying us our fundamental human rights by preventing food and medicine from being delivered and blocking the free passage of our family and community members—humiliating those who wanted to go to work or purchase food outside the community. They made it impossible to leave and go home. For example, the SQ would make community members wait in the sun for hours at checkpoints, forcing chemotherapy patients to also stand in the hot sun for hours; intimidating people, causing food to rot, and they confiscated people's belongings, all at gunpoint. When the army came, it wasn't much different.

SEAN: Can you tell me more about your dealings with John Ciaccia? He spent time working with the Department of Indian Affairs before becoming the Minister of Indian Affairs for the Quebec government. He passed away recently, but in the twenty years after that summer he gave quite a few interviews that were critical of the SQ, the Quebec government, and the Canadian Army.[1] Did you feel like a negotiated settlement was possible, having the ear of someone like Ciaccia?

ELLEN: John Ciaccia was a very kind person, it's true. He was the only person that actually reached out his hand to us when things got really tense. I found him to be approachable and very compassionate, despite the fact that he was the provincial government's Minister of Indian Affairs. He brought in food for us at one point, which was greatly appreciated.

I think in some ways it was a big learning curve for him as well, even though he had lots of experience in negotiating with Indigenous Peoples, like with the James Bay and Northern Quebec Agreement (1975). He was with the Chrétien government for quite a long time, and he was a career politician. But it was exceptional for a government representative to show compassion and good faith the way he did. I got to know him years after the barricades came down,

Blockade shack, March 1990.

Leaving the scene of police fire, July 11, 1990.

July 12, 1990, the first day of negotiation: heading to a press scrum with Indian Affairs Minister for Quebec, the late John Ciaccia.

Signing the pre-conditions for negotiating in the Pines of Kanehsatà:ke.

Early August, negotiating team with the late William Kunstler, famous lawyer for the AIM.

Indigenous delegation presenting to the European Parliament, November 1990.

The Siege of Kanehsatà:ke, 1991.
Acrylic on Canvas, 4 × 6 ft.

and we had many honest discussions about what happened and what could've been done differently that summer. There was an understanding between him and me, of always trying to maintain the peace.

He was a peacemaker and I wanted to uphold The Great Law of Peace. That was my key focus after July 11. I didn't want anyone else to get hurt or be killed. But, as well, I wanted to protect our land from the development. It was difficult to remain focused on the original reason for the barricade and remind everyone of why we were in the situation we found ourselves in.

John Ciaccia was sincere and genuine in his offer of help and wanting peace to prevail too, but he was alone amongst his cabinet members—as opposed to Premier Robert Bourassa, who, from the beginning, wanted to call in the Canadian Army. When John Ciaccia passed away in 2018, I was one of three people to give a eulogy at his funeral. I felt very honoured to have been asked to speak and tell how much I had admired and respected him as a human being.

SEAN: John Ciaccia often talked about the pressure of that summer, of disagreeing with what was happening, the impacts on his own health and view of Quebec and Canada. Do you empathize with his position?

ELLEN: Well, he was still representing the Government of Quebec, but he agreed that what was happening was wrong and tried to help by using his power as a minister over the situation. That is really important to remember in the history of this event. He genuinely tried to help but was pushed aside and betrayed by members of the Quebec government. I know that hurt him deeply, as he thought that finding a peaceful resolution was in everyone's best interest. Unfortunately, Premier Bourassa and members of his cabinet thought otherwise.

At John Ciaccia's funeral his wife talked about how she remembered me calling and waking them up at three in the morning one night that summer. The SQ were shooting at night trying to provoke an incident, so I would have to call to tell him what was going on. I'm sure he didn't get much sleep either, but he always took my calls. I don't think his wife realized how urgent our situation was, or knew about our agreement to call when a crisis popped up. He was always gracious and never angry no matter what time I called him. He understood that the SQ were out of control and lives were at stake.

I was also a liaison between the community and the SQ for the first few weeks of the Mohawk Crisis, so I spoke to him daily. Eventually I gave up that position because the SQ became more aggressive and belligerent. It was very stressful, it felt like we were at war—which essentially it was a war, I mean this was Canada, right?! We never expected this to happen to us in such a brutal way. Mr. Ciaccia understood that, and since no one could control the SQ, he knew that evenings were worse for us. But his hands were tied by his cabinet.

Life behind the barricades was hard and the situation was getting more and more complicated as time passed. Prime Minister Brian Mulroney would say outrageous statements, like it was Canada who was "under attack" and so they wouldn't negotiate with "a gun to their heads." In reality, we were outgunned, we didn't have the kind of resources Quebec and Canada had. But some people in government and in the public wanted to see a massacre so they could open the Mercier Bridge and things would go back to "normal," at the expense of the lives of the communities of Kanehsatà:ke and Kahnawà:ke. It was maddening.

As the summer dragged on, there was always this looming sense of a major attack. I wasn't really sure if any of us were going to be able to leave, especially for the men on the frontlines. The issue of criminalization was always in our face, we felt it from the government, and it was presented that way in the media, and so we had to stick together to show that this wasn't a group who had taken over the community. The Kanehsatà:ke and Kahnawà:ke Siege was a continuation of long-standing historical land disputes caused by colonial laws, by racist laws, to dispossess Indigenous Peoples of their lands.

As the situation evolved, it felt like our only options were going to be either death or jail. That's how it felt at times, honestly. Especially since negotiations were not advancing and the government did not negotiate in good faith. I tried not to think about that too much. My focus was on the land, the safety of the people, and carrying out my role with honour. It was for our ancestors who had fought so hard against the evil of the Seminary of St. Sulpice and their brutality to remove us from Kanehsatà:ke.

I was fortunate to have two really exceptional Elders, Thelma and Walter David Sr., who took me under their wings and comforted me during this time. They shared their

Ellen with the late Walter David Sr.

knowledge, and they encouraged me as I struggled with what to do. I'm very grateful for their guidance, teachings, and support. They really helped me get through that difficult summer and to be able to process it afterwards.

SEAN: How did you feel when the SQ was withdrawn, after they lost control of the situation, and the federal government called in the Canadian Army to Kanehsatà:ke?

ELLEN: To be clear, the SQ never left. They simply moved their barricades back a bit, while the Canadian Army supposedly replaced them—only that wasn't what happened. Later, we were to find that they created new barricades with tanks and attempted to provoke an incident throughout the day and at night. Their advance into our community was really intimidating for many. For others, we became more determined to resist.

The SQ remained throughout the summer, in fact they're still here. They were very scary, unrestrained, and acted as if they were above the law. No level of government could control them, that was the problem. But I think it was convenient for Quebec to allow the SQ to be out of control. They could claim that this was strictly a police operation, just as the Canadian Army did—they told me that this was a military operation, and their attitude was we were the enemy and needed to be punished. It's scary to see this and know that they had the power to destroy us, to kill us!

Like the SQ, the army were trying to provoke us every night as well, to worsen the conflict; they tortured people, spoiled people's food, and detained people for hours in the hot sun. The whole premise of the army coming in was the acknowledgement by Quebec, as told to us by Minister Ciaccia, that the government had no control over the SQ. And so, it was announced that the army would replace them before something more serious happened. It was also a way for the Quebec government to wipe their hands clean and say, "this is a military operation now, it's out of our hands." It was just a ploy to try to deceive the public, promising that the army would be more reasonable. But they were just as bad, and they hid behind their weapons and tanks. That's not a fair fight. In fact, the Canadian Army was waiting to step in since the beginning.

The Canadian government wasn't much better. In the end, Bourassa's desire to bring in the army was fulfilled. He was always for the use of force over diplomacy from the start anyway. Prime Minister Brian Mulroney added to the dysfunction when he refused to recall Parliament back to session in the summer, to debate how Canada should respond, even though the opposing parties were demanding that Parliament be resumed to resolve the situation peacefully. It was easier for the government to simply use the police and the military as muscle—to do their dirty work, criminalizing us publicly, instead of taking responsibility for creating the situation. It was far easier to capitalize on the stereotypes that depict Indigenous people as inferior and violent.

John Ciaccia was an exception. He never gave up on trying to find a peaceful resolution, while all the other government officials were calling for the continued use of force and dragging out the standoff to make an example of us, discouraging other Indigenous people from standing up for themselves and protecting their lands. Canada knew it could, at any time, order another attack if they created a situation where force was justified. Canada and its political leaders wanted to emphasize that the outcome was really up to them, not us. They needed to show that they were in charge. The government wanted to, once again, get rid of the "Indian problem," to put us, and all Indigenous Peoples, in our place and keep us down.

SEAN: Okay, what about Tom Siddon, the federal government's Minister for Indian Affairs? He had just been reshuffled in Mulroney's cabinet from the Fisheries and Oceans to Indian Affairs portfolio that spring. It seems like he didn't really understand the situation or have a mandate to actually resolve the land issue. How do you understand Siddon's role in what happened?

ELLEN: Tom Siddon was cold and unfeeling to me, like he was putting on a show, but he really didn't want to be there. He viewed us Mohawks as inferior and criminals. During negotiations, we kept trying to bring the discussion back to our land issue, but it was completely forgotten, pushed aside for the dismantling of the Mercier Bridge barricade and for the death of Corporal Marcel Lemay. The July 11 raid transformed everything into a standoff, which became the focus and was used as government propaganda to say that we were the unreasonable ones. For Kanehsatà:ke, the answer was resolving the land issue, but government officials weren't interested in that. Siddon ignored us, he did nothing throughout the summer except to spout propaganda.

Siddon was never officially part of the negotiations, but he was part of the behind-the-scenes rush to resolve it militarily. The federal government sent Bernard Roy to be their negotiator, but he never had a mandate to negotiate or resolve anything about the historical land issues. The only negotiator that actually had a mandate was Alex Paterson. His focus was on dismantling the barricade on the Mercier Bridge, which was a key point in negotiations. The government knew that in order to weaken our position here in Kanehsatà:ke, they had to get rid of the Mercier Bridge barricade. This barricade was the only thing that prevented a second attack by the SQ, put a pause on the Canadian Army from moving in, and prevented a massacre in Kanehsatà:ke.

The whole goal for the government had always been to ensure that their feigned concern for the inconvenienced motorists' needs were prioritized. From the settler state's perspective, this would clear the way for a successful "end" to the Mohawk Crisis. The government's goal was to save face, look strong, and make sure that no Mohawks nor our allies would be seen as legitimate and reasonable. Given the amount of solidarity protests across Canada, I don't think they succeeded at that.

To hide their culpability in the root cause of the problem, government officials were focused solely on ending the stand-off and the Mercier Bridge blockade, citing the inconvenience for motorists without making any concessions concerning our land. They had no interest in resolving our land issue, which was at the heart of things. There was a lot riding on the economic interests of investors of the golf course and condo development. But that all got lost and was likely the government's strategy to continue their divide and conquer tactics.

Some people thought a peaceful disengagement required the issue of amnesty, but we didn't think amnesty was appropriate because we had done nothing wrong. Government wanted us to give up our weapons without any guarantee for our safety or freedom from prosecution, but we felt we were perfectly within our right as a Sovereign Nation to defend our land and our people.

The army wasn't better, and they were even harder to deal with, as they had tons of human resources, weapons, and tank guns pointed at us. There were also Canadian ships surrounding both Kahnawà:ke and Kanehsatà:ke. The army restricted media access at many times to try to win the public relations battle. They tried hard to make the Mohawk People seem guilty in the court of public opinion. The death of Corporal Marcel Lemay early on was used strategically to justify the increased SQ presence and condone the torture and beatings of Mohawk men and women. But this propaganda, promoted by the army and SQ, sent a message to the public that our lives are disposable and we deserved the impending violence, should they decide. Our lives were in their hands, so what else were we supposed to do?

John Ciaccia suggested that the army could do a better job than the SQ. He hoped the army would help calm everything down and create a path for peace. We were somewhat hopeful that that could happen, and hopeful the army would live up to their reputation as "peacekeepers." We assumed wrong, that simply wasn't the case. The soldiers were just as brutal as the SQ, guilty of numerous human rights violations. The Canadian Army continued the psychological warfare started by the SQ, using intimidation and provocation. It was hard for people to wrap their heads around that.

Amongst us there were army veterans of both the Canadian and American regiments, some recent, some from older wars. I remember being moved and concerned by some of the older veterans who were disgusted with the behaviour of Canada. Some of them wrote letters to the government in protest of the use of the Canadian Army against the Mohawk people. Their behaviour was to intimidate the Mohawk people and to send a message to Indigenous people across the country that Canada is willing to exert its violent colonial power and control. Like, all of this for a golf course and condos? It was ridiculous, unbelievable. But solidarity came from people from all walks of life actually.

Combined with the letters from veterans, the protests we saw on TV lifted our spirits up as, at first, we felt very alone. We didn't have control over what would happen next, but seeing protests in solidarity across Canada gave us some hope. There were Québécois sovereigntists, union leaders, Jews, Palestinians, and other Indigenous Peoples in our support, and it really lifted our spirits up to know that the citizens of Canada did not condone this absurd situation.

SEAN: Yes, that's the power of solidarity. So, the arrival of the army brought little change, as the resistance dragged on into August and September?

ELLEN: The army made things worse, in a way. All of a sudden, we were surrounded by two thousand troops—which was more than Canada sent at any one time to Kuwait during the Gulf War (beginning the last few weeks of the Siege). The army occupied our small community and were present in Kahnawà:ke as well, with all of their personnel, heavy-duty equipment, and weapons. It felt like an invasion. A number of international human rights observers witnessed the way the army was treating our people. The International Federation of Human Rights, based in Paris, France, documented thousands of human rights abuses. We were all relieved that there were witnesses to what was or could happen. There were also members of faith-based entities who volunteered to be witnesses as well. So, people understood that this was a human rights issue and shouldn't be considered a criminal or military operation.

The army, like the SQ, tortured several men who they arrested, seemingly for no reason other than being Mohawk. We were outgunned and outnumbered, which Prime Minister Brian Mulroney knew full well. The intimidation tactics and psychological warfare used belied the many inflammatory statements by politicians and some of the media outlets claiming we were the violent ones. With their armoured vehicles and tanks with cannons, they aimed their weapons at us constantly, as a reminder of their might and power. It was a show of force, for sure. They put razor wire all around the community at every hundred metres to try to hem us in and restrict our mobility. When the Canadian Army moved into Kanehsatà:ke in August, the community tried to block them, but with no success. I tried to block one of them from installing their blockade on our land and was met with a lewd gesture, which I though was just juvenile and rude.

When I alerted some of the journalists there, they had been turned away watching the tanks moving slowly towards us. In Kanehsatà:ke, we had the Royal 22nd Regiment (an infantry regiment of the Canadian Army commonly called the Van Doos), based in Loretteville near Quebec City, who were on the frontline, and they were arrogant. They did not hide their contempt for us. They vandalized and stole from the homes they occupied here. Once they moved in on September 1, 1990, there was no protection for community members anywhere. So, no, there was little change when the Canadian Army arrived. It was just more government authorities who outnumbered the Mohawk communities to provoke fear and intimidation. To make people within the community want to leave, they coerced them with money, which meant there would be few people left by the time the military operation was in full swing.

They were just as abusive as the SQ were, it was more of the same from the Canadian soldiers. We were all very disappointed that the army was just as bad as the SQ behaved, and this caused more fear in our communities. We also found out that there were CIA and FBI agents up here because some of the guys were from Ahkwesásne (and some had fought in Vietnam). It was a big operation to undermine our safety and to discredit us, causing an escalation in fear and intimidation pretty quickly. We were surrounded and outgunned but we were "winning the PR war," as a member of the Quebec government stated later. Good-minded people could see that this wasn't a situation that came out of the blue, but that ongoing colonialism was the root cause. So, the demonstrations across Canada boosted our morale.

SEAN: Do you think the federal government was using the siege of Kanehsatà:ke and Kahnawà:ke, the 1990 Mohawk Crisis, as a way of looking strong to Canadians? Mulroney and his Progressive Conservatives were down in the polls, and because of Elijah Harper's blocking of the Meech Lake Accord, perhaps Canada wanted to make an example out of Indigenous leaders and Land Defenders, to deter further actions?

ELLEN: I think that was true. As the army expanded operations in September, we started winning what Mulroney and Ciaccia called the "public relations battle." There was a changing tide, I think. We could feel it from our interactions with the media. There were growing solidarity actions across Canada, especially here in Quebec, like blockades and protest marches—by Indigenous and non-Indigenous people—and all that started to shift the strength of our resistance.

Canada was being shamed for their actions on the international stage, through the work of Kenneth Deer who is part of the Haudenosaunee external relations committee. Kenneth Deer was at the UN in Geneva telling the global community about Canada's actions to deny us of our fundamental human rights. It was a blemish on Canada's reputation of being a defender of human rights.

A peacekeeping nation and defenders of human rights don't use their army domestically, right? Especially not to support the expansion of a golf course and luxury condos. We were fortunate that our request for international observers was granted, and they documented thousands of human rights abuses cases by the SQ and the Canadian Army. An international human rights body witnessing the negotiations confirmed that the government was wrong in its actions. I think it all started to become a bit of an embarrassment for Canada and Quebec, but the international observers (in their final press conference in August 1990) witnessed the negotiations and saw the farce it was as it became apparent that things were ending in a stalemate. The International Federation of Human Rights stated that Canada did not negotiate in good faith.

On September 26, 1990, when the people walked out of the Treatment Centre, they stated that it wasn't a surrender but simply a decision to return to their homes, despite knowing the strong possibility that they would get arrested. The Canadian Army's heavy-handed approach made the optics look even worse, as the media witnessed the brutalization of the people—men, women, and children—who just wanted to go home, to their families.

I think it caught the army off guard with that strategy, of refusing to acknowledge their authority. And in the chaos of trying to apprehend the people as they left, they stabbed a young girl—Waneek Horn-Miller—in the chest with a bayonet. The famous picture that was snapped from that day, of Waneek crying out after being stabbed by a soldier while trying to protect her four-year-old sister, Kaniehtiio, changed the narrative further.

Canadians were appalled at what they were seeing on their TVs and reading in their newspapers. They maybe didn't understand what we were doing or why we were standing up, but they did not like seeing the army being used as thugs. It was a conflict of conscience for a lot of Canadians, as it should have been. Canadians started to see their country in a different light, they started to see how it treats Indigenous people, that is, as an aggressive bully, an oppressor. They sent in the army! What did they think was going to happen? We received a lot of mail from people across the country who were angered by the violence happening—all for a nine-hole golf course expansion.

Those 78 days changed the way I saw Canada, too. It was a steep learning curve for me that summer. Being an introvert and then speaking for my community was an extreme shift for me personally. But I had support and that made all the difference.

The resistance brought a lot of people together, it woke people up. It motivated a lot of Canadians to pay attention to Indigenous issues and learn more about what was happening and what needed to change in Canada. There were some positive shifts, for sure. It was also a moment that brought a lot of Indigenous people together in solidarity. That was really heartening and important for us. We could see a future in which we, as Indigenous Peoples, were no longer invisible. That summer taught us about how to stand up for the land, for our Nations, for our survival.

I don't regret our actions at all. We were defending ourselves, our Homelands, our sacred pine forest. I'm very sad that a police officer was killed for the greed of a few and the refusal by the Municipality of Oka to halt their project. As well, the federal government did not negotiate in good faith even before July 11. But we have always believed he was shot by friendly fire.

I was disappointed that our three-hundred-year struggle for the land was lost and criminalized due to the chaos of government propaganda, with the sensational photos and images of men with weapons. The story became about "warriors" in camo gear, bridges being blocked, and inconvenienced motorists annoyed by our actions, when it really should've been all about our land struggle and the root causes as to why things had escalated to this point. It should have been about why two Kanien'kehá:ka communities were meant to suffer because the government used a racist doctrine to justify the persistent land dispossession of Indigenous Peoples—along with the blue bloods from France, the Seminary of St. Sulpice.

The story should have been about the land and our people, the multigenerational cry for justice, and the centuries of resistance and the resilience of our community. The root was—and continues to be—the settler colonial project that continues to undermine the rights of Indigenous Peoples in Canada to this day.

The resistance may have changed Canada's relationship with Indigenous Peoples. But today, Kanehsatà:ke still struggles against land dispossession, and we have lost more land since then, so there is no end to this story. While there were many ripple effects and ways that our struggle informed other struggles, we still have a long way to go before there is any resolution to the long-standing historical land issues in Canada.

One of the major impacts of 1990 includes the Royal Commission on Aboriginal Peoples (RCAP), which was a direct result of the Mohawk Resistance, for example. For me, though, the legacy of that summer is that Indigenous people are finally awake, we're still resisting the colonial project, and we are reclaiming the narrative being told about us. We are visible and we are not accepting the lies and violations of our human rights.

We still don't have a resolution for our land and so the struggle continues. Our land is sacred, and under our own laws and Constitution of Kaianera'kó:wa, we're obliged to defend our lands. We must defend it for the faces not yet born, those future generations to benefit from the work we do today. I hope our efforts of resistance inspire new generations who can learn from our experience in our community and in other Onkwehón:we communities, to defend their lands and territories against corrupt companies and governments, including band councils and municipalities. For us, as Indigenous people, it's part of our survival, a multigenerational resistance against oppression.

First Spiritual Gathering, one-year anniversary of July 11, 1990, with
Kelly White, the late Milton Born with a Tooth, Danny Billy,
the late Thelma David.

Summer of 1990, at the front gate.

4

ECHOES

SEAN: Let's turn now to the legacy of the summer of 1990. For the twentieth anniversary, Leanne Betasamosake Simpson and Kiera L. Ladner published an edited collection of writings that speak to the enduring legacy of the blockades.[1] In thinking about the influence of the Mohawk Resistance that summer, Anishinaabe scholar Damien Lee writes,

> the Onkwehonwe mobilization at Kanehsatà:ke in 1990 is echoing through time and space as Dibaajimowinan [or teachings roughly translated into English as echoes]. These echoes link the past with the present with the future because they resonate through our landscapes and within the implicate order, uniting us in a common resistance, in a common world.[2]

Lee also states: "We learned at Kanehsatà:ke about our oppressor and about our vitality as Onkwehonwe. . . . These echoes inform us how to live our lives and to address challenges without losing our identity."[3] With these words in mind, what do you see as the main lessons, or echoes, from that summer?

I think a lot of people see the Kanehsatà:ke and Kahnawà:ke Resistance as an inspiration, as a resistance movement to hold up and celebrate. You also mentioned, though, that you see the legacy of that summer as more of a mixed one. Can you explain why?

ELLEN: Yes, some people say it was a victory, and in many ways it was. The proposed golf course and condominium development was halted, the golf course and parking lot over our ancestral burial ground in the sacred Pines didn't go ahead as planned.

For that, I'm truly grateful, and for all the brave people from other Kanien'kehá:ka communities and our allies, for uniting to protect our ancestors' resting place. They protected the people, stood up against the bullies, and exposed Canada and Quebec for their collusion to defraud the people of Kanehsatà:ke of our Homelands. Because of this kind of solidarity, we were a formidable force against the corrupt governments and their authorities.

But what most people don't realize is that our land struggle became lost in the narrative of the 1990 Mohawk Siege. It became a military operation to cover up the ways in which all levels of government (municipal, provincial, and federal) colluded to commit land fraud. The root issue—getting our land back—was overshadowed by images of Mohawk men with masks and weapons facing off against a barrage of Canadian Army personnel. They forgot about the role the women played in keeping people safe and in the decision-making process.

I mean, officially, the Mohawk Crisis ended on September 26, 1990, but the Canadian Army didn't leave right away. We were still under their occupation for many weeks later. While the federal government promised to resolve the land issue after the barricades came down (through a statement by federal negotiator Bernard Roy), we have yet to resolve the issue of our land dispossession. Canada claimed it bought our cemetery for one dollar from the Municipality of Oka. Under the Indian Act, the pine forest we fought to protect is there for our use and benefit. It's so frustrating because we're treated as wards of the state, because this is the status quo and part of systemic racism.

Once the cameras left and our allies went home, the public assumed everything was resolved, but it wasn't. The government didn't deliver on their promises of negotiating with the Rotinonhseshá:ka of Kanehsatà:ke. We went from the Siege, to remaining occupied by the SQ and army. Then there were the trials of community members and our allies for standing with us to protect the people and lands. We experienced increased harassment by the SQ and the invasion of our privacy by the authorities, like CSIS[4] who labelled us as terrorists. So, it did not end after 78 days. In fact, the two Kanien'kehá:ka communities of Kanehsatà:ke and Kahnawà:ke didn't have peace from the harassment for years after. Today, we are still struggling with the same issues: our long-standing historical land dispute.

Personally, I feel that the legacy of 1990 is mixed, largely with sadness, because of how things are in the community today, with lawlessness, colonial-rooted social and economic problems, and the fact that rather than resolving our land issues, the "rights" of local municipalities persist in trumping Onkwehón:we rights to self-determination. However, during the Siege, Canadian society took notice and started learning more about what has been happening to Indigenous people since the creation of the Indian Act.

I think it helped to create a more informed view of Indigenous Peoples. But not for the community of Kanehsatà:ke, with all the turmoil within, ongoing systemic racism, and the chaos that now exists in the community— with government turning their backs on the community. I feel as if we're being punished for tarnishing Canada's international reputation. Our land dispute has never been resolved, with more colonial laws being imposed if we want land back. There is more development stealing our lands, and even in the community schools this major historical event isn't taught. There are extreme trauma reactions whereby the land is abused, divisions between community members distract from the ongoing land issues, and people are racing on our roads and behaving in ways that threaten our peace and security as a community. I no longer recognize the community I grew up in.

Nevertheless, our resistance in 1990 had a number of important ripple effects. It's important that the narrative be reclaimed by those of us who stood up for the land—not historians and not government and not certain media outlets who perpetuate the propaganda and create new stereotypes.

The 1990 Siege changed the trajectory of Indigenous Peoples' resistance in that all the history, the acts of resistance, motivated people to become more aware of the insidiousness of colonization. Starting with the 1990 Standing Committee on the "Oka Crisis," we recommended that the government create an RCAP in response to that summer. The commission's work and report (1996) brought to light a lot of the abuse and the impact of Indian Residential Schools, its legacies, and all that led to the important work of the Truth and Reconciliation Commission (TRC) in 2015 and the National Inquiry into Missing and Murdered Indigenous Women, Girls, and Two Spirited People (MMIWG) in 2019.

During the immediate aftermath of 1990, we thought that things would change. When the RCAP was announced we were happy because there seemed to be some hope for change. But an individual from our community who was working on the RCAP was also working with the police as an informant in 1990 and betrayed us. The RCAP was supposed to come to Kanehsatà:ke, but, last minute, they changed it to Montreal instead, stating that there were warriors who were threatening this individual or something. This was a lie. I believe it was more his shame that caused him to feel threatened. And so, the commissioners actually never came to our community to talk about our issues, which is unfortunate. I think it would have benefited the commissioners to understand our experience of the events, like that the original barricade was on a secondary dirt road, not a highway.

When the commission delivered its report, I was still optimistic. We had hoped that it would bring about significant changes to the way the federal government deals with Indigenous people and land issues specifically. But it didn't. RCAP was a blueprint for massive change, but it has been ignored for the most part; placed upon a shelf to gather dust like all the other consequent reports. Canada's colonial project continues on its violent path.

It's disturbing that the government drags its feet to implement any recommendations from the TRC or the Final Report on Missing and Murdered Indigenous Women, Girls, and Two Spirited People (2019). Indigenous people use these reports to help in our advocacy, but we face challenges with government bureaucrats and political agendas that block progress, all due to concerns about how much justice for our peoples costs. Their key recommendations to change our relationship with Canada are essentially ignored. While there has been some attention to the recommendations of the TRC, it's mostly Indigenous people who are the ones bringing up these recommendations and demanding change. Canada knows what needs to be done: return our land and honour its international human rights obligations. It must stop its ongoing land dispossession.

While Canada passed legislation to implement the United Nations Declaration on the Rights of Indigenous Peoples (UNDRIP) in June 2022, Canadian and provincial laws remain rooted in these racist doctrines to continue land dispossession and occupation.

There were a lot of changes for other Indigenous people after 1990, but for us things became worse in every aspect of our lives. While the resistance brought people together and made them more aware of the issues, it also created new stereotypes, building on the historical image of the "violent Indian." We're still feeling the repercussions of the event, both positively and negatively, in our community. But, for the rest of Canada, it made people more aware of the history and the realities faced by Indigenous Peoples. While on the surface it appears that society is more aware of Indigenous resistance movements, there remain many challenges to educate the public servants and the public in general. It seems like things changed in our relationship with Canada, but in reality, it has increased pressure on Indigenous people to accept a repackaging of colonialism.

There are moderates amongst us who benefit from the work of frontline activists, and who side with corporate agendas for resource development. This causes increasing divisions, but it's always the moderates who government sides with.

The 1990 Kanehsatà:ke and Kahnawà:ke Resistance demonstrated that Indigenous Peoples couldn't be pushed aside or silenced anymore. We must be taken seriously, as it's not only a matter of justice and respect for our human rights, but it's a matter of protecting the land and water for present and future generations.

Our stand in 1990 became a seminal moment in centuries of Indigenous resistance. It happened during a moment in time when society didn't give us a second thought—thinking that we were conquered, that we were dependent upon government to tell us what to think. But we have always resisted, not just today, throughout history. I think our ancestors would be proud. But I also wonder, how much has really changed?

As a Kanien'kehá:ka person, I'm very aware of our history, our experiences as Onkwehón:we Peoples, and of how the impacts of colonization controlled our families' lives and how it influences the reality of the community's existence.

It's the multigenerational trauma of being an Onkwehón:we person in a society whose foundations are genocidal.

SEAN: I mean, as a historian I see these big flashpoint moments, whether it's the 1990 Siege or Idle No More (2013), and there is that catalyst for change, the promise of change, but then very quickly the colonial status quo snaps back and reasserts itself through government inaction and Canadian indifference.

ELLEN: Yes, it's very frustrating. I see that happen again and again; however, the struggle for justice requires patience, education, and compassion. The fight is long-term, and people need to understand that. It requires commitment and discipline.

For example, I see what is happening in the United States, with the murder of George Floyd, and Black Lives Matter, and the outburst of frustration that led to protests during a time when the COVID-19 pandemic was in its early stages, and I can relate to the anger. It took a lot of courage to take a risk and express indignation and disgust with George Floyd's murder, to expose, dramatically, the impacts of systemic racism that permeates society. I also know how difficult it can be to suppress your anger in the face of injustice, to get people to listen, because one's anger can be used against you to make things even worse. I don't agree with violence for the sake of violence. Society must be educated and made aware that the violence against Black people, Indigenous Peoples, and people of colour has always been initiated by the state and its authorities. People must learn how to effectively protest against corrupt powers of government and corporations whose economic agenda affects us all.

When Kanien'kehá:ka people talk about Kaianera'kó:wa, there are three aspects or principles of our Constitution: respect, strength or courage, and love and compassion. When combined, these three elements bring peace. That means a person must do things in a dignified way in spite of what the enemy is doing or throwing at you. It doesn't mean we're perfect but that we must always strive to uphold these principals. Given the challenges we have faced from the colonial machine, there will be frustration, there will be anger. As human beings we are not perfect. But for Onkwehón:we people, there is an urgency for some sort of justice, something which has eluded Indigenous Peoples in general.

You always have to find ways to channel that frustration into knowing what your rights are and what your goals are. Indigenous Peoples have experienced multigenerational trauma and continue to live under oppressive, paternalistic systems of governance. We're dealing with the continued effects of the Indian Residential School system and other genocidal projects.

From the moment we're born, we're taught how to be "good little Indians" through the educational system. We're expected to remain peaceful, and we do, but when police do the dirty work of government politicians, they often initiate the violence, then we're forced to defend ourselves. Yet we are the ones considered "violent." Government propaganda continues to criminalize us. This puts a lot of pressure on Indigenous people to be patient, to be peaceful during our protests in order for our voices to be heard. And if we don't, the government might send in the police, the RCMP, or the army to intimidate us like they did in 1990.

Our resistance has been used as an example to discourage Indigenous people from sticking up for their Homelands. To control the narrative, settler governments and corporations denounce us as either violent or irrelevant and illegitimate, measuring us against what is considered the acceptable image of "progress." The government knows that our grievances are legitimate. But the government is well resourced, both financially and with human resources. So, Canada can afford to play the long game. That is the nature of colonial oppression. They drag out issues and they use stall tactics, divide and conquer, hoping that they will wear us down because most communities cannot afford to take Canada or corporations to court. At least that's their strategy, hoping that Canadians won't get involved and side with us. But our allies are an important part of helping Indigenous Peoples achieve resolution to our long-standing historical grievances. Solidarity is key.

We have to remember at the end of the day that this is an imperial, racist system that works as it was intended to do. People say the system is broken, and it is—the imposed band council system does not work either. However, the system's not broken from the perspective of the colonial settler government that benefits the most from the chaos it created. It's a racist, patriarchal, corrupt settler colonial system that works for corporations who plunder the earth and get rich by exploiting the gaps within the racist colonial laws that allow and support continued land dispossession and profiteering. It's a racist system that facilitates the ongoing dispossession of Indigenous Peoples from our lands and results in our shrinking land base—which means we lose the ability to be Onkwehón:we, to protect our future.

When we fight back to protect our inherent rights, our human rights to self-determination, we are viewed as being too radical. We know that people here in Kanehsatà:ke and Kahnawà:ke always had this in the back of their minds, how the threat of violence will be carried out, which the settler government has used time and time again. They're keenly aware now, that no one wants a repeat of 1990—I certainly don't—but they use this sentiment to exploit the fear and intimidation that we feel is always around the corner, resulting in people staying silent when they should speak up or protest. The government then relies on that fear, and they use that fear strategically and wield it as a weapon to keep

Indigenous Peoples oppressed and the colonial status quo in place, using our own people to succeed.

The struggle for the land is tethered to these racist settler colonial laws, as it has been for the past five hundred years. Be it the Doctrine of Discovery, originating from the Vatican's Papal Bulls,[5] or the effects of the Indian Act, we aren't able to progress economically. We're dependent upon government funding agreements made with band councils. And these are taken, mind you, from a trust fund created over a century ago for Indigenous Peoples, from the minerals and resources taken from our Homelands, but which we have no control over. Meanwhile settlers all around us make money from developing our Homelands while we suffer and struggle. As we continue to wait for supposed "progress," and respect for our human rights, more land is stolen. That's what colonization is like today, and what it has always been. It's imperialism, capitalism, and Indigenous people stand in the way.

SEAN: Those motives—greed and profit—are core features of settler capitalism that continue to drive development in Canada today. I remember Dene political theorist Glen Sean Coulthard writing a piece around the time of Idle No More where he argues, "For Indigenous nations to live, capitalism must die. And for capitalism to die, we must actively participate in the construction of Indigenous alternatives to it."[6]

ELLEN: Absolutely. Canada, though, isn't willing to change the status quo. It costs too much to decolonize. Canada's foundation remains tethered to racist doctrines of superiority, even though it has many international human rights obligations and domestic law that recognizes, although it does not respect, our rights to self-determination. Even if it passed a law in June 2022 to implement UNDRIP, the status quo continues. Rhetoric in support of reconciliation is cheaper than action, and it enables Canadian officials to placate the

Canadian public. We, as Indigenous Peoples, are outnumbered by the hundreds of employees in Indigenous Affairs, Indigenous Services, and all the different departments in Canada which are part of the Indigenous industry to weaken and deny us our human rights. It's a big bureaucracy we're up against. Indigenous Traditional Laws, including the rights of Mother Earth and all our relations, must be included in the decolonization of Indigenous Peoples' realities.

We, as Indigenous Peoples, are strong because we've had to be, but we remain vulnerable because of ongoing colonization. The uncertainty, threats to our safety, and lack of opportunity that my ancestors experienced continues to this day, because we do not have free access to our traditional Homelands and our land base is shrinking. You know it's hard to defend the land when you start from a disadvantaged position, disadvantages caused by centuries of colonization. Canada is well aware of this. Despite government rhetoric, they don't want us to succeed in practising our traditional governance structures or protecting our languages and cultures. They want us to be perpetually dependent on the colonial government for everything, to spin new and acceptable forms of assimilation. If we're dispossessed and poor, fighting back and resisting is difficult. Our resistance means that they haven't entirely succeeded with their assimilation attempts to erase us from history. However, the nature of colonialism hasn't changed, it's just been repackaged.

It's a challenging situation, because now settler governments are working with assimilated Indigenous people to push forward corporate agendas, to surrender our human rights to self-determination. There is a lot of money involved, so they can coerce Indigenous people to agree to their agenda. There is nothing wrong with people wanting a good life, a better life for their children. But since we cannot practise a way of life that our ancestors did, people in the community, like everyone else, need money to survive. The struggle is so stressful and difficult. So, people accept things the way they are. Complacency and compromises are made because the colonial project has reached a certain level of success, they've worn people down and everyone just wants to survive. There remain many people who are continuing this multigenerational struggle and who have been trying hard to create change; however, many of us are women, and because of the impacts of patriarchal culture, Indigenous women are still not taken seriously.

People in power, mostly men, don't want to hear the voices of women. They tried to silence our voices, dismissing our concerns and experiences. The view that we should deal with "domestic issues," like conjugal violence or murdered and missing Indigenous women, signifies that there remains much work to do within our own communities. But it is changing, although like justice, it is slow. We've been saying that for a long time, and we know the solutions. We, as Nations, need to discuss them together, and there must be good faith and good will to begin the process of decolonization. We have the framework of Kaianera'kó:wa and this can be complemented by UNDRIP. We need to brush the dust from our colonized minds and look at our ancestors' teachings on how to protect our human rights through Traditional Laws, and see how we can implement change together.

History does repeat itself in colonial societies like Canada because the truth isn't being taught. Settler society must learn its colonial history. Without a greater awareness of this history, then new generations will continue to make the same old mistakes over and over again. I have been trying to work on the issue of how to raise awareness, how to reclaim the narrative, so that the youth can really understand what actually happened in 1990, what the root causes were. This kind of knowledge, the understanding of Indigenous Peoples' history and experiences, is crucial. Truth is paramount. It's a key to the changes needed for our survival today and for the future.

SEAN: In terms of processing the events of 1990, do you think Québécois have confronted what happened? I recently watched a film called *The Oka Legacy*, and Francine Lemay, Corporal Marcel Lemay's sister, was interviewed and she had a lot to say about the importance of understanding the history of the land struggle.[7] I didn't realize that she actually translated *At the Woods' Edge* into French to help spread awareness about your struggle. She admitted to not really knowing the history of Canada, the history of Quebec—and virtually nothing about the Kanien'kehá:ka People—prior to 1990. But she has since dedicated herself to education, to learning, in hopes of sharing that wisdom with others so that peace and reconciliation can be achieved. She basically feels like her brother died unnecessarily.

ELLEN: Her brother Marcel did die unnecessarily, that's what's so sad. And all for a golf course. The root cause of this tragedy remains the ongoing systemic racism against Indigenous Peoples. The SQ tried to deflect their ineptitude and responsibility for what happened, by calling the Kanien'kehá:ka Peoples "terrorists" and making us responsible for Marcel Lemay's death. They took their anger and frustration out on the community. They enacted a kind of revenge in which they did not listen to government and became a law onto themselves. In truth their anger was misdirected, it should have been at their own government whose lack of good faith, honesty, and racism were responsible for the 1990 Mohawk Crisis. They used violence to protect the private interests for a golf course on stolen Kanien'kehá:ka land. It's a tragedy that could have been avoided. But it was history repeating itself.

SEAN: But Francine's anger is directed towards Canada, right? I mean, I guess if she can become educated and fight for change, anyone can do it, you know? Settlers need more role models like that, I think.

ELLEN: Francine Lemay has become a strong voice for reconciliation. That's a positive impact of 1990's legacy. It created a number of important leaders outside of our Kanehsatà:ke community, which is really heartening. Decolonization will require settler help, as they become educated in their own colonial history and its impacts. We need support from people like Francine Lemay who has become an ally, a voice speaking to Québécois about Indigenous issues and that is *powerful*. The depth of her understanding is just amazing. She's so open, kind, and compassionate.

I often wonder, though, if it had been one of us that had been killed, would there have been such a public outcry. That's not to take away from Francine's loss or the good work she's doing. If we look at the shooting of Dudley George by the Ontario Provincial Police and his death in 1995, for example. The Ipperwash Standoff is barely spoken about and not really taught in history. That happened just five years after the 1990 Resistance was supposed to change Canada's relationship with Indigenous Peoples forever. There's also the use of force at Gustafsen Lake in British Columbia which happened at the same time, in August and September 1995. Most Canadians don't know anything about the extreme use of force used by their country against Indigenous Peoples, but the media always reminds people about Marcel Lemay's death. Again, that's not to diminish the loss of Lemay's life, but it's to say that we live in a racist society where Indigenous people's lives really don't matter. That's the injustice that really annoys and worries me.

Canada's sovereignty is based on this racist Doctrine of Discovery that, in its eyes, legitimizes ongoing dispossession, and Canadians must push their government to end the implementation of this racist doctrine. Wider solidarity is needed to spread education and awareness, so that land is returned, so that land dispossession stops. It's part of the decolonial framework that is sorely needed to transform Canada, to become a more just society that respects the human rights of Indigenous Peoples. Canadians have an important role to play in realizing decolonization and reconciliation, but it must be done through education and discussion, understanding the root causes of colonialism and the genocide it committed. Reconciliation is a Canadian responsibility, including every institution and employee of the federal, provincial, and municipal governments. Just as the Truth and Reconciliation's "Calls to Action"[8] states.

SEAN: In saying that the legacy of 1990 is a mixed one, you mention that the land issue was not—and is still not—resolved. Can you explain what's been happening in Kanehsatà:ke since 1990?

ELLEN: While the resistance ended in 1990, the struggle to protect our Homelands never stopped because the land in Kanehsatà:ke is valuable, considered "Crown land" by Canada. They have said that the land is for our "use and benefit," so essentially they are saying that we are able to live in Kanehsatà:ke because of their good graces! Canada only recognizes the entity it created, the band council, to undermine traditional governance under the Longhouse Rotinonhseshá:ka. Therefore, the Longhouse people persist in contesting the land theft, but our voices are ignored by the colonial entity. So we lose more land from inside, through land grabbing and land theft from land speculators.

Many Kanien'kehá:ka and our allies were criminalized and jailed, and we had to organize fundraising events and concerts to raise awareness in order to get funds to cover their legal costs. Justice is costly in every way imaginable and is only for those rich enough to hire a lawyer who understands international law, not criminal law.

There was and remains hope that the land issue will be resolved. During negotiations in 1990, the federal government promised that they would sit with the traditional government under the Rotinonhseshá:ka, and address the long-standing historical land issue. The focus then was the dismantling of the barricades—not resolving the land dispute.

Today our rights to our land are still not being respected. In 1990, the International Federation of Human Rights was witness to the lack of good faith by the federal and provincial governments. The government quickly returned to the status quo once the cameras left, and we were still reeling from the collective trauma. In essence, we were all dealing with post-traumatic stress from what happened that summer in 1990.

We remain stuck in this position today with local community members whose actions and reactions are affected by trauma. We hear gunshots daily, racing cars up and down the roads of the community, and there are divisions within the community for various reasons, and all the while developers continue to steal our lands.

Today, as always, the Municipality of Oka has more rights than we do on our land. They continue to hand out permits to developers to build new homes on our territory. The barricades may have come down, but the barriers of systemic racism remain. Nothing has changed in that respect. The golf course project was stopped, yes, and we were able to stop Oka from removing our ancestors from their graves, but the core issue remains unresolved. Things have gotten worse in every way. Land speculators continue to profit from ongoing land theft in our community. When we ask the federal government to intervene, they claim that they cannot tell Quebec or Oka what to do, but they have no problem telling Indigenous people what to do!

In 2001, the Kanesatake Interim Land Agreement[9] was created, but this is controversial. It's a terrible, racist law that sees the Municipality of Oka as having more rights than Kanehsatà:ke. It was passed by two votes, by one quarter of the community who voted, meaning one quarter of eligible voters voted. The Longhouse people did not vote but we stated our opposition to Bill S-24 to a parliamentary committee. Under the Indian Act, any Act of Parliament must pass by 50 percent plus one by all eligible voters. The government decided to go ahead to unilaterally break their own "rule of law" anyways because they knew the Longhouse people wouldn't vote. This was a way to bypass our inherent rights to our lands and governance, to ignore the laws under Kaianera'kó:wa in order to legitimize land dispossession. The Act also contains the insidious component of "fee simple,"[10] which is detrimental to our rights to the land. But it goes deeper than a questionable voting system. The Act gives priority to Municipality of Oka bylaw over any traditional system of land use and has been shrinking the borders of our "reserve land."

We have expressed our opposition to the Paul Martin government, the Stephen Harper government, and now the Justin Trudeau government, but all administrations refuse to act, refuse to acknowledge our land rights. We don't recognize the authority of the Kanesatake Interim Land Agreement because it's another way of forcing Kanien'kehá:ka to cede our land to the Municipality of Oka. This struggle is just one of many, we're not even including the other nine municipalities that are on our Homelands building luxury homes.

Every year we lose more and more land. It's very frustrating, and as Rotinonhseshá:ka we have been unable to find lawyers that will take our case. Nobody wants to take our case. There is a small pool of lawyers who are capable of understanding the complexity of our issues, and those capable lawyers are associated in some form or another with the band council, so there is a conflict of interest for them to take our case. We wrote a letter to Prime Minister Justin Trudeau about the former Minister of Indigenous Affairs (Carolyn Bennett) being part of the problem, as she ignored our requests for a meeting. His response was to suggest we go to the band council to deal with it. But the band council system is a colonial creation, it is not my government! I don't vote in band council elections, and I don't recognize their authority over our traditional Homelands.

As a result, we remain in the same situation. A lot of land that could be used by our people today must be protected and maintained for future generations. The Mayor of Oka and the Government of Quebec prop up their development agenda by criminalizing Kanehsatà:ke Land Defenders, like we're disposable human beings. Meanwhile, the federal government repeatedly says, "our hands are tied, we can't interfere." That's the depravity of colonialism whereby there is no equality, no respect for international human rights, particularly for the Kanien'kehá:ka of Kanehsatà:ke. And the band council goes along with this because they've been co-opted. We see this evident when a band council leader travels out west protesting pipelines but then refuses to support his own community members trying to protect further settler development here in Kanehsatà:ke.

During negotiations during the summer of 1990, the federal government promised to work with the Longhouse people and the community to resolve the historical land issue. Instead they fraudulently sold a piece of the pine forest to a land speculator who has admittedly stated that he's aware of the history of Kanehsatà:ke's land issue but who knowingly continues to sell disputed land. His claim, that he was "in reconciliation mode," was a joke as his hidden agenda was to have the federal government purchase land that was illegally sold to him—a piece of land that the late John Ciaccia had urged the federal government to also purchase.

People need to understand that this type of land fraud and dispossession has been going on for over three hundred years. Whether it's the Sulpicians, land speculators, or developers, the destiny of our land is not in the control of the

Kanien'kehá:ka Nation. This is why we must maintain the struggle to protect our land.

This is how Oka was created. Our Homelands were fraudulently sold out from under us by the Sulpicians who colluded with the British Crown and Canada to commit land fraud and create the Municipality of Oka. It's annoying when I hear people say that Oka is near or around Kanehsatà:ke. Kanehsatà:ke is Oka. Oka *is* Kanehsatà:ke. Kanàtakon is founded on the displacement and land dispossession of the Kanien'kehá:ka people. Without telling the truth about Oka's foundations, colonial amnesia works to erase our presence in Kanehsatà:ke for millennia.

The current Mayor of Oka, Pascal Quevillon, continues this collusion because it benefits Oka economically and promotes the tourism industry. By increasing development there are more property taxes which can be collected, and that of course benefits the municipality. This is how Canada operates the free market economy. Canada steals land from Indigenous Peoples and fraudulently sells it—at a profit—to settlers and developers and then they tax that land and use the money to support more colonization and development. Meanwhile, Indigenous Peoples must go to Canada's court system to try to stop the constant land grabs, but the process continues while negotiations and court cases drag on. People think the new developer's so-called gift of some of our land will end this story, but it's just another chapter in the saga of settler colonialism in our community.

SEAN: Right, I heard the developer Gregoire Gollin is making an "ecological gift," promising to return some of the disputed land. Can you explain a bit more about this gift and what you think about it?

ELLEN: Well, it's not a gift at all, really. It's just more colonial trickery. The so-called gift comes with terms and conditions that only furthers colonization—it's a form of extinguishment. First, because it's an "ecological gift," the land will continue to be controlled by the federal and provincial government guidelines and not by Kanien'kehá:ka of Kanehsatà:ke. Sure, there can be no development in the Pines, which is good, but our land isn't being returned to us. The "gift" will be subject to provincial laws and colonial-imposed rules and regulations. There will be a board of directors that we don't get to choose. Again, we will have no say what happens with our land.

Second, the developer's so-called gift will give him a hefty a tax break. He's a businessman and wants compensation from the federal government in exchange for his purported philan- thropic gesture. He's playing the system. He knows we will always resist development of the Pines, as we did in 1990, so he's trying to cut his losses in the face of our persistent resistance.

We protested his development project in the summer of 2017, and he stopped the work temporarily, I'm guessing to see if the federal government would bite on his offer to sell our land. He wanted to receive compensation to recover some- thing for his investment. Most notably, he claimed he was "gifting" Kanehsatà:ke with 60 hectares of Kanien'kehá:ka land, but he was manipulating the public, trying to force the government to buy his other 150 hectares at a profit. He shouldn't have been able to purchase that land in the first place. His claims are supported by Canada and Quebec to further dispossess Kanehsatà:ke of our Homelands.

This offer has failed since Gregoire Gollin's conditions were unreasonable and were rejected by the Longhouse peo- ple. His condition was that we could have the forest—our land and two parcels of land at the development site—as long we would agree that he could sell more land.[11] The community divisions and weak leadership caused the offer to be withdrawn, and so Gollin continues to sell our land, despite being sent a lawyer's letter, from the Longhouse peo- ple, to stop. In fact, the development site is almost now full of expensive homes and so all our efforts were for naught. Gollin wants to be in control of everything, but our condition was that returned land would be under the jurisdiction of Rotinonhseshá:ka, not government, and not some foundation under his control. But especially not for our "use and benefit," as this is what happened in 1990 when the federal government bought our Pines and our cemetery from the Municipality of Oka for one dollar.

Non-Indigenous people and land speculators are profiting from the human rights gaps rooted in systemic racism under the Indian Act which permits Canada and Quebec to claim jurisdiction over our Homelands. While the government insists that Terra Nullius[12] did not apply in Canada, their arguments over Indigenous Homelands are rooted in the Doctrine of Discovery—which they claim they repudiated with the bill to implement UNDRIP.[13] The unilateral decisions they've made allow them to restrict access and authority over our Homelands.

Corporations are profiting from Canada's lack of respect of our inherent rights, and they stall progress by exploiting the dysfunction within the community. Government officials continue to allow development to proceed regardless of international human rights laws. As a result, more of our Homelands are sold to settlers to build homes in our traditional village: in Kanehsatà:ke, or "Oka Park," and our Homelands. Our people were forcibly removed from their homes to create what is known as Oka today. The collusion between the Seminary of St. Sulpice, the British, and Canada enabled the violation of the Kanien'kehá:ka of Kanehsatà:ke, of our rights to our Homelands. And it was done in a brutal way. My maternal grandmother's family was forced out of their homes by the security forces of the Sulpicians and they were only allowed to take the clothes off their backs. So all of the village of Oka is a result of forcibly removing Kanehsata'kehró:non from their homes.

But that's how Canada's theft of our Homelands proceeds even today. An empty field is worthless to the colonizer unless there is a building on it. Whereas the so-called empty fields have the potential to feed our people; these lands are home to our four-legged relations, birds, and where our medicines are found. We need to protect them so that future generations, and this generation, may enjoy the land. As it is, all our community land is being chipped away by settlers, and assimilated Mohawks who don't respect their own Traditional Laws. Land fraud is the legal norm when it pertains to Indigenous lands under dispute.

Gollin wanted to profit from his "investment" in infrastructure, so his version of a "gift" was hypocritical. Had he been genuine about his purported gift, there wouldn't have been any conditions, like the one stating he wanted compensation from the federal government for his construction of infrastructure and his investments. This rich man did not make this gesture altruistically. Gollin has bought land in "Oka" and surrounding municipalities, so he owns a lot of land, and he's adept at playing the divide and conquer game within the colonial framework.

In the end, and I can't stress this enough, people need to understand that this is our Homeland. We never relinquished or surrendered our jurisdiction over our Homelands; and today, the land is still being stolen from us. To take the matter to Canada's colonial courts will require us to prove "occupation since time immemorial," which no settler is required to do. Think about it, we are forced into the colonizer's expensive court system, a system that has allowed the ongoing theft of our lands and the theft and murder of our children in Indian Residential Schools. And now Canada's legal system allows the repackaging of colonialism to make it more palatable to Indigenous Peoples, to placate their constituents, and to appear as if there's reconciliation going on. But there's not.

Going to Canada's courts, in fact the first stage is provincial courts, is an exercise in futility and requires us to have all kinds of "experts" who are usually funded by government agencies. We can't find a lawyer or an archeologist to testify on our behalf. Once they take a look at the situation, most say "it's too messy and complicated." Meanwhile, the Longhouse people's voices are silenced, as we are kept outside of negotiations. This stems from Canadian legislation in 1924 that outlawed traditional Indigenous governments as illegal. The federal and provincial governments' rhetoric states that the only legal entity they recognize is the colonial-created band council system, which does not have treaties with foreign nations. The band council may seem like a government, but in actuality their jurisdiction goes as far as financial agreements for services for community members.

We're also battling this mythological creation, by archeologists and anthropologists, who say that Kanehsatà:ke "was" the Homelands of the St. Lawrence Iroquois. They don't acknowledge us as descendent of the original people who have lived in Kanehsatà:ke for millennia and that we are their people. Our language is their language. Our pottery is their pottery. It's frustrating how many hoops we, as the First Peoples of Turtle Island, have to jump through with a state like Canada that is persistently violating our human rights to self-determination.

SEAN: What is the role of federal government here?

ELLEN: The bottom line is that the federal government and politicians don't really care if the land is transferred, even though they promised to do so after 1990. If we had the resources to take Canada to court, we could bankrupt Canada easily, just this community alone, because of the land fraud and land dispossession committed by so many players for over three hundred years. The brutality of the Sulpicians against the people of Kanehsatà:ke, the collusion with the British and Canada, has caused generations of oppression and poverty—although that aspect is changing now. But for so long, so many things have been taken from us and we have been denied access to our Homelands.

Canada has never upheld the honour of the Crown, especially here in Kanehsatà:ke—and indeed in many other cases on Turtle Island, affecting other Indigenous people. Our rights are always trumped by the settlers. Their concerns receive priority from Canada, over that of the people of Kanehsatà:ke and Onkwehón:we people everywhere. The government's most pressing concern is the opinion of their constituents, to garner their votes for the next election. They don't care about Indigenous Peoples. We need only look at how they've acted on important issues like murdered and missing Indigenous women or implementing the recommendations of the RCAP and the TRC.

If there is to be any kind of reconciliation, people must understand that there needs to be reparations as part of that process. That makes the public nervous because they think we want the keys to their homes. But we don't. We want our lands back, we want safety, we want a healthy environment. To stop the land dispossession, which is designed to help this country's economic agenda, the truth must be told about how people are living on occupied land. My mother's family was dispossessed by the Sulpicians who forcibly removed and kicked out families from their homes in the late 1800s. They were only allowed to leave with the clothes on their backs.

Canadians need to work with us on this together, nation-to-nation and stop thinking it's up to the government for the process of reconciliation. Right now, negotiations are lopsided with government holding all the resources and power, while the band council holds secret, closed-door meetings to bow down to government's wishes. This goes against the wishes of the majority of the community to restore and recover our Homelands. Canada has created a hierarchical process which it demands Indigenous communities follow. It's a very authoritarian process for Indigenous people; when it comes to protecting our lands, we're not allowed. We're expected to go to court if we don't like what the government has to "offer." That's not what a nation-to-nation relationship looks like to me.

Gollin has been allowed to continue to sell more land, with the blessing of the federal government and Mohawk Council of Kanesatake. In the meantime, while the federal government drags its feet, we continue to lose more land. We're stuck between a rock and a hard place. If we say no to this so-called gift, then we'll hear "oh, you guys don't want a resolution? You're just violent people." That's what I remember the Mayor of Oka and many others saying in 1990. Just like back then, the current Mayor of Oka creates a similar atmosphere with his incendiary remarks telling his constituents that he's afraid that Mohawks will surround the people of Oka and that they will lose taxes. He doesn't care about our history or perspective. He told me in a public meeting, organized by Oka around 2017, that it's an insult to the Québécois culture for me to say that "Oka" is Mohawk Land!

Throughout history our rights to land have been ignored, denied, and violated. Across the Americas, colonizers committed genocide on behalf of their sovereigns. Which means this society has succeeded and exists because of these genocidal acts. But we're framed as the unreasonable ones, and we're supposed to accept the crumbs thrown our way. We have no control over our destiny. We're still treated as wards of the settler state.

The Mohawk Council of Kanesatake falls in line with whatever the federal government tells them to do because, if not, they won't have a funding agreement. But they don't communicate well with the community about what is going on with land negotiations. Instead, they hold secret discussions causing tensions within the community to rise. It's very frustrating that in the years since 1990, after the Kanehsatà:ke and Kahnawà:ke Siege, we're still dealing with the land issue. The federal government had an opportunity to do something about it in 1990 but did absolutely nothing to change it. Canada continues to commit land fraud. They've sold our land to a developer again, as they did in 1990. They sold contested land to a private individual, so they should be compensating the people (in Oka) that they fraudulently sold the land to, but they won't acknowledge or take responsibility for creating this mess.

The public and people, like the Mayor of Oka, demonize us for wanting our Homelands back. They claim we want the keys to their houses, but that is absurd, really. Canadians need to direct their outrage at the right people: the Sulpicians, the Municipality of Oka, the provincial and federal governments, settler-colonialists themselves. They all need to be held accountable for their ongoing complicity in land fraud and land theft at Kanehsatà:ke. And, indeed, for the land fraud committed against all Indigenous Peoples in the Americas.

Peace and reconciliation will require sacrifice and change, and that can benefit all of us. It can and will be painful because truth-telling is a painful process. But in order for there to be peace between our Peoples, the acts of genocide committed by colonizers against Indigenous Peoples must be acknowledged. More importantly, there needs to be reparations and restitution.

Instead, everything is regressing. It's like what we see in the environment, everything is off balance, and Mother Earth is trying to bring balance back by cleansing herself. People are asking important questions right now about how to protect the biodiversity and how to protect the land from exploitation and contamination. This is important because we rely on the land for our medicines, for our health, well-being, and spirituality. Indigenous Land Defenders are implementing those teachings of our ancestors that helped us survive for centuries. We're obliged by our Onkwehón:we laws to be protecting the land for all of our relations: the birds and animals that live in the forest, and the waters and all its inhabitants. But our lands and waters are being contaminated so present and future generations cannot enjoy them fully. But we are really far from resolving anything.

SEAN: Arthur Manuel, before he died, talked about how Canada suffers from a base-case of colonialism. This sounds a lot like what you're describing.

ELLEN: Colonialism is a sickness of the mind because it's based on European superiority—over Indigenous Peoples, among other Peoples and beings. Corporations influence governments with lobbying and manipulation which affords them even more power in influencing government legislation.

For Indigenous Peoples, it's an imbalanced playing field. We are constantly in survival mode and constantly trying to overcome the impacts of colonization, but we can't compete with corporations and their financial resources—which are used to buy politicians, lawyers, and judges so that they can take whatever they like from the land. Most Indigenous people are more concerned about sustainable development as opposed to corporations, which never leave the environment in a way that will be usable for future generations. So we have no choice but to push back. Our resistance is essential to the survival of our Homelands, our languages, our cultures, our traditional forms of governance.

SEAN: This fight against colonial and capitalist development is playing out clearly in Western Canada right now with Indigenous resistance to pipeline projects and extractive resource development. In thinking again about Lee's concept of "echoes," Leanne Betasamosake Simpson credits the Mohawk Resistance as a flashpoint moment for her and many Indigenous people. She says,

> When I think of the "Oka Crisis" I think of the hundreds of Kanien'kehá:ka women from Kanehsatà:ke, Kahnawà:ke, and Akwesasne and across the country who organized the logistics to support the blockades. I think of the food, the medical supplies, the childcare and the worry. I think of their tremendous spiritual and political influence. I think of the principled leadership Kanien'kehá:ka women showed us from behind the barricades. I think of Ellen Gabriel, and how during the summer of 1990 she taught me about righteous anger, love, and to come at injustice from a place of unapologetic strength.
>
> The summer of 1990, for me and many other people of my age, was the most profound political education of my life. It has influenced my professional, artistic, and activist life in a way I couldn't have predicted. I learned the value of direct action. I learned the value of articulating our histories, perspectives, and realities in a clear way. I learned what it looks like when Indigenous peoples live and act by using our own political traditions, systems of governance, and values. I learned what principled action looks like. [The summer of 1990] was never a crisis; it was a radical transformation—and to realize the full potential of that transformation, when Indigenous peoples act with such conviction, we should all listen and ask, What can I give up to promote peace?[14]

With these words in mind, what lessons does 1990 hold for Land Defenders today?

ELLEN: First, thanks to Leanne for saying that, I'm honoured by her statement. Throughout my life as a Land Defender, I

have been guided by Elders who taught me that the goal of all
we do is to promote peace.

The 1990 Kanehsatà:ke and Kahnawà:ke Siege was a
wake-up call for Indigenous Peoples. When we look back
at that time, we were all sleeping not knowing what was
next because Canada never took us seriously. The resistance
movement was always there, but I think this was the seminal moment when people realized how bad of a situation we
were really in. It began an Indigenous resistance movement
that still resonates today.

All the blockades across Canada and the protests by
Indigenous people and our allies, I don't think that we realized how powerful we are. The 1990 Siege was that moment
that woke us all up, we were reminded how important our
history, teachings, and Onkwehón:we laws are, how these
can be used as tools to strengthen our resistance. It's about
honouring our ancestors, creating a state of mind that has a
vision of the future, that helps the present and future generations live and survive on Mother Earth. This is more powerful
than money; money won't save us from the things to come in
the cleansing of Mother Earth. But if you have a clear vision
and goal, for justice and peace, you can stay grounded. For
Onkwehón:we Peoples, the land is precious and priceless, it
contains all aspects of our identity.

The divide and conquer strategy that colonizers like
Canada use comes from an ancient playbook that has been
adapted over time. In this so-called era of reconciliation, the
colonizer attempts to rebrand colonialism to make it more
palatable to Indigenous Peoples, to make their constituents
believe the propaganda that Canada is trying to decolonize.
Instead, what they're really doing is a form of increased pressure, placed on Indigenous Peoples, to help keep the colonial
machine going and fed. They control education, social services, health care, and our Homelands.

Indigenous Peoples are still reeling from the impacts of genocide that have affected multiple generations. We are out-resourced as the government has the financial and human resources made up of hundreds of bureaucrats making policy decisions affecting our daily lives. Colonization is ongoing and has not ended; it continues to impact our daily lives.

As an Indigenous Land Defender, I often wonder how we can build a better future, where Indigenous Peoples' land, culture, and languages will flourish. We need the opportunity to start by rebuilding our nation-to-nation relationship. We need a chance to heal from genocide, ongoing colonization, to reconcile amongst each other from the laws and policies that attacked our identity, our spirituality, our sexuality, our traditional forms of government. Onkwehón:we Peoples are Peoples of the land, we belong to Mother Earth and Grandmother Moon, who was the first human-like form on this beautiful blue planet, according to our Creation Story. We're made from this land, and she's our mother. She's beautiful, she's priceless.

All we have ever wanted is to prosper, to live in a safe and secure environment. But we cannot do that when the Government of Canada continues to steal our lands and control our lives and our lands through their funding agreements, laws, and colonial policies. And if Canadians want to pressure their governments—municipal, provincial, federal—to do something, if they really care about peace in this country, then they must learn their own colonial history. They must take the time to learn from Indigenous Peoples' perspectives and the oppressive state we have been forced to live under for centuries. This kind of knowledge can help change our relationship for the better.

We have so little land left from our original Homeland. We live on tiny pieces of postage stamp-size land. We're not asking for much. We're asking for justice. We want our human rights to self-determination to be respected. This means that

Canadians need to become educated and active, they need to be part of the solution of peace, understanding that their prosperity has been at the expense of Indigenous people's prosperity, identity, Homelands. Canadians must understand that colonization isn't over, that it continues with brutality and trickery under the guise of the "rule of law."

SEAN: Right, it's an ongoing process as well as a structure. How did the Siege shape your activism beyond 1990? What keeps you going and hopeful for radical change?

ELLEN: I was privileged to have patient and generous Elders and lots of support around me during those challenging times. When you go through something as traumatic as being shot at by a paramilitary force, being a target of the army and police on a daily basis, constantly being in the crosshairs, and seeing the brutality of the colonial state, it's an awakening. All of the stories of racism and police brutality, as told by the older generation, are just manifesting in front of you, and you think: Is this really happening? It's a shock to the system.

As a result of my experiences during the resistance, I became more determined to defend our land and get justice for our Nation, to have our rights to self-determination respected. I love the land and the energy that it brings me. Protecting the land is a reason to keep resisting. You know, previous generations thought about us through their decisions and fought the oppression that tried to make them feel less than. They fought hard to leave a legacy that their children and grandchildren could survive. They fought hard against the genocidal policies, land dispossession, and poverty. We owe them so much for thinking of us and for fighting as hard as they could for us.

For me, I'd like to see future generations enjoy the land, have a good quality of life on the land, respect and cherish the land, and not have to go through what we had to in 1990.

That's what motivates me, because I think this has been going on three hundred years too long.

Reconciliation is about having uncomfortable conversations, but we have to sit in the discomfort and get through it to have a better future and learn from the past. Only then can we deal with righting wrongs and telling the truth. But in the end, it benefits everyone, it leaves a legacy of peace, love, respect, and understanding—that people in this time were brave enough to face oppression and learn the truth. I keep thinking about the next generations, and I feel so bad for the little ones right now because the climate crisis is just a beginning of the changes yet to come on Mother Earth. I really hope that they will have their human rights respected and for them to be able to survive and live in a world whose foundation is peace, love, and courage. They have to be given the chance to see the beauty of Mother Earth and all our relations. So many things are changing faster than we realize, and our struggle is far from over.

But you can't fight alone. You have to surround yourself with people who are good-minded. People who are compassionate and understand what you're going through and who will guide you when things become difficult. In order to undo the trauma that colonialism has caused, we must remember our history—where we have come from and why we are in the position we are in today—and we must have a vision for the future. Memory and the oral stories from our ancestors are key to having a vision for the future.

We need Elders to guide us, but you also need people who are like-minded and committed to peace and lifting each other up constantly. Because the resistance of 1990 wasn't just one person's stand, it was the struggle of two Kanien'kehá:ka communities along with the help of people from Ahkwesásne. But it also was a worldwide Indigenous struggle against oppression. It woke Indigenous Peoples up and encouraged people to tell their stories and their Elders' stories of the genocidal Indian Residential School system. From the siege of 1990 came events, commissions and reports like RCAP and the TRC, because the Kanien'kehá:ka took a stand. We rose together with other Indigenous Nations and scared the colonizer with the realization that the resistance from hundreds of years ago still lives and breathes in this generation. But colonialism isn't finished. It remains the root cause of so many deaths and social problems for Indigenous Peoples today. So we must continue to resist, and another generation is obliged to carry on the fight to protect our lands and human rights to self-determination.

So, I think that's what the youth need to remember. Being mentored and learning the history of Indigenous Peoples— our traditions, our languages, our culture—and the importance of our relationship with each other, the land, and all our relations, this is an important part of Indigenous advocacy. We need to support each other in our fight for change, to envision and create a better, beautiful future.

5

THE ART OF RESISTANCE

SEAN: So far we've talked a lot about your activism and your role as a Land Defender in the 1990 blockades. These are things, I think, you're well-known and even celebrated for, but you're also an incredibly talented artist as well. I don't think as many people know that side of your work. Can you talk more about how you became an artist and why you've made art such a big part of your life, especially after 1990. I think you said you had just finished your Fine Arts degree at Concordia just before the Siege happened, and obviously that event shaped the trajectory of your life. But let's talk more about your art, how you got started, and why it's still so important to you today.

ELLEN: Yes, art has been a constant in my life. This comes from my early childhood when I would sit and draw for hours at a time. My parents recognized my talent and nurtured it by buying me sketchbooks, pencils, and paints, all kinds of art supplies, which I'm very grateful for. They were the best in supporting each of us (me and my siblings) in our talents, and I feel so fortunate to have had them as my parents.

As a kid, I always felt happiest making art because I never liked school much. So, art was a great escape for me. My parents encouraged and always praised me for my drawings. That was a precious gift. Still, I really wanted to go to art school, but my mother, being the practical person that she was, wanted me to find a more stable way of making a living and do art on the side. So I tried a number of other things in my early life. I studied nursing for a while at Dawson College.

After my parents passed away,[1] it was difficult because, while we were young adults, my siblings and I became orphans. It was devastating for us to lose both our parents, who were young when they passed. It was then I realized I needed to go back to school. So when I was twenty-six, I went to Concordia University and studied studio art, which I loved. I also learned about art history, and "the masters," but I was disappointed that Indigenous art was viewed as "folk" art, almost as if it were inferior or not "real" art. I wanted to study Norval Morrisseau, Daphne Odjig, and other Indigenous artists, but I couldn't. Still, it didn't stop me from taking out books about Indigenous art in the library or buying them from bookstores. I wanted something that reflected my identity, and in my refusal to accept that Indigenous art was inferior I learned about other Indigenous artists. It was great being immersed in art.

Human beings are responsible for the care of Mother Earth and all our relations. We must take only what we need so it does not have a serious negative impact upon future generations. This is the philosophy of the One Dish, One Spoon. When we honour Ohén:ton Karihwatéhkwen, we bring into our discussions and decisions an acknowledgement of all our relations—who we live with and rely upon to nourish us. Our actions and decisions impact all life. For me, art conveys this philosophy of life, of the Onkwehón:we Peoples in a way that is non-threatening while also provoking thought. Art can bring people into discussion in ways that conventional politics simply can't. It's been said that artists are the conscience of society. Art is an important medium and tool to express our cosmovision, the roots of our identity, our history, our perspectives, and our realties.

I became frustrated with people who thought that Indigenous art is "folk" art or some obscure, stylized form of art that was only suitable for collection and placed in museums and galleries. Indigenous art from various cultures can feed our souls; it reflects our worldviews and illustrates so many of our realities and experiences that have been silenced and ignored for too long.

Back when I was in school, I believed that Indigenous art should be viewed alongside any other art form or art movement because all art is a form of expression and storytelling. But Western culture likes to compartmentalize and measure everything against itself, as the standard, the ideal. Their culture is the one, we're told, that's the standard, lording their values as higher than all others. Fortunately, things have come a long way in this regard. Indigenous arts are now valued and respected, finally. But I've always understood that art has the power to convey who we are, as Indigenous Peoples, and it can be a way to reclaim the narratives and stories told about us.

I enjoyed my time at Concordia University and appreciated the opportunity to learn, from my professors, about different styles of art and develop my skills. In May 1990, I graduated from Concordia with Bachelor of Fine Arts degree, majoring in studio art.

I'm really an introvert at heart. I was very shy as a kid and even as a young adult. The summer of 1990 shattered my shyness, you could say, out of necessity, and threw me into a whole new world. Afterwards, because of the trauma of that summer, I had a mental block in my creativity, even though I still wanted to paint and create. Somehow the enjoyment was gone. Today, I have my inspiration back, and I love creating. For me, art is very meditative and calming.

For millennia, Indigenous Peoples have communicated their values and their cultures creatively. Even wampum belts, agreements and reminders of the values of our culture, those I consider works of art. Not to take away from their meaning, but my respect for the work that went into the creation of one wampum belt, they are astounding works. Whether it's with a pen or paintbrush or needles and thread or music or writing, art is part of the richness of our cultures, and you can't help but be drawn to art. At least I was. I always wanted to learn about the richness of my culture, not just focus on the dysfunction caused by colonization and genocide, you know? I wanted to make a positive choice to connect with my culture and feel connected to my family and my ancestors.

I think that's how art has helped me to understand it on an existential level. Art can be a way of expressing the world as we see it—but also the way we want it to be. Art creates a message of some kind. Whether you're trying to understand your reality or letting the medium dominate your work, resulting in a work of art that surprises you, and many other elements in creativity all are important. Art, for me, brings me hope. It's not necessarily about money or fame, but about creating a better world somehow.

After the summer of 1990, and going through what I went through behind the barricades, my view of the world changed, even though I had a creative mental block afterwards. Art really became a safe space for me. It's your own space, and you do it in your own way and time. Because I've always loved doing art, I persevered and continued to paint even though sometimes the final work wasn't satisfactory to me. I think it took about five years or so to finally feel creative again.

Creating art is a big part of who I am as a human being. I always felt uncomfortable about selling things, as I create an attachment to my work. Quality art supplies are expensive, but having them anytime I want to paint or draw is reassuring. When I was younger, I didn't have high self-esteem and so I initially didn't want to show my art. I was content more with the process of making it—of expressing myself. I think that's why I ended up focusing more on my activism, but I have always been creating. I just haven't shown much of it. But I've been an artist for most of my life, so I continue to create no matter what is going on in my life.

Art and activism are a lot alike actually, they're connected for me. In both art and activism, you're really trying to tell a story or share a reality, trying to help people understand the world from a different perspective. Art really is like the social conscience of society. While some people might see my art as a diversion from my activism, I see it as being connected, as being another mode of expression. To me, being an artist is equally as important as my life as an activist.

SEAN: I find it interesting that you finished art school around the same time as the resistance began, again speaking to the continuity of your education informing your art and vice versa.

ELLEN: Yes, I graduated university in May 1990, as things were getting started. I was going to the barricade when I wasn't studying, starting in March 1990. Once I finished my classes, I was in the Pines full time.

SEAN: It must have been quite something to go from art school, thinking about how to represent life and talking about things like perspective and representation, to then having journalists and filmmakers interviewing you, trying to represent you and what you were fighting for, all the while filtering things through their own perspectives. So, perhaps, it's not surprising that after the conflict you turned to art to figure out your perspective and create a view of the world as you saw it to share with others.

I know that shortly after 1990 you contributed a number of illustrations to *At the Woods' Edge*, and I've seen a number of your paintings about the Pines and your land. And, of course, we recently collaborated on a poster depicting the July 11 Siege for the thirtieth anniversary as part of the Graphic History Collective's radical poster series. It seems like empowerment is a key theme in your work. Has that always been a focus of your artistic practice?

ELLEN: Empowerment is a good word. Someone called it "in your face" type of art. I think the therapeutic part of art is what you see: from anger and frustration, some great works of art are created. We need only look at anti-war paintings, or Kent Monkman's pieces on the Indian Residential Schools.

I was fortunate to have been invited to several art shows after 1990. I had been invited by the Eskimo Art Gallery in Montreal to do a solo show before all of this happened. It was delayed by the Mohawk Crisis, but it still went ahead and held my first solo show in 1991. I also was given an opportunity for another solo show at the University of Northern British Columbia. They included paintings that I had done before and after 1990.

I love doing art, I love what it gives me. At the end of the day, I can show the world what I'm thinking, what I'm doing, what I care about. Even if it's just a landscape or a portrait or something. You're giving back somehow. It's part of a legacy that I think everyone wants to leave behind. And I think that's what artists want to do: give back to society and give people an alternative way at looking at life.

Art is an outlet for the persistent feeling of being voiceless which colonial oppression sometimes makes you feel. It's a very personal thing to be an artist, but there is also a collective element. It can be difficult to allow your work to be sold and to be shown in public, it's like exposing a private personal part of yourself. As an artist, you can't control how the audience will interpret your work or prevent your creations from being exploited. But that's just part of the reality of being an artist. I'd rather take the chance to have my work mean something to someone and bring someone joy.

SEAN: Can you speak more about that tension, between art and consumerism in a colonial and capitalist society? I imagine that ends up shaping your art and artistic process immensely, no?

ELLEN: Yes, you have to be prepared to be judged as an artist, and as there is a lot of pressure to fit into the status quo and the idea of what an Indigenous artist is. There was a time when people, even Indigenous people, thought that our culture had to be represented in every aspect of our work. But what does that mean when you paint a portrait, landscape, or say for instance a hockey game? You're Indigenous and you just happen to also be an artist. The world of art and society like labels, but I just go with what is important to me and not what the art world thinks I should paint.

Just like being an activist you have to get used to judgment and criticism, but unless you take the risk, you won't be part of the change you want to see. That's another similarity between being an activist and being an artist. There is that struggle to have your message received and taken seriously. Figuring out the best medium to do that effectively is always a challenge. I like to explore new media and figure out how it helps my creativity. My latest endeavour has involved documentary filmmaking as a storyteller.

SEAN: Yes, your multidisciplinary range is impressive. What have you learned about your artistic process over the years, as you engage with different styles and media?

ELLEN: Well, documentary filmmaking helped me to understand story structure much better than I did before. And I have come to appreciate the power of icons and symbols of my culture. As an artist you get to choose the structure of how things are represented. It's all about the choices you're making in your mind and the power you have in the creative process. Your mind and the heart are involved when you're creating as an artist. And the thing for Indigenous artists is that we can sometimes feel invisible—that we're only now reclaiming our own narratives and telling our own stories and history. I mean, we've always done that, but today we're taken more seriously as self-determining People and to me that's important.

Art is a really powerful tool to create with, and a powerful way to use icons and symbols that we feel represent us. I like using a variety of media. I admire and respect artists who use painting, dance, poetry, and writing. For example, the Warrior flag created by the late Louis Hall of Kahnawà:ke is now known as the Unity flag. It is used all over the world as symbolic of Indigenous resistance movements. This flag was flown during the 1990 Mohawk Crisis. It's amazing that something created by a Mohawk artist, Louis Hall, is now a recognizable icon for Indigenous Peoples, even internationally.[2]

Artists influence how people feel and think, how they identify with society and their Nation, either collectively or individuality. And this is especially true for Indigenous people right now. So, art is a really powerful medium to support a message. Art can help break through the barriers people might have on challenging issues. You have that freedom to create and represent your vision to the world. I think that's why so many activists are artists and so much art is used in activism.

SEAN: I think there are a lot of connections there between dreaming of what might be and fighting to bring that vision of a better world into being. Do you have a particular artistic genre or style that you prefer? I've seen your photography, drawing, painting, but do you feel most comfortable in one, or what's your weapon of choice in terms of your artistic expression?

ELLEN: It depends. There are times when painting is all I want to do, acrylic mostly. Although I love oil painting, my house is too small for that, and you need good ventilation to paint with oil. But I love painting with oil because of the richness and the texture you can get from it. You can blend differently with oil paints in a way that really accentuates a piece. It's a very special medium.

Then there's drawing, which is something that I've done since I was a child. I love drawing with pencil crayons and black felt-tip pens, which I used in many of my illustrations. You can blend pencil crayons in almost the same way as with paint. Watercolours are trickier but the end product is beautiful, and it gives you a different kind of look. It requires you to approach a piece with more thought and preparation because watercolours can be unforgiving. It challenges you as an artist to envision your work before you begin. I love it! I enjoy using different media as each one has its own challenges, so I choose a medium depending on the message I want to convey.

However, painting with acrylics is the medium where my activist messages are created. I haven't painted this kind of theme in a while, though. I have to be in the mood because life as an Indigenous person is challenging on a daily basis. Painting a landscape or a portrait is meditative and peaceful for me. But I love using different media because I learn something new creatively each time.

I really enjoy photography as well, going out into the woods and taking pictures of the land, the plants, the medicines, and recording them with each changing season. I feel that it's important to document the land as it looks today because it's changing so quickly—from climate change and careless people cutting the Pines for their personal gain, to

Ellen, 1990.

urban sprawl, which is another form of land dispossession. Photography helps me feel less hopeless in my advocacy. It's like being in another world where the beauty is like a gallery just for you.

I'm also enjoying documentary filmmaking, a new medium of artistic expression for me. I've just released my first film, *Kanàtenhs: When the Pine Needles Fall* (2022), which I directed during the height of the pandemic. The film is about July 11, 1990, the first day of the Kanehsatà:ke Siege and the role of the women on that day. It's about correcting false narratives that have been imposed on us. I wanted to regain the narrative and present the truth and show the role of the women behind the barricades that did not get media attention.[3]

As storytellers, we try to honour the people we interview, their experiences, and acknowledge the truth about our history and experiences as Indigenous Peoples. Indigenous cultures have always had storytellers as part of the foundation of our cultural identity, the stories that we listen to, our legends, our Creation Stories, the cosmology, those were all handed down to each generation. It's about strengthening the link to our ancestors, their stories, their language, their experiences, and understanding of our cosmovision.

It's just amazing to think about, there's so much power there, in our Oral Traditions. They shape our identities. For instance, we don't know how many generations have heard the Iroquois Creation Story or all the other legendary stories that have been passed down to us as Indigenous Peoples. But it's those storytellers that have given us that creative ability to imagine our history, our worldview, our cultural values, and there is even more of an impact from these stories through the words of our Onkwehón:we languages. Our languages describe in a visual way which colonial languages cannot. This inspires and motivates our creative minds to picture what those experiences might have looked like.

To me, everybody's an artist, be it with crafts, words, painting, drawing. Together these different art forms are able to fill in the gaps and inspire discussion as to what lies between the lines. I draw a lot of my inspiration from our stories and from Mother Earth as well. The natural world embodies such inspirational and amazing designs—how the sun gives shape to what we see. I think that for Indigenous artists there is no lack of inspiration.

SEAN: How did your experience in the 1990 Resistance shape your art and artistic practice, the story or message you want to covey?

ELLEN: The 1990 Siege was a traumatic event, and I had PTSD afterwards, like so many people in the communities. It caused me to not feel very creative and so I wasn't able to paint in peace for quite a long time. Not the way I wanted to, anyway. So it affected me deeply by interrupting my creativity. I guess it was like a kind of writer's block. For a while it felt as if I was still processing the trauma from that summer. I had to sort through what I experienced and continued to experience with all the legal matters: the harassment by the police and invasion of our privacy through monitoring our mail and phone calls. It was difficult to prioritize my healing, but I had a lot of support and love from my family so I'm fortunate to have a loving family. I mean, they themselves had their own traumatic experiences from 1990 but they were there for me.

My niece and nephew, who were young children at the time, they were good medicine to help me see the beauty in life, along with participating in sweats and having wise counselling from Elders who guided and supported me. I've been an amateur photographer since my parents gave me a small Kodak camera when I was a teen, so I used that medium to help me focus on the good in life. I took many walks in the Pines and I'd ride my bike, and when I saw something interesting, I would stop to take a picture. But it was difficult to enjoy completely because there were people in the community who disagreed with what we did. They would harass me while I was on my bike, and sometimes drive me off the road, so I had to stop riding my bike for awhile. But I'm stubborn, so I found other ways.

There was so much going on after the barricades came down and we all had a lot on our plates. I was frustrated by the misrepresentation of the Mohawk People in 1990 by the media, and all the propaganda that twisted the story of what had happened really frustrated me. That motivated me to find an outlet, a different way of using my voice. Art was a vehicle for me to tell my own story, in my own way.

Photography allowed me to regain a bit of control over my experience, and I was invited to many places to give talks about what happened to Kanehsatà:ke and Kahnawà:ke in the aftermath of 1990. I started taking pictures of my family, home, and landscapes plus the horses I grew up with. I had a friend who was an amateur photographer, and he helped teach me about the basics. I really enjoyed it. During 1990, I was supposed to be taking photos as part of my duties. I had rolls and rolls of film that I gave to somebody for safekeeping, just in case I was arrested, and they buried them somewhere in the Pines. At least that's what they told me. It just makes me want to cry when I think about it, because I had tons of film that I lost from that summer. Those rolls are lost forever.

Photography is really interesting when you start learning about the artistic ways of composition, like when you're painting, and you know how important even the smallest details are. The technological advances in AI nowadays make it even easier for people to get into photography, which is just great. Smart phones are the cameras of today—that's not to say that they're replacing analog cameras. But these new technologies, like DSLR cameras, allow for more people to share their lives, and that can be a positive thing or negative depending on your perspective. Now that we don't have to develop film, we can just go home and upload our photos or videos to our computers. So we can represent our reality instantaneously.

Technology is making things easier for certain things in our lives. In activism, that immediacy and ability to show your perspective and what is going on in your Homelands is powerful, such as going live on social media platforms. Indigenous people have a new tool to instantly post their messages to the world on these social media platforms and reclaim our narrative. Overall, I think that photography with any kind of camera is a wonderful medium for artists to use and to explore.

SEAN: Tell me more about your new work with documentary filmmaking. Do you see it as a continuation of your artistic practice? What kinds of issues are you looking at in your work?

ELLEN: I think filmmaking has enhanced the tools that I have as an artist to tell a story that means something, has relevance, and is a lasting legacy for Indigenous voices. It's an accessible medium and there are many YouTube tutorials to help understand the medium more. Studying documentary filmmaking has helped me understand the structure of story-telling. I've learned how to create a production book to guide my filming and how to write a script to enhance the story-telling. One of my instructors gave us this little question, a tip to help us know if we're on the right track, and that is, to ask myself: What is the dramatic question of your story? The story must have an arc: a beginning, a middle, and an end that concludes the story. Using the strengths and richness of Indigenous culture to convey my story, from an Indigenous woman's perspective, is key in my motivation.

The government and mainstream media have persistently hijacked the narrative and distorted the realities of Indigenous Peoples. Well, documentary filmmaking is a tool that will hopefully push back against the colonial narrative and bring about a kinder, more compassionate understanding of who we are as human beings.

I'm also learning a lot about soundscapes and how to use it to evoke emotions. Just like in Hollywood blockbusters, music creates tension in a dramatic moment or a soothing sound when the story is emerging from a darkness. My niece, Eliza Kavtion, is the musician who has written all the original music for my projects. The relationship between sound and story is interconnected, they enhance and complement each other.

After understanding the whole process of making a doc-umentary film you realize how a story has many moving pieces that combine to create a story. The smallest detail is important in your storytelling and the choices you make can trigger certain emotions for the audience. Sound can either lift your spirits, make you feel sad, or make you want to learn more. So sound is extremely important.

SEAN: Speaking of the importance of sound, sometimes when we talk, I can hear birds chirping outside your house in the background. I really love that. They're part of our conversations.

ELLEN: Yes, I love listening to the sounds of birds. They're so smart and amazing to watch and listen to. Sometimes, if you sit still while listening to their songs, you can almost understand what they're saying. They have their own languages and songs that change from the morning to nightfall and also with the seasons.

Everything in nature has a rhythm, as do we, and when you're outside you sync with the natural world, its own sounds and rhythms. The energy the earth gives off, along with the trees, the plants, and air, is absorbed even if we don't realize it. It's easy to understand if one stops and listens often, it helps you enjoy and appreciate nature. If you immerse yourself in the environment in a way that breaks down the barriers of our human world, you can learn and hear things from the earth. We just need to learn how to listen. That can help us to understand how connected we are all to Mother Earth; we come from her, and while we may not understand the language of all our relations, they understand us through their own extraordinary senses. Life is beautiful and amazing.

Indigenous people are multigenerational survivors of genocidal projects and overcoming that oppression is difficult. From the impacts of the Indian Residential Schools to living under the systemic racism of the Indian Act, it takes a conscious effort to undo all the cultural shaming of being Indigenous, of being displaced from our Homelands, of the persistent criminalization of Land Defenders, defending our sovereignty.

Under Indigenous laws, it's about embracing kindness, compassion, and listening, understanding, and respecting ourselves and others. We all have our own beat, our own rhythm, our own families. The earth, too, has its own rhythm and its own beat. I think that the animals and the birds, the plants, the fish, amphibians, the four-legged animals, and waters have always stayed in time with Mother Earth and her rhythm. It's us humans who have been walking out of beat because we've been oppressed by those who believe they're superior to everyone and everything. Society is out of rhythm, and we need to find our way back.

I think for artists, that's what we're trying to do, in our own humble way. We create things that hopefully help connect us with ourselves and others. Art is about relationship building, infused with all the courage, compassion, and respect we can muster. It's kind of like a really beautiful window into someone's soul. But it's also a really complex and interesting way to express your experience of being alive in this world and sharing that with others.

Indigenous people have never been allowed the time to heal from the ongoing trauma of genocide. It seems as if we're just surviving one crisis after the next, perpetually. Many of us live in what feels like a permanent state of crisis, and so I think for some of us art is a way to deal with that reality, by helping others see what we experience. The process of making art is often solitary, we create a world as we see it. We're in our own bubble when we're creating. Art is very personal and expresses our reality and vision within the world. It can be powerful and healing not just for the artist but for the viewer as well. Indigenous artists who include the stories of historical injustice, the challenges, but choose to highlight our ongoing strength and resilience, rooted in our land, language, and cultures, can make art a powerful medicine of healing and reconciliation.

Opposite: *Astral Traveling*, 1989.
Acrylic on canvas, 3 × 4 ft.

Doda Elizabeth, 2000.
Oil pastel on Stonehenge paper, 30 × 42 in.

Great Grandfather Tekahonwénhsa, 1989.
Oil paints on canvas, 2 × 3 ft.

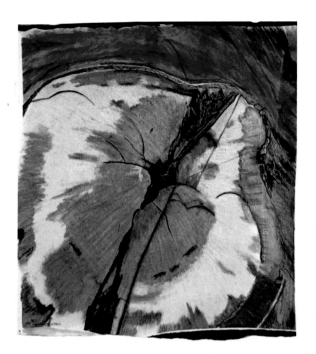

Top: *Stump*, 2000.
Oil pastel on
Stonehenge
paper, 2 × 3 ft.

Bottom: *Grandfather
speaks*, 2000.
Oil pastel on
Stonehenge
paper, 26 × 30 in.

6

WOMEN'S RIGHTS

SEAN: I think there is a risk of narrowing your contributions just to the summer of 1990, so I'd like to talk more about some of the incredible work you've done since the Mohawk Crisis, and I want to start with your work advocating for women's rights. You talked earlier about patriarchy and your experience as a female student at Concordia, of being aware of the *École Polytechnique* tragedy, and seeing how the media chose to focus more on the men in 1990, instead of the women at the heart of the struggle. Could you talk more about what your role as the spokesperson in 1990 taught you about women's rights and why you decided to become an advocate for women in and outside of your community in the years since?

ELLEN: It's true that sometimes I feel like my whole life as an activist has been confined to 1990, but I've worked on many issues advocating for Indigenous Peoples. My life has moved on since that time and I learned many lessons that summer that shaped my path. Most of the Elders who taught me were men, although many women have taught me as well. But the importance of the role of the women amongst Haudenosaunee Nations is to protect the land, which is exactly what we did in 1990. I've always been surrounded by strong women who were my role models. I grew up with a strong bond and love for my grandmother, mother, and sisters, and with my aunties too.

When I joined the Longhouse, I saw that the women of the Longhouse played a strong role in the decision making. I was in awe at how strong they were, and in learning how, under our Traditional Laws, women were given the role to be protectors of the language and land. There were many strong Indigenous women who have been on the frontlines of resistance movements, especially in 1990. The men were always looking to the women for guidance on what to do and how to respond to the police and the army, not the other way around. It was the women that calmed the men down when things seemed very volatile. This nurturing role that most women have is deeply embedded in our cultural protocol, and their leadership skills are connected to our responsibility to protect our Nation and our lands.

During the 1990 Siege, the women did not carry weapons. We knew we needed to guide and support the men on the frontlines—especially since stress was causing an adrenaline rush because the police and army were provoking us daily. The police and army were looking for an excuse to attack us, that's what they were hoping for. If the men responded, that would have risked the safety of everyone in the communities. As women, we needed to be strong and show our courage, determination, and leadership skills.

Colonial and patriarchal beliefs created the stereotype that Indigenous society is a hierarchy where the Chief is a man and decides everything for the people. It's actually quite the opposite. Decolonization requires the understanding that there is diversity among Indigenous cultures and protocols and that women have important roles within our governance systems. For the Haudenosaunee, under The Great Law of Peace, women are equal and are entrusted with holding the titles of each Chief in order to choose them. We transmit our Clans to our children. The Clan Mothers are the ones who declare war, and they appoint a war Chief who works for them. Women form the foundation of our Nations and governance systems, from inheriting our Clans and transmitting our languages to protecting the land and leading.

Like Mother Earth, we give life and nurture it. In our Creation Story the first two people on this planet were women: Sky Woman was pregnant with a female child who was born on this planet. So, the role and importance of the women in Iroquois culture is important. Our culture honours and respects these Origin Stories and respects the role women play in the health and well-being of our Nations.

SEAN: You've also spoken a lot about media bias and how it served to silence the role of women in the resistance in 1990. Can you expand on how that experience shaped your views?

ELLEN: Yes, people watch Alanis Obomsawin's film, *Kanehsatake: 270 Years of Resistance*, or they see news coverage from that summer, and they think they know the whole truth. They think the story has been told, but they're wrong. The focus was on men with weapons wearing face masks in camo, and this is what people still think when you mention the 1990 Mohawk Crisis. Images of warriors facing off against Canadian soldiers were sensationalized and helped sell newspapers. But this representation drew attention away from the real issue of ongoing land dispossession. The men, to be clear, played an extremely important role, but it's only a part of the picture.

The men and women behind the barricades worked together to come to a consensus on strategy and decisions. The two Kanien'kehá:ka communities directly affected, Kahnawà:ke and Kanehsatà:ke, tried to practise traditional democracy during the 1990 Siege, but democracy during war is challenging especially if there are people who don't possess the Traditional Knowledge of their culture.

Men cannot make decisions that exclude the women. There are certain roles for men and there are certain roles and responsibilities for women. But when it came to discussions and decisions during this time, traditional people in Kanehsatà:ke and Kahnawà:ke understood how important the role of the women is and that it's as equally important as the role of the men. And that wasn't captured by journalists, so I'm glad you're asking me about this.

It's important for people to know that women played a key role in the resistance and that they were key decision makers at the start of the barricades and throughout the entire summer. I want future generations to know that Indigenous women were and are at the heart of the resistance, not in the margins, as the media and government portrayed us. In terms of media bias, you have to remember that in the context of 1990, most journalists at the time knew nothing about Kanien'kehá:ka or the history of colonization by Canada.

SEAN: Michael Orsini, a journalist with *The Montreal Gazette* that summer, has written about how he was "parachuted into the story" with "little in the way of background knowledge" about Indigenous Peoples or the land struggle at Kanehsatà:ke.[1] Isn't that a key part of the problem?

ELLEN: Journalists had no clue about our culture, our history, our language—or Canada's colonial history. Nothing. They showed up framing the Mohawk Crisis solely as a criminal event and eager to talk to some scary-looking men with guns to get a dramatized news story. There were exceptions, however. Some journalists were sincere, open to learning, and were concerned about what was happening. But I think for many it was a culture shock and there was a cognitive dissonance amongst journalists regarding the history of Canada. They were reporting about us without understanding us at all. Today the media is a bit better. That said, every anniversary of 1990 I still get asked what happened that summer because the narrative is still being controlled by mainstream media and the government. It's frustrating because while society has become more educated, there is still a long way to go.

Nevertheless, in the summer of 1990 women demonstrated that we're an integral part of the struggle to protect our Homelands and resistance in our communities. We don't accept colonial patriarchy and marginalization. We as women are on the frontlines of Indigenous resistance and are central to these struggles. Building on the work of women, such as Sandra Lovelace Nicholas and Mary Two-Axe Earley, we carry on the fight for Indigenous women's rights.

The changes we're seeing now didn't happen overnight. Indigenous women had to fight for them and overcome a slew of challenges like misogyny, patriarchy, and the devaluing of our work in our Nations, even amongst our own people. Much of this oppression is rooted in settler colonialism, experienced in Indian Residential Schools, the cultural shaming and patriarchal, religious ideologies that are rooted in misogyny. However, there have been gradual changes because of the efforts and courage of Indigenous women. I was conscious of all that as I took up the role as spokesperson that summer. As I said, that experience helped me to find my voice, so to speak, and afterwards I was determined to continue to use my voice to speak up for the land, women's rights, and for our human rights, something we were told we did not have access to in 1990.

SEAN: I know a lot of Indigenous women see you as a role model. Quebec Idle No More co-organizer Melissa Mollen Dupuis has talked about growing up and watching you on TV during the summer of 1990 and being inspired. Your stand served as a catalyst for Melissa, and I'm sure countless others who watched you that summer. How does that make you feel?

ELLEN: I'm truly honoured and humbled, of course, and I don't think I can take much credit for it because I just did what I was asked to do and I had support from my Elders, particularly Walter David Sr., my family, and my aunties. I don't feel like a heroine. I'm a Kanien'kehá:ka woman who cares deeply about our land and I want a better future for the generations to come.

I know people focus on me because I was in front of the news cameras on a daily basis, but it really was a collective effort in 1990. If Indigenous women see me as a role model, then that is an incredible honour, but I want them to know that I was encouraged and supported by my own role models in my life, especially the women who fought before me. We stand on the shoulders of the women and men who came before us, and it's necessary that we acknowledge them. In 1990, I wanted to make my ancestors—my role models—proud, too.

SEAN: In terms of learning to use your voice to fight for women's rights after 1990, I'm wondering if you can explain how you became involved with Quebec Native Women, specifically, and what your involvement with that organization taught you?

ELLEN: Right, well, after 1990, I decided to join Quebec Native Women. I had known about the organization previously, as my mother, my aunties, and my grandmother were all part of this movement in the 1970s for equality for Indigenous women. And even my father talked about that in the brief time that he was a band councillor in our community.

I had knowledge of the inequalities facing Indigenous women in Canada. In my family, my aunties who married non-Indigenous men were denied their rights and/or their status—as a result of the Indian Act. For me, that was the norm, but we knew it wasn't right. I didn't question that when I was young; however, when I got older, I took it upon myself to learn more about our culture and history. Then Bill C-31 amended the Indian Act in 1985, and I could see the impacts that colonialism had had on my own family: denying my aunties and cousins access to their ancestral communities and people.

I felt that Quebec Native Women was an organization that could make a difference and I wanted to bring something positive to the fight, to the struggles of Indigenous women and their families. I served as vice president for a while and I really enjoyed the work, so when an election came around and the president was leaving, I became acting president. After thinking it over, I decided to run for the position, and I was elected. I was president of the organization for six and a half years, and it was one of the most interesting and wonderful periods in my life. I had the best team to work with, in regards to research, knowledge, and administration. I was so thankful to be surrounded and supported by so many amazing women, during my time as president. It was a pivotal time as well, as there were many issues affecting Indigenous people.

In 2004 the Stolen Sisters report came out which brought to light the issue of Missing and Murdered Indigenous Women in Canada.[2] Then there was the TRC that travelled across Canada gathering the stories of Indigenous people. And, at the same time, I participated at the United Nations Permanent Forum on Indigenous Issues where I talked about human rights and gender equality. It was an enriching experience which taught me a lot about the power of women, and women organizing, especially Indigenous women's strength as leaders. Today, I remain good friends with the people I worked with at Quebec Native Women.

We needed strong Indigenous women in leadership, like Beverley Jacobs, who was President of the Native Women's

Association of Canada at the time. We were able to push back against some of the Indigenous leadership that didn't see the struggles of Indigenous women as a priority or important in rebuilding our Nations from genocide. When Stolen Sisters came out in 2004, the work was thought to be a domestic problem, so women like Beverley Jacobs and Terry Brown were pivotal in providing strong leadership at the beginning as we began to educate the public and our own people about this issue.

The leadership role I shared with Beverley Jacobs pushed it out there and we worked to strengthen the voices of Indigenous women. I did many presentations at the National Assembly in Quebec and in Parliament, which had its own challenges. I met amazing people through this work, and I'm grateful to have had that opportunity to serve. I'm honoured to have represented Indigenous women in Quebec.

SEAN: Speaking of your work as an advocate for Indigenous women, I recently came across a speech you gave in the House of Commons in Ottawa, Ontario, on May 7, 2013. This was in relation to Bill S-2, an Act respecting family homes situated on First Nations reserves and matrimonial interest or rights to structures and lands situated on those reserves (Appendix A).

ELLEN: I remember that day, and it's sad that Indigenous women constantly need to fight to have their voices heard in spaces like the House of Commons. The issues affecting Indigenous women remain a low priority for governments, which delays justice for any positive changes in our advocacy efforts. But we must persist if we're to undo the impacts of colonization.

SEAN: Absolutely. Can you explain more about the kind of work and projects you were involved in during your time with Quebec Native Women?

ELLEN: Our focus was always on improving the lives of Indigenous women in Quebec and in Canada generally and working in solidarity with Indigenous Peoples across the globe. In organizing and in life, you always need somebody to plant the seeds and push from the grassroots. In my role as President of Quebec Native Women, that person was Beverley Jacobs. Our collaboration helped me focus my work on important issues that weren't being addressed by the national Indigenous organizations at the time.

Quebec Native Women was very independent as an association, though it was a member of the Native Women's Association of Canada. When I was president, we received Consultative Status to the United Nations Economic and Social Council (ECOSOC)—an essential status granted by the United Nations to Indigenous non-governmental organizations (NGOs). I felt it was important for Quebec Native Women to obtain ECOSOC status because we were becoming involved in many global Indigenous issues—biodiversity, women's rights, climate justice, education, and self-determination for instance.

These issues are all intertwined, so, as part of this work, my team and I attended the Convention on Biodiversity, the Nagoya Protocol.[3] This was an extremely challenging situation because member states and companies like Monsanto, who participate as NGOs, seek to deviously steal the Traditional Knowledge of Indigenous Peoples through influencing Western governments. There are some Indigenous people who are gatekeepers and support, for different reasons, certain member states' exploitation of Indigenous Peoples' Traditional Knowledge because they feel that we cannot upset UN member states if we contest and remind them of their international human rights obligations. The rationale is that the state controls the narrative and decisions. So, Indigenous people must tread lightly, or risk not being allowed to sit at the table—a table, mind you, whose power dynamic is unbalanced, as currently Indigenous people are more observers than actual decision makers. It's extremely frustrating.

All of the work on Indigenous Peoples' human rights, the acknowledgement by the UN that racist doctrines are morally condemnable,[4] helped justify our arguments to participate at UN meetings. However, we still have a long way to go. But that global solidarity piece is essential. Quebec Native Women became part of the Intercontinental Network of Indigenous Women of the Americas, and making those global connections helped highlight the common issues and solutions for Indigenous women across the Americas. So that was something that the team at Quebec Native Women put together. I'm proud of our accomplishments, and I hope that future generations can continue to benefit from the work that has been done.

Beverley Jacobs and other Indigenous women, and many NGOs like Amnesty International Canada, were successful in pushing forward with the momentum surrounding MMIWG. That was a huge undertaking to convince people that it was important and to educate them that this issue is rooted in colonial laws and attitudes.

It was a challenge to get genocide (femicide) any kind of attention, especially in Canada. Racist and misogynistic colonial attitudes, which have affected us all our lives, led to a lot of indifference when it came to the issues of Indigenous women. It makes me sad that it took so long for the issue of MMIWG to be treated seriously and it was only after the Native Women's Association of Canada received a huge funding grant to do research that everyone took notice.

When I went to my first vigil in Montreal, which was actually organized by a young Mohawk man named Irkar Belkaar, there were only about twenty people there. I thought, wow, more people are becoming aware of how this phenomenon is negatively affecting our women. Prime Minister

Stephen Harper once said that the issue wasn't "high" on his radar, and former Quebec Premier Jean Charest once told me he wasn't going to do anything about the issue because he "wasn't going to tell an Indigenous man what to do in his own home." I had to tell him that this wasn't solely a domestic issue but one rooted in colonialism. These are just the same old excuses colonial politicians make to ignore our issues and marginalize the voices and experiences of Indigenous women.

I told Charest that he didn't understand the issue, that it's not just about domestic abuse. The issue of men's violence against Indigenous women goes further than that. It's about the attitude of disrespect towards women and a history of disregarding our rights. We're not trying to hide what happens in our communities. What we're talking about is systemic discrimination and its violent nature that is disproportionally affecting Indigenous women, and widespread gender discrimination stemming from the Indian Act which is wrapped up in racism and genocide. That's what we're talking about with regards to the issue of MMIWG. There are over a thousand women identified as murdered between 1980 and 2012. All of their lives mattered, and they deserve justice. Their families deserve closure because these women were mothers, sisters, daughters, friends, cousins. It doesn't matter what walk of life they came from, what path they chose. It doesn't matter. They were all human beings.

At the beginning, trying to humanize Indigenous women was quite a battle, that was a big part of our work. We'd hear so many disrespectful statements from ignorant people, saying "yeah but she was a prostitute," "she deserved it." Horrible things. People can be so ignorant and cruel, you know? It shouldn't matter what path a woman is on, there are many factors that play into the paths we choose, no one deserves to be murdered. Each woman was a human being. When she died, when her family lost her, they grieved for her. As our Elder said, at the first vigil we held for

MMIWG, "she was someone's daughter, someone's sister, aunt, wife, friend."

So, there was a lot of education that was required to get society to care about this issue, and it's still difficult sometimes to break through the indifference that persists. There is so much more work to do, to follow through on the MMIWG inquiry and Final Report (2019) and its recommendations.

For me, I always think about Helen Betty Osborne. This nineteen-year-old, beautiful young woman had dreams of becoming a teacher and living a fulfilling life. Instead, she was brutally raped and killed by a group of white men in The Pas, Manitoba, in 1971. The RCMP, who were complicit, knew who her killers were for years but they did nothing simply because it was the norm for these kinds of violent actions and murders to go unanswered. To them, Indigenous women are not a priority. Today crimes against Indigenous women continue with impunity. To me, that's not only disturbing, it's outrageous. It's a racist, systemic norm that is unacceptable. We know that police are complicit in the violence against Indigenous women, as Human Rights Watch stated in their 2013 report titled "Those Who Take Us Away."[5]

Authorities continue to defend corporate interests, brutalizing and criminalizing Indigenous people who are defending their rights to self-determination. It's disturbing that this still goes on. It's a crisis for our communities, and Canada doesn't really care. We needed action decades ago, and, in my work with Quebec Native Women, we tried to raise the profile of this issue to protect our communities and our women from further harm. I think we were successful in that our communities and society have become more aware, but there is so much work ahead. The struggle continues.

SEAN: You mentioned earlier that you were aware of some of the sexism of the Indian Act and the efforts by previous generations of women in challenging that. As part of your

work with the Quebec Native Women, how did you confront
the Indian Act and its gender discrimination?

ELLEN: Colonization uses an age-old strategy which is to
divide and conquer Indigenous Peoples so that they can continue to steal our lands and resources; to annihilate the First
Peoples of Turtle Island by chipping away our rights to self-
determination. The Indian Act implemented policies and laws
based in gender discrimination to succeed at this mission. As
a result, the colonial ideology and its propaganda has created deep divisions in our communities and has succeeded
at making many of us feel inferior. It gave men a superficial
political power, which was contingent upon the Minister of
Indian Affairs' approval, while Indigenous women were (and
still are) marginalized. While it may be changing incrementally, there is still a long way to go.

The Indian Act undermined and criminalized[6]
Indigenous Peoples' traditional governance structures like
Kaianera'kó:wa to justify the theft of our Homelands and our
children. The band council system was created by Canada
to continue to control and assimilate us but always with the
necessary rubber-stamping of the Minister of Indian Affairs
(now Minister of Crown-Indigenous Relations).

The difference between band councils and traditional
governing systems is that one is colonially created (band
councils), the other existed pre-Contact and has survived
colonization (traditional governance). Leaders were chosen
by the Clan Mothers, who would select their representative
based on their character, their knowledge of the language and
ceremonies, and whether they were good listeners or kind.
While leaders were chosen under traditional governments,
it was always a democracy that seeks consensus. It isn't a
hierarchy like the band council system. That's how our traditional governance works according to The Great Law of
Peace. The colonial-created imbalance, which is a hierarchical

characteristic of a band council system, is an imposition upon our communities. Patriarchy and gender discrimination has been absorbed into our ways of being, just as the colonial project intended, and it wreaks havoc in every aspect of our lives. Weakening us from within.

But Indigenous Peoples have been fighting back against this kind of assimilation and colonization. They're starting to see how colonization has disrupted and affected our lives, causing dysfunction in our traditional governing structures and teachings. This has led to so many problems for Indigenous women and people due to the double discrimination of being a woman and being Indigenous in a patriarchal and white supremacist society. It's sad to say but addressing the issue of murdered and missing women isn't moving fast enough to save Indigenous women and girls from violence. This is a direct result of the impacts of Canadian colonization and indifference.

When we consider how much apathy there was amongst even our own people when we began the MMIWG campaign, and to see how far we've come on the issue, I think that the movement to confront violence against women and girls is gaining strong momentum. But challenges remain in educating society that this is a real problem rooted in colonialism and that more work needs to be done. The Indian Act still creates divisions from within, bureaucrats coercively waving the carrot of funding agreements that benefit government's agenda and not the needs of the community. Canada drags its feet, using the approval of the Treasury Board of Canada as having the final say, to place the cost of anything that we do to try and undo the impacts of colonial laws and policies. Annual vigils remind us that the issue of violence against Indigenous women remains a priority, as it is often a marginalized issue. At the international level, it is among many topics of priority for Indigenous Peoples, who themselves have a diversity of priorities. But we continue to fight to keep our sisters and families safe.

This is another effect of the Indian Act which, insidiously, was created to get rid of the "Indian problem." As long as the Indian Act exists, our human rights will be placed to the side and this "nation-to-nation" rhetoric will be just words by politicians to placate their constituents and public. The Indian Act will continue to control us, to the advantage of the colonizer. The Indian Act has never been for the benefit our communities but for the benefit of Canada. It keeps us divided, placing us in constant survival mode, in crisis mode, because the colonial-rooted social issues are so huge. Time is needed to overcome the effects of Canada's genocide. This includes ongoing land dispossession, which chips away at our land base—especially here in Kanehsatà:ke. In other words, the Indian Act is a management tool designed to keep us oppressed, dispossessed, divided, and disempowered, and that facilitates the continued theft of our lands, waters, and resources.

SEAN: You have received a number of impressive awards, including the Golden Eagle Award from the Native Women's Association of Canada (2005), the Jigonsaseh Women of Peace Award (2008), and the International Women's Day Award from the Quebec Bar Association, to name only a few. As a leading voice on these issues, what do you think the next steps are in the struggle to advance the rights of Indigenous women?

ELLEN: We have all the research—the commissions and reports—we need to create different kinds of policies and solutions that will oblige police and authorities and government institutions and entities to respect the rights of Indigenous women and Indigenous Peoples. Now we need to implement change and hold society, the authorities, and governments accountable. Solutions must be based on Indigenous laws and teachings, and the needs of Indigenous Peoples in order to help educate the public and our own people that violence against women is not part of our culture. Curriculum in all schools must change to teach the truth about the brutality of colonization. That would be a start.

We also have a lot of work to do within our own communities. I think that when we look at some of our colonial-created dysfunction, the government consistently uses the divisions as an excuse to continue the violation of our human rights—so they can carry on with the stealing of our lands and defending corporate interests. We need to break that cycle, to decolonize our relationships, and do better for our communities and future generations. Not just with Canadians but with each other; those of us who have shared this collective pain and the collective resistance of many generations of Indigenous Peoples.

A revolution requires people to understand what freedom and justice means, in a larger sense. We know that the system is archaic and is broken. Internalized capitalism and the unfettered free market economy that promotes and protects corporate rights over human rights and women's rights is the problem. Human rights, education, health care all get put on the back burner and are sacrificed for corporate greed and profit as Mother Earth is destroyed. People are trained and rewarded through capitalism; they're trained to not think about how this society is tethered to a way of life that is not sustainable. As long as we continue being good consumers, then we can continue looking away and thinking it's someone else's problem or responsibility to do something.

Justice is slow and costly, and it's evident by the way Canada's feet are dragging on this issue, and that the issue of MMIWG is low on the list of priorities. This has endangered the safety of Indigenous women and their families, our communities, and the ecosystem we depend on for survival. Resource development and urban sprawl continues to shrink our land base, as does the creation of man camps near Indigenous communities without our free, prior, and informed consent. These practices destroy the environment, and future generations won't be able to enjoy the land and its resources.

SEAN: Speaking of the planet, a lot of Indigenous women activists are connecting Canada's violence against Indigenous women and the violence against the land and waters and non-human relations. How do you make sense of these connections?

ELLEN: We know what the answers are. Again, we have all the reports and commissions that tell the story of colonialism and genocide. We have hundreds if not thousands of recommendations which outline the frameworks needed for social change. Economic prosperity, or the bottom line, is the underlining concern of colonial states. It's another example of the systemic racism and gender discrimination that Indigenous women's advocacy has faced since the early days of contesting the inequalities in the Indian Act in the early 1970s. It's frustrating because our voices aren't respected. As I mentioned, it's a double discrimination in this society, when you're a woman and Indigenous in Canada.

There's nothing wrong with conducting research studies; reports like RCAP, TRC, MMIWG have given Canadians and Indigenous Peoples alike guidance on how to implement the recommendations and in understanding settler colonialism. Research and reports alone have not brought about the changes we need, even though they are evidence based. These reports must be grounded in efforts to teach the truth about Canada's genocidal history against Indigenous Peoples—not just a footnote in a history book.

For centuries Indigenous people have been calling on colonizers to stop hurting our people, to stop hurting the land and contaminating the waters, to stop stealing our children and killing our women. Yet, we're still waiting for the colonizers and their governments to act with honour. Instead, Canada just drags its feet hoping that our issues will be forgotten until the next election.

We know the connection between the rape of the land and the abuse of Indigenous women, symbolically, they're the same. The destruction of our Homelands—like the toxic waste dump in Kanehsatà:ke, which causes the land to be unusable for thousands of years,[7] like the tar sands and its terrible tailing ponds—it threatens the quality of life for present and future generations. The impacts of our lives and our decisions will affect seven generations from now. What we're missing is *true* reconciliation: action to repair our relationship with one another and Mother Earth. We all need to heal from the genocidal project. But reconciliation must come from Canada and its citizens and must not be placed upon the shoulders of Indigenous people.

SEAN: That was a key teaching of the Idle No More movement, right? That all of these issues were connected, and that people need to take direct action to confront colonial injustice, violence against Indigenous women, disrespect of the lands and waters. It was, as Dene political theorist Glen Sean Coulthard has argued, an example of what "resurgent Indigenous politics might look like on the ground."[8]

For me, Idle No More was a key moment of consciousness raising and organizing.[9] I was living abroad at the time, in London, UK, and I remember occupying the British Museum with some comrades in solidarity with the transnational Idle No More movement.[10] There is a great collection of essays and poems about Idle No More by the Kino-nda-niimi Collective called *The Winter We Danced*.[11] You have a piece in there, originally a Facebook post from January 2013, talking about Attawapiskat Chief Theresa Spence's hunger strike and her courage. What do you remember about Idle No More and its power to make all of these connections and inspire a new generation, especially of Indigenous women, to be leaders and use their voices?

ELLEN: Well, I think it was a very tough time to be an Indigenous person, at the peak of Idle No More, because of the disrespect by Stephen Harper, who was prime minister at the time, and others like him who don't think much of Indigenous people.

So, Idle No More, which started in 2012 with four women in Saskatchewan, was part of that process of denouncing the systemic racism that Harper epitomized. Refusing to be "idle" or silent about ongoing oppression, it was very inspiring to see the number of young people, especially young women, who stood up against Harper's omnibus bill, Bill C-45, which weakened environmental rights and excluded consultations with Indigenous Peoples and undermined our inherent rights.[12] It was a big awakening for people and brought many people together. Like 1990, it was a spark in the ongoing resistance movement against colonization. People saw the government's proposed legislation as an attack on Indigenous Peoples and the land, and it was really inspiring to see that there was another generation willing to stand up and be vocal in their opposition. But many of us who had been active for decades thought "we've never been idle," but we understood and supported the movement of Idle No More.

At the same time, there was Attawapiskat Chief Theresa Spence's hunger strike. Witnessing on social media all the horrible things being said about her and Indigenous women generally, it was disgusting. I remember seeing people post about her weight and her motivations for the hunger strike. How ignorant and disrespectful! Women have to put up with this kind of disrespect all the time. Our bodies are constantly being dehumanized, in a mocking manner, expected to fit an image that suits the colonizer. In a way I'm glad there wasn't social media during the 1990 Resistance because the vitriol would have been so toxic. I would have preferred to not be bombarded by what was being said about me by racists that summer.

When we get labelled as activists or Land Defenders, which government equates as being criminal in many instances, it's often done without any context. This is part of our daily struggle because if we don't fight it, we will disappear and become part of the melting pot that is Western society. It would be turning our backs on all the efforts by previous generations to give us our languages, our cultures, our values. It's part of the status quo to label Indigenous people as troublemakers or criminals. It's a way of delegitimizing our struggle for justice. We saw that again during Idle No More. This is just part of our reality. Unless we want to become footnotes in history, and see our Homelands be chipped away until we can no longer use the land, these are necessary acts of resistance, it's what we have to do to ensure our survival as Indigenous people, as Indigenous women.

People may assume it's easier to give up and assimilate and say, "okay, I will accept the colonizers' wishes, whatever it takes to not have to struggle. To believe that it's someone else's responsibility to create change, not mine!" But we have the responsibility to continue to push back against our oppressors. Previous generations did it for us, it's now our turn to do this for future generations.

I think Idle No More showed the power of Indigenous organizing and the brilliance of Indigenous women to yet another generation who will be inspired to take up the struggle. The unity was heartwarming, and the ripple effects of all of these resistance movements continue today—from the AIM in the 1970s, the international work of Indigenous people like Deskaheh Levi General, and the Mohawk Resistance in the 1990s to Idle No More. We see in our communities that another generation is standing up for their rights and that colonization isn't over. There are a lot of young and brilliant leaders coming out of these moments. We see the continuation of these resistance movements which began centuries ago because we haven't entirely forgotten our traditional teachings and our history. It's the colonial state who persistently refuses to respect our rights to self-determination and so we have to remind them of their international human rights obligations.

SEAN: It's interesting that you say that, because *Chatelaine* just selected the Wet'suwet'en matriarchs and Land Defenders as the Women of the Year for 2020.[13] These Land Defenders, who were arrested by the RCMP, are being celebrated in *Chatelaine*.

ELLEN: Really? It's very telling that the ordinary citizen has a different perspective than the colonial governments.

SEAN: Do you see something like that—mainstream recognition—as a positive change in the way that Indigenous women are treated by the media, in some ways?

ELLEN: Well, having good allies is really important in the progress of Indigenous resistance. And it's necessary for non-Indigenous people to become educated on how laws like the Indian Act have impacted Indigenous people, especially Indigenous women's human rights. It's crucial in making progress, that society realizes how important Indigenous women are within the struggle for justice. It's heartening that things are changing in this regard, but the resistance to create real change is coming from all levels of government. And it doesn't end there. Is *Chatelaine* supporting the Wet'suwet'en in the fight to get their land back? Are the readers helping to support the organizing, are they contributing to legal defense funds? You know? It needs to go beyond a feel-good news story. Although I think this is great and helps expand the reach of our issues.

It's great that *Chatelaine* is highlighting what these brave women are doing to protect their Nation's right to self-determination, it's a national magazine with a big reach for sure. But it's also a collective effort. History has shown that awareness alone won't end the crisis in our communities. It's great to have that momentum for this year, to have these matriarchs spotlighted for the courageous work they're doing. But at the same time, land dispossession continues happening on a daily basis. I hope people realize how insecure and difficult it is to be an Indigenous woman and to live the consequences of double discrimination under Canada's colonial systems.

The genocide that began on our lands five hundred years ago hasn't changed. Racism and the theft of our Homelands has remained constant. It's the resilience and strength of Indigenous people, and the work of Indigenous women in particular, in the continued fight against oppression and colonization, that that needs to be recognized. *Chatelaine*, and other media outlets, should continue to cover Indigenous issues to strengthen Indigenous women's voices and help us to gain control over our own narrative. Media should take an active role in reconciliation. To get our land and respect back, Indigenous voices need to be heard. Indigenous women's rights must be respected. Our efforts for justice and equality and our historical influence on the women's rights movement must be acknowledged.

7

INDIGENOUS INTERNATIONALISM

SEAN: In his recent book about the Standing Rock protests and the history of Oceti Sakowin resistance in the United States, *Our History Is the Future*, Sioux historian Nick Estes builds on the work of Michi Saagiig Nishnaabeg writer Leanne Betasamosake Simpson and talks about the "long tradition of Indigenous internationalism."[1] He argues that "far beyond the project of seeking equality within the colonial state, the tradition of radical Indigenous internationalism" imagines a different kind of world that respects Indigenous sovereignty and human rights.[2]

In 1990, you experienced human rights violations as the police and military denied people behind the barricades in Kanehsatà:ke food and medical supplies among other things, but you also experienced support and solidarity from Indigenous Nations around the world. How did your experiences shape your understanding of the concepts of human rights and Indigenous internationalism and why you think they're important for people today?

ELLEN: Yes, both Kanehsatà:ke and Kahnawà:ke experienced thousands of human rights abuses in 1990, and no government entity was ever held accountable. That changed the way I see things today. We were all feeling the full weight of the state and the authorities plus the army on us, so to see to what degree the governments were willing to go to squash our resistance, even before 1990 happened, that changed my whole outlook from that point onwards. During that summer Elder Walter David Sr. taught me that our rights are at an international level because we are Nations with sovereign rights to our Homelands.

After 1990, I became interested in what was going on at the international level to protect Indigenous rights, especially the struggles of Indigenous Peoples around the world. At one point, we heard that the Zapatistas had been following our fight and used some of our media strategies in their struggle. And so I wanted to learn more about other Indigenous struggles around the world too, because we're all similar in that we're all struggling for the land.

I became more involved in international issues during my time with Quebec Native Women, and in 2004 I went to the United Nations. I knew people like Kenneth Deer had been going there for decades, so there was already a presence of Indigenous people to rely upon.

It was also during the time when UNDRIP was still in draft form and there was a lot of opposition from colonial states like Canada, the United States, New Zealand, and Australia. Stephen Harper was prime minister then, and there was a lot of opposition being directed towards Indigenous Peoples during the final stages of passing the UNDRIP. Even though Canada was a member of the UN Human Rights Council at the time, it voted against adopting UNDRIP. It was kind of interesting to see, because people on the international stage saw Canada as a great defender of human rights, although Indigenous Peoples were revealing to the world that Canada failed and continues to violate the human rights of Onkwehón:we Nations.

As Indigenous Peoples of Turtle Island, our Homelands are occupied by settler colonial Canada, whereby addressing the colonial-rooted problems remains challenging. The perspective of society is we live in a rich country like Canada, so we must then be fine. But we're still struggling against land dispossession and the impacts of genocide.

To us, Canada isn't a benevolent peacekeeping nation at all. Canada treats Indigenous Peoples poorly and its history of genocide continues. In 1990, we tarnished Canada's "peacekeeper" and "defender of human rights" image. Canada cannot use the army against Indigenous people without expecting its human rights reputation to take a hit. I was hearing from many people at the international level that Canada's squeaky-clean image had been tarnished. So they undertook a lot of damage control, a strategy which included damaging the reputation of Indigenous people involved.

When I travelled to the UN, I learned a lot about how Canada is viewed internationally. I think a lot of people are shocked when we speak on the global stage of how Canada persistently violates Indigenous Peoples' human rights and their international human rights obligations.

On the world stage, all states play the same game of professing to uphold the minimum standards of human rights protection, though some don't even try. States attempt to present and promote themselves as forthright, compassionate, and honest, a kind of best version of themselves to the international community. Many states proudly boast about their human rights record and how they follow the rule of law, but it's all propaganda at the end of the day. All states persistently violate human rights, especially when it comes to Indigenous people. Then they claim Indigenous Peoples are criminals to justify their oppressive racist laws.

Stephen Harper once said at a G8 summit that Canada has "no history of colonialism" and that it was open for business.[3] I mean, maybe he thought that wouldn't get reported, but it did. It just sounded like nonsense because Indigenous people vigilantly try to protect our rights to self-determination on a daily basis, and live with colonization on a daily basis.

However, the UN provides us a platform to have our voices and issues heard at the UN Permanent Forum on Indigenous Issues (UNPFII). While there is more work to do, so that Indigenous Peoples can have full and effective participation at the UN, this is a space for Indigenous people around the world to bring international attention to our issues. And this forum teaches us that there are many parallels with our issues even if we're not from the same parts of the world. We, as Indigenous Peoples throughout the world, are fighting colonial oppression and discrimination. There are common issues linking our human rights struggle for water and shelter and protection from land dispossession, systemic racism, and oppression. This includes countries that are celebrated on the world stage for their tolerance and commitment to human rights, like Canada. There are many wonderful human rights declarations and conventions, treaties that provide a framework for states to uphold their international human rights obligations. These are the tools we use to critique states like Canada. But it has to be more than words on paper. The UN must provide stronger mechanisms to hold states to account for their violations of Indigenous Peoples' human rights. Opportunities to tell these stories of our realities must be held with as much importance as the discussions in the UN General Assembly. Otherwise it is tokenism, and states like Canada will always be believed that they know what's best for us.

The UNPFII provides space for Indigenous people to report human rights complaints and has heard many complaints against Canada's systemic racism and the failure at upholding their human rights obligations. It's a platform where numerous human rights abuses against Indigenous people in Canada are linked to the implementation of systemic racism embedded in the Doctrine of Discovery.

Ellen at the United Nations in New York City, for the UN Permanent Forum on Indigenous Issues, 2010.

Colonial entities in the Americas have been brutal towards Indigenous people, not just in the past but today as well. The assumed sovereignty over Indigenous Homelands is part of the implementation of the Doctrine of Discovery, even though the UN has declared such doctrines legally invalid and morally reprehensible. Yet, domestically, judges are still using it in their decisions regarding Indigenous Peoples and Land Defenders. The genocidal project continues.

SEAN: Can you expand a bit more about the strategy of working with the UN? And as you say, there is a history of Indigenous leaders travelling abroad to press for justice. I'm more familiar with the West Coast and people such as Skwxwú7mesh Chief Joe Capilano who exhausted efforts domestically and then went to England to speak to the King directly in the early 1900s. Or the work of Secwépemc leader George Manuel who sought to unify Indigenous Peoples with the Constitution Express between 1979 and 1981, which sent a delegation to the United Nations in New York and another to Europe as well.[4] So, there's this long history of Indigenous Peoples organizing outside of Canada. Can you explain more about why it's so important to advance calls for human rights and Indigenous people's rights on an international stage?

ELLEN: The Iroquois Confederacy was one of the first to actually send an Indigenous representative to meet with global leaders. In 1923, Levi General, under the title of Chief Deskaheh Levi General representing the Iroquois Confederacy, travelled to Europe to talk to the League of Nations (which later became the United Nations) in Geneva, Switzerland. The League, however, urged by Canada, the United Kingdom, and the USA, refused to hear him and made his life difficult, calling him "crazy." However, he did have friends and allies in the city of Geneva, but he became ill while he was there. He came back home and delivered a famous speech, known as "The Redman's Appeal for Justice."[5] But Canada, when they made traditional governments illegal in 1924, they also issued an arrest warrant for Deskaheh Levi General, claiming he had stolen the wampum belts which Canada claimed belonged to them. These are wampum belts he had entrusted to him as a Traditional Chief and he was in his right to hold them. So these made-up stories by Canada caused Levi General to never again return home, and he was forced to spend his last days away from Six Nations, his home, because there was an arrest warrant for him in Canada. Levi General spent his last days in the home of Clinton Rickard of the Tuscarora Nation. So, there's a history of resistance that we are building upon that goes back even further than the AIM and Red Power organizing in the 1960s. Internationalism is something that goes back many generations.

Like Deskaheh Levi General was saying to the global community one hundred years ago, we are Sovereign Nations with a land base that is occupied that has been stolen through ongoing colonization and land theft. We have a government, we have a land base, we have a language, we have a culture, we have a Constitution. The Iroquois Confederacy is one of the oldest "league of nations" there is.

That Deskaheh Levi General, one of our own people, our own Chiefs, went abroad to represent us, and he was treated so poorly at the behest of Canada, the United Kingdom, and the United States, well, that just goes to show how weak and fragile the colonizer's position really is in regard to their sovereignty. Because, if we weren't such a threat, why would they be going to the lengths that they have for so long to continuously try to discredit us and ignore us? That's why talking to the international community is still important for us, for our struggles. We need to press on the world stage as well as at home.

With the UNDRIP the international community opened the door to having Indigenous Peoples' human rights respected and recognized. In its preamble, it condemns "racist doctrines and policies and practices based on or advocating superiority of peoples . . . [that] are scientifically false, legally invalid, morally condemnable, and socially unjust."[6] It did not give Indigenous Peoples new rights, but instead, reinforced the fact that Indigenous Peoples have always had these rights. Since Canadian laws places Indigenous Peoples, or "Indians," under the Indian Act as wards of the state, the international arena helps us reveal the violations impacting our human rights, which is something I think Deskaheh Levi General would have been happy to see—that we have not relented and are following in his footsteps. Leaders like Deskaheh Levi General are important to remember in the history of Indigenous Peoples at the international level because if we put things into context, the work he undertook was powerful, even if during his lifetime he did not succeed in his mission.

There is the older generation who taught me that we should go to the Queen, to the King and the Governor General, that kind of thing, which is the protocol in Canada for dealing with Indigenous people; however, that hasn't really gotten us anywhere. Pleading to our oppressors hasn't been a winning strategy. Deskaheh Levi General realized that.

Nevertheless, I still think that the UN, especially since the adoption of UNDRIP, is a place to take our grievances and push them into the international spotlight. The doors are now open to us, and we're allowed to use the complaint procedures of the United Nations to talk about what Canada is or isn't doing. That's important because Canada isn't listening and seems to have no interest in meaningful reconciliation. It's just a big corporate conglomerate that uses coercive methods to divide and conquer Indigenous people and communities so that they may continue to dispossess us of our lands and resources to satisfy their greed and make money. Canada's court system continues to implement colonial laws and policies, to protect settlers' control of Indigenous people and our Homelands. When it comes to protecting our rights to self-determination, the "justice" system isn't for us. While there have been some small wins, there are many more challenges to face, as we've seen recently with recent Mi'gmaq fishing rights and the struggles in Wet'suwet'en territory.

All levels of government in Canada consistently side with their constituents and so the norm is to trample over

Indigenous people's rights; colonial laws have been designed to protect settlers' rights, not Indigenous people's. It's up to Indigenous Nations like the Mi'gmaq and Wet'suwet'en Nations—and many others, just like the Mohawks in 1990. If we didn't stand up for ourselves and say "no" to development without free, prior, and informed consent, we would be swallowed up whole by the colonial machine.

The government loosely interprets Supreme Court decisions, or it stalls on implementing decisions that could create change. And when Indigenous people try to move forward on the small wins, when we do get wins, it seems that Canada and third-party corporations increase their efforts to undermine our rights. And so many of these decisions are never fully implemented. Government and corporations have the human and financial resources to delay justice in order to keep us oppressed, under daily threats to our personal safety and ongoing destruction of the biodiversity of our Homelands. To protect their economic interests, they try to discredit Indigenous people and create suspicion around those who are standing up for their rights and sovereignty.

We know that domestic laws are not on our side; Canadian courts interpret our human rights through a racist doctrine rather than a human rights lens. As well, it's costly, takes a great deal of time and energy which stresses the already limited resources we have. That's why the international stage is an important one. The UN may not be perfect, but we have an international audience who is listening and documents our interventions. This helps us amplify our voices. It's really a unique kind of platform whereby Indigenous people from all over the world are there to call out different colonial states on their failure at upholding the highest standards of human rights. Some UN member states don't even uphold the *minimum* standards of human rights in their own backyards, those being: freedom, security, and recognizing the dignity and worth of a human being. They can't even do that. The UN, as I see it, is a necessary arena for us to be in and will continue to be a venue where we can push for justice in this world to overcome centuries of genocide.

SEAN: What's the experience like at the UN as an Indigenous person? Do you feel like people there are listening and interested in putting pressure on Canada to change and do better today?

ELLEN: The UN Permanent Forum is an excellent venue to discuss the rights of Indigenous people, as is the UN Expert Mechanism on the Rights of Indigenous Peoples (EMRIP). The UN Convention on Biodiversity is more toxic, its focus has been on access to benefit sharing and the commodification of our knowledge systems, causing threats to Traditional Knowledge. If Indigenous people are at the table, we can monitor who is a friendly state and identify the Indigenous gatekeepers working for states. But really, we have little say in what happens to our Homelands' biodiversity.

But the UNPFII and EMRIP are important spaces to have your issues heard. You can either do a verbal intervention or a written submission. In my experience, it can feel a bit chaotic at times because of the protocols and time limits—you're given three minutes to say your intervention. There are so many issues to discuss, and it can be frustrating if you don't get on the "speakers list." So sometimes issues can easily get overlooked as a result. Participating at the international level requires being prepared, organized, and assertive to make sure our issues are heard.

SEAN: Yes, I recently came across a speech that you gave as President of Quebec Native Women at the United Nations Permanent Forum on Indigenous Issues on May 19, 2009 (Appendix B).

ELLEN: Thank you. I'm glad someone thought to preserve that speech. I'm proud of the work I was able to do with my team at Quebec Native Women. The best part of the experience at the UN, though, is gathering and meeting other Indigenous people from around the world and learning about their realities. That has been so enriching for me, coming from a small town like Kanehsatà:ke, with all its challenges in our struggle for justice. So it's refreshing to meet other people who are also experiencing similar things or to see that it's possible when people get together and fight for the same causes. That solidarity is really heartening.

But there's a lot of apathy in many of our communities, which is one of the results of colonization. It has taken away the ability for critical thought, for empathy, for respect for all our relations. The Indian Residential Schools did a real number on our identity, our values, as well as the impacts of government laws and policies which perpetuate colonialism on a daily basis.

Like most Western democracies, the attitude by its citizens is that it is the responsiblity of the politicians to deal with issues like reconciliation or changing curriculums to expose the truth about the genocide that happened in the Americas. Participating at the UN is refreshing, as it feels as if our voices are being listened to. Not only do you have an opportunity to reveal issues affecting your community or Nation, but you also learn about other Indigenous Peoples and see how we're all connected in our beliefs and struggles. But there are frustrations because we're dealing with an international bureaucracy too. In the international arena, Indigenous Peoples aren't seen as Sovereign Nations but rather like NGOs belonging to UN member states. But the "s" in "Peoples" signifies that we have the right to self-determination.

In some ways, it's another level of colonization as we're thought of like an NGO, which can be frustrating. However, the door has been opened, although we're still fighting to protect our human rights and self-determination. In some respects, we have progressed incrementally, but we have not reached the goal that Deskakeh Levi General intended, which is to be respected as Sovereign Nations. For me, it's useful to learn about the UN system and how it can help promote our struggle and protect our human rights. I hope new generations continue to go there and learn about the international efforts to protect the human rights of Indigenous Peoples, and that they will be more successful.

SEAN: You mentioned the UN Declaration on the Rights of Indigenous Peoples, or UNDRIP. Can you say more about your thoughts on this, and Canada's commitment to implement it? Different provinces, such as British Columbia (2019), have recently adopted it and Canada has adopted it as well in 2021. Are you hopeful that this will bring about meaningful change?

ELLEN: I know there was debate on the issue, and not everyone will see it the same way. My perspective is that UNDRIP isn't perfect, but for twenty years Indigenous Peoples have negotiated with states to have it passed. Brilliant Indigenous Peoples and allies fought hard for it, and its implementation is a chance to actually break with the colonial status quo. That's how I see it. In 2021, I argued that Bill C-15 is a chance "to actually break with the colonial status quo."[7] I'll read you what I wrote:

> I have great admiration for all those champions who continued this fight, year after year, until the UNDRIP became a consensus document at the UN.
>
> What resulted is the first international human rights instrument to clearly recognize what we have been saying all along—that Indigenous Peoples have the inherent right to self-determination. Throughout its provisions—there

are 46 in total—the Declaration sets out in detail the obligations of nation-states, public institutions, corporations
and more to honour and respect our inherent rights, our
homelands, our identities, and in every aspect of our lives.

Like most Indigenous land defenders, as history has
shown us, I view anything the government does with skepticism. We have witnessed many Indigenous-led movements
that spark resistance to colonialism be quelled by promises
that wind up broken. Recommendations to improve and
respect the inherent human rights of Indigenous Peoples—
such as the TRC's Calls to Action or various Supreme Court
decisions remain words on paper. While many Canadians
agree with the various reports, in reality, Indigenous peoples must fight to protect their rights.

As a piece of government legislation, Bill C-15 deserves
our skepticism. But considering what we have to deal with
under the Indian Act, many see Bill C-15 as a positive
development. I feel strongly that its passage into law would
represent the best chance we've seen in a very long time to
actually break with the colonial status quo.[8]

But here's the thing: there has to be political will from
government. Now that UNDRIP has been adopted, how is
Canada going to do things differently? There has to be a
better understanding of what human rights are and what
the state's legal obligations are. Declarations may be aspira-
tional, but they comprise international human rights norms
which are supposed to be absorbed into domestic policy.
Canada resists upholding its legal obligations, jeopardizing
Indigenous Peoples' human rights for its own economic gain.
I mean, they're playing this game where they pretend that
they want to decolonize and get rid of the Indian Act. But
in reality, it's all a very sneaky way of pushing more assimilation and pressing for the extermination of our rights. It's
colonization repackaged.

The Government of Canada and its provinces in particular are filled with bureaucrats who work full time to try to undermine Indigenous Peoples' human rights. They talk about UNDRIP but do they really understand what it means? When you implement something, that means you understand what it's about, not just picking and choosing what you want to implement. You must understand the spirit of its intent, making the words come to life off the paper, opening the hearts and minds of the people. It provides a framework for change and justice.

It's unfortunate that we live in a society where human rights are expendable for the sake of economic benefit. It feels like a war, the rich against the poor. It's a very dysfunctional society in which racism is the accepted the norm and whereby systemic racism and environmental destruction are justified for corporate profits. I think that is the key reason why there's so much resistance to change: Land Back will mean less money in settlers' pockets and the coffers of the state—hence the lack of political will to implement meaningful change on issues of decolonization and reconciliation. Canada's economic prosperity has always been at the expense of Indigenous Peoples' lands and our human rights.

It's really frustrating when you live day in and day out with that kind of oppression and chronic stress. The politicians and bureaucrats who are making the decisions aren't doing it with human rights in mind. They're basing their decisions on what kind of social or economic benefits they're going to have. International human rights norms and obligations, like the those stated in UNDRIP, have as a foundation the Universal Declaration of Human Rights that has been absorbed into domestic legislation by the majority of UN member states around the world. It goes back to the question of how you bring people into understanding, recognizing, that justice is needed and human rights are universal.

We shouldn't have to take our fight to colonial courts to be able to protect our lands, ways of life, and rights to self-determination. In fact, Indigenous people are the only ones who must go to the colonizers' court system to protect our human rights. We have the right to a quality of life and health in our territories, just as anybody else who is living in this country. And we have the right to access our Homelands.

But the cognitive dissonance about Indigenous Peoples' human rights continues to benefit the economics of settler states. Canadians who are indifferent to our plight and history seem oblivious to the fact that their prosperity is built on the backs of Indigenous people. They're getting rich from developing our lands, which they've stolen, and their developments are protected by colonial laws. So, naturally, they stay quiet and benefit from the racist norms they're oblivious to in order to justify their inaction on key issues, such as those that the RCAP and the MMIWG inquiries have laid bare.

In reality, we just want to be treated as human beings and to be able to live on our lands, using the teachings of our ancestors, and preserve our language and health—things most people take for granted. To live in peace and safety, it's not much to ask for.

SEAN: I agree. Can you speak more about the kinds of work you have done on the international stage about climate justice from an Indigenous perspective and some of the lessons you think we still need to learn in this moment?

ELLEN: Yes, I think the rights of Indigenous Peoples are intimately connected to the fight for climate justice, just as women's rights are tied to human rights and climate justice. It's all interconnected.

Part of my participation at the UN, in addition to advocating for the rights of women and the rights of Indigenous Peoples generally, has been spent trying to make international connections between Indigenous issues and the climate crisis. Our human rights are interconnected to the rights of Mother Earth. My hope is that new generations will start to fully understand this connection and find a way to break through all the barriers we face. I think the youth today have a right to be outraged and angry, frankly, at the ineffectiveness of laws and corrupt governments actively destroying Mother Earth for the sake of economic gain. It will take hundreds if not thousands of years for the planet to recover, if it ever will.

As you know, the Haudenosaunee have something we call Ohén:ton Karihwatéhkwen, or The Words Before All Else, and before we start a meeting, we acknowledge all of the natural world: all our relations. We greet the water, the fish, Mother Earth, the birds, the trees—all life we co-exist with and who support and nurture us. We greet and thank them for all that they provide us. It's very important to calm our minds and remind ourselves that in all our discussions and decisions we're also bringing in these connections to the natural world. All our decisions impact the land and all other beings. And those are the things that I think are really important for people to understand and connect to, in order to form stronger relationships with the natural world.

Capitalism is dependent upon supply and demand, and sadly, on the military war complex, which many Western states' economies are reliant upon. We as consumers are part of what's driving oil companies to continue contaminating and exploiting the environment, destroying Indigenous Homelands and, thus, preventing present and future generations from enjoying the land.

Western society has it backwards when they do environmental assessments before a project is started. They only think of the minimum human impact upon the environment. They fail to consider the biodiversity, other beings and their rights to protect their habitats too. That is why Ohén:ton Karihwatéhkwen is so important to keep us focused on our relationship to the land and strengthen our relationship to Mother Earth and her right to health. Western society is based on a free market economy with one goal: money. But the American/Canadian dream is contributing to the destruction of our planet, Mother Earth.

Changing our direction on this planet is a challenge. Our future depends on what we do now about these issues. It's not too late, but we need to act now. If someone doesn't have a relationship with the land, then we need to increase awareness campaigns. There has to be an awareness of the interrelatedness of everything and everyone.

There's also the Haudenosaunee philosophy of One Dish, One Spoon. There is one dish and one spoon that everybody uses for their survival, to take only what they need and not be greedy and take someone else's portion to survive, that is how we all get to live well. You only take what you need. You don't take more from someone else's part. And that, I think, is what surviving the climate crisis is all about. It's not about people taking more than what they need to create a false economy that isn't only destroying the environment but is destroying the very fabric of society too. People don't seem to get it—leaving their cars running when they're in a store because it's too hot or cold outside.

In some ways the resistance to change is understandable, people have become comfortable and know only one way to live. But given the amount of pressure and changes in lifestyle needed to help future generations and the young ones to survive the ferocity of the climate crisis, things need to change quickly. It's easy to place all the responsibility on the government "to do something," so in the meantime everyone can carry on as usual. Many feel like it's someone else's responsibility. But it's everyone's responsibility and we need to figure out how to act collectively to transform things, and fast.

The reason I continue in the struggle is to create change for the Elders, for the children and young people—or the next seven generations—so that they will have a fighting chance to survive the climate crisis. We need to challenge the power that corporations have over us, and which influence governments to ignore human rights and look the other way as the environment is being destroyed. Sometimes it makes me want to cry when I think of how many species have gone extinct, or even to know that species are becoming extinct almost on a daily basis. We humans have an impact on everything that we do. Our human rights are interdependent yet interrelated and interconnected with the rights of Mother Earth and all our relations. It's not just human rights that are interrelated, but the rights of the environment will affect all other rights because we're dependent upon each other.

If we treat the environment in a respectful way, then we too will have a good life and we will be able to pass on our Traditional Knowledge so future generations can use and enjoy the land. But we need to keep pushing back against corporate greed and the oil companies who want to protect the status quo and their stakeholders' profits.

We need to help the new generations understand this, see that they can be more aware of what is going on in the world, to remain vigilant and make choices that will help build a sustainable society. It shouldn't fall completely on their shoulders, though, and that's why I'm trying to raise awareness on these issues. I want to do my part to create a better legacy than the current path we're on. I want a better world for them, for all our relations.

I'm glad that some people, like you, are willing to listen and fight. I saw the climate strikes by high school students, before the COVID-19 pandemic. That was really great and inspiring to see. But I think that a lot of the environmental NGOs, and even some of the human rights NGOs, don't quite understand Indigenous Peoples' perspectives and the urgency we feel. The Elders I have spoken with in my three decades of travel and activism have said that we're living in the prophecy times: a time when Mother Earth will be cleansing herself. They say that we have to prepare ourselves to survive what is coming, from this cleansing. We as a species need to understand our place in this changing world. We need to renew our relationship with the natural world. We need to listen to Mother Earth, observe the small changes in the land and animals. Understanding our place can help us act and make change.

Indigenous people have always been leaders in the fight against the climate crisis. We come from rich cultures who knew how to survive sustainably on the land. We know how to respect the natural world and understand how to be stewards of our lands and waters, and how this is paramount to our survival. Our Traditional Knowledge teaches us this. Some environmentalists are just starting to understand the importance of Indigenous Traditional Knowledges in combatting the climate crisis. Land, a healthy land, is key to the survival of our species and others. Indigenous people have always advocated not just for their rights, but for the rights of the environment too.

There is a slight difference in how Indigenous Peoples are approaching the climate justice movement. A greener, sustainable capitalism won't work, as many of us have been saying. People get resentful towards Indigenous Peoples, for us wanting to include not just our rights but also undoing and unpacking some of the impacts of colonization and capitalism on the natural world. But that's what needs to happen for us to have a fighting chance to survive. It seems pretty obvious at this point, right? I mean, people celebrate the Industrial Revolution for all of these great inventions and things, but we're only now seeing the devastating effects it had—and is having—on Mother Earth and the biosphere.

For some, there's a comfort to the kind of numbness enabled by not acting or being part of the solution, so some people are deep in denial. But you cannot leave your rights in the hands of others. You know, voting is important, but people also have to be aware of what's going on in a larger sense, on a global scale, and how it affects everyone. People need to be part of their democracy and know what their government is doing here and abroad.

It's concerning that some people are just focused on "taxes," for example, when the world around them is actively being destroyed. It's disturbing to see how fundamentally tied Canada is to corporations and to the oil industry, in particular. It was, and continues to be, about greed and power at the expense of vulnerable populations: poor and marginalized and people of colour as well as our non-human relatives. Most often, it's Indigenous people's human rights and self-determination that are sacrificed.

I don't think anything will change unless people educate themselves, know their history, and have a vision and concern for the future generations. They need to actually voice their concerns at a universal scale. We need to end the dependency on fossil fuels, to start with. Considering all we know about human beings' role in the climate crisis, we still have a lot of work ahead. The youth are our big hope. I think the youth are doing a better job of meeting the moment. They're intelligent and connected to the issues. They're learning and showing tremendous leadership.

But, again, it has to be inclusive, it can't all fall on their shoulders: people of all ages must be part of the solution. It also can't just be on Indigenous people, either. It has to be a larger movement of all people willing to acknowledge the truth and embrace the responsibility of becoming agents of transformational change. We have to find ways to build bridges and work together, for the sake of each other and the land and the seven generations to come.

8
RESURGENCE

SEAN: We've been witnessing an increasing number of police raids of Land Defenders on Wet'suwet'en territory in recent years. We've also seen a resurgence of direct action to defend the land as well as the rise of a solidarity movement called Shut Down Canada, with major social disobedience actions and blockades. We've been talking a lot about the colonial past so far and your experiences fighting for the land and Indigenous Peoples' human rights, but how do you respond to these kinds of actions—much like you lived through—playing out today? What happens when you wake up to reports that the militarized RCMP has, yet again, forcibly raided Wet'suwet'en territory, with attack dogs and snipers? How do you respond to these events?

ELLEN: It reminds me that colonialism isn't just in the past; we're living it every day, be it the Wet'suwet'en on the West Coast or here in Kanien'kehá:ka territory. The kinds of attacks we're seeing out west provoke a lot of anger towards the governments of British Columbia and Canada and the authorities who protect corporate interests over Indigenous Peoples' right to self-determination. In some ways, everything that is unfolding is predictable and formulaic, because that's how corporations and governments have been responding for centuries.

When the police come in early in the morning under the cover of darkness, around 5:15 a.m., it's a paramilitary force. That's what they did to us in July 1990. It's the same sort of tactic. The police have learned from the "mistakes" they made in Kanehsatà:ke, and they're using the same strategy in different Indigenous communities today. The government feigns innocence and claims they've tried to speak with Indigenous people. But at the end of the day, the reality is that they're not listening at all. They're just sticking to the same old colonial playbook. Their strategy is to delay and force us into accepting crumbs, trying to force us into going to their courts to get an injunction, which we never win. Meanwhile, they justify the plundering of land and trampling on Indigenous Peoples' rights for their own economic gain.

That's what they did to us in 1990 and that tactic hasn't changed—it's just window dressing to make it look like a new relationship is happening. So, it's worrisome to see a repeat of the sneakiness of colonial governments happen all over again, despite all of this recent talk of "reconciliation" and strengthening nation-to-nation relations.

But the use of force by policing authorities is a symptom of the problem. Police are doing the dirty work of corrupt politicians whose rhetoric upholds corporate greed, they're constantly repeating to themselves that they need to "balance" the so-called rights of all "stakeholders," which is just code for pandering to businesses and corporations while justifying the human rights violations of Indigenous Peoples. It should be understood that Indigenous rights are human rights, that we are more than just stakeholders, we are rights holders.

I consider Prime Minister Justin Trudeau's words about reconciliation to be empty, meant to placate Indigenous people and the public. Trudeau says that no relationship is more important to him than Canada's relationship to Indigenous Peoples. But that's not what it feels like to me. His actions, or the lack of actions by his government, prove that little is changing in this country and that reconciliation is simply colonization repackaged.

It all makes me wonder if Canadians are really paying attention. Are they willing to learn about their colonial history and how their country is built on the ongoing genocide of Indigenous Peoples? Canada calls out other countries where human rights abuses are being committed, but in their own backyard Canadians ignore the issues affecting Indigenous Peoples. There seems to be a lot of apathy concerning Indigenous Peoples' rights in Canada because we remain a "problem" and threat to the economic prosperity of Canada.

It's really unfortunate that people don't realize that the colonial formula of divide and conquer continues today to the benefit of government and corporations. There are those constructed as "good" or moderate Indigenous people and then there are those framed as the "bad" or radical ones. The radicals are on the frontlines, defending the land and protecting it for future generations, refusing to be bought or bribed, but are often criminalized by the settler state. The moderates are the ones who listen to government, are propped up by it, and don't like to make too many waves. Assimilated Indigenous people are those promoting unsustainable economic development, for the sake of what they see as "progress." Meanwhile, the radicals are critiquing capitalist exploitation and privatization. The spin-doctoring of the semantics used by government is the same today as it was in 1990. It's the same racist and paternalistic attitude that we were up against.

SEAN: For me the most frustrating part of watching/listening as new events unfold is, we just went through this at Unist'ot'en (in 2019) where there was an armed RCMP raid.[1] As a historian, one of the things that keeps me going is that we can all learn from the past to make better decisions in the present. And yet, when I wake up and see these same images, it's very frustrating. It's anger, but also profound disappointment. It seems that Canada is incapable of change, despite its promises to build stronger relations with Indigenous Peoples.

ELLEN: Well, the problem is systemic. There are judges, lawyers, politicians, the whole parliamentary system, who accept the racist, colonial norm and act in ways that perpetuate oppression.

As a person who had a similar experience—of being surrounded by a paramilitary force and shot at while defending Kanien'kehá:ka Homelands—I know there is a lot of trauma for those involved on the frontlines. I think about those people who have been traumatized by what this paramilitary force has done in the name of public security. The invisible hands reap the benefits, like the CEOs who are sitting comfortably in their offices while Indigenous people, who are trying to protect the land from an unsustainable and very dangerous kind of development, are suffering the brunt of this violence. All to increase the investments of stockholders, and all the while using the police to do their dirty work.

Canada's economic prosperity is based on unfettered capitalism, and it's a real danger from a perspective of sustainability. Globalization forces Canada to be competitive in the world market and it's always at the expense of Indigenous Peoples' human rights and the rights of Mother Earth. It has been like that since Contact with Europeans, killing and enslaving Indigenous people for gold and other resources. Colonial violence is insidious and violates all of Canada's human rights obligations.

People think that going to the court system to fight is the more progressive and civilized kind of response, but it's not really civilized, is it? The cards are stacked against Indigenous Peoples. We always have to prove occupation from time immemorial in order to have our title to the lands recognized. No one else in Canada has to continuously protect their human rights on a daily basis. Colonial laws don't recognize or respect the human rights to self-determination of the First Peoples of Turtle Island. Why should we even bother playing by their rules? Who benefits most from those rules? It's an imbalanced relationship with the colonizer holding all the cards and making all the rules.

The rule of law is based upon colonial perspectives—but Canada forgets its international human rights obligations when it comes to Indigenous Peoples' human rights, which are protected under international human rights laws. Why would we want to go to colonial courts for help when it's a foreign government's laws ruling the system? The courts weren't made with Indigenous Peoples' laws in mind, only for the benefit of the colonizers. Justice seems to be for people rich enough to afford it. Therefore, the law is not neutral but implements discriminatory laws founded upon the Doctrine of Discovery: a racist and legally invalid doctrine, condemned by the United Nations. Right now it's mostly rhetoric and double standards, so that Canada may continue its justification of dispossession of Indigenous Peoples from their lands and resources, while criminalizing Land Defenders.

SEAN: On the subject of the law, Canadians follow "the law" as if it's ironclad and natural rather than an imposed tool of colonialism. They think the law is cut and dried, black and white. So, you often hear Canadians speaking about "the rule of law," using it to justify violent, coercive dispossession to facilitate capitalist development. The police arrive with a court injunction, and it needs to be enforced so people are kept safe, but the people they're claiming to protect aren't Indigenous people. The majority of Canadians have no conception of Wet'suwet'en territory as unceded, no idea about Wet'suwet'en governance structures and laws. They don't know about the Delgamuukw v. British Columbia Supreme Court of Canada ruling. Ignorance seems to perpetuate colonialism and protect the status quo.

ELLEN: These were the same kinds of arguments and positions we presented to Canada and Quebec in 1990, that we are Sovereign Nations with a right to protect our Homelands and people. The negotiators totally ignored all of that, mainly because they were intentionally ignorant of Indigenous Peoples' rights and sovereignty. Our lives have always been dispensable because of Canada's economic agenda.

The rule of law is based on an archaic, outdated form of governance that works for the rich and oppresses the dispossessed and marginalized, more specifically Indigenous Peoples. Colonial laws are designed to fool people into thinking that they live in a democracy, but it's really about how the rich and powerful can use the law and manipulate it and steal from Indigenous Peoples, because they have the human and financial resources to afford lawyers to defend their case. For Indigenous people, when we talk about the Constitution Act of 1982 and Section 35, "inherent right" means pre-Contact. We're not dependent upon Canada or Britain or France to grant us our inherent rights, yet we're forced to go to their courts to get our rights protected. So, the rule of law to me means the protection of settler rights, not Indigenous human rights.

Colonizers invoke the "rule of law" when they're losing the public relations war, so they threaten us with the use of force and then inflict acts of violence against Indigenous Peoples. A human rights-based approach is freedom from fear, freedom from violence, and freedom of speech. Unfortunately, the rule of law in a colonial society is always used as a weapon to oppress and further erode Indigenous Peoples' inherent rights. We must remember that this is the same "rule of law" that led to the deaths of thousands of Indigenous children in Indian Residential Schools and sanctioned the genocide of our ancestors. Colonizers continue to this day to treat us as wards of their state. It's not a rule of law that is made for us; it's the colonizer's rule of law to protect their interests, their economy, and settler society.

What could help is if everyone in society used a human rights-based approach, but Canada isn't even respecting their own laws and is unwilling to use this approach. Canada isn't respecting any of their international human rights obligations that oblige them to respect our right to self-determination.

SEAN: It's quite hypocritical that Canada is saying, "we need to follow the rule of law" and yet they're deviating from a nation-to-nation understanding of Indigenous-settler relations that suggests that Canada should work with Indigenous Nations and choose diplomacy over force. Particularly in the case of the Wet'suwet'en, they're just ignoring the Delgamuukw decision, the fact that much of British Columbia remains unceded territory, according to Canadian law, and that all of this sets the stage for conflict and disagreement.[2]

So, I see the "law" as a kind of shield to continue colonization. You know, you see this as police officers were smashing windows at the Wet'suwet'en camp early in the morning, with the RCMP letting all of these Coastal GasLink vehicles roll into unceded territory. It rids you of any illusions of the role of the RCMP. They clearly continue to serve and protect Canada's colonial status quo—as the force, originally the North-West Mounted Police, were created to uphold.

ELLEN: That's what the RCMP were created to do, over a hundred years ago, yes. Clear the land of the original inhabitants, the First Peoples of the land and brutally deal with the so-called Indian problem. That continues today. The police are used as a paramilitary force, just as they were on July 11, 1990. There is a standard practice to these kinds of violent actions—authorities learn from each other and pass along tips and strategies using their colonial playbook. From Northern Ireland and South Africa to Canada, these events don't happen in a vacuum. The military industrial complex needs to test its weaponry to sell them as battle-tested. So those they test these weapons on are the marginalized, poor, and people of colour.

In 1990, Canada and Quebec prevented journalists from telling the truth and pilfered their films. Journalists had to sneak out tapes for their producers, as the government and the authorities didn't want to show the world how the police and the army were treating us behind the barricades. The big difference is that, today, people have cellphones and can live stream on social media to show you what is happening. That makes it all the more difficult for Canadians to ignore and dismiss what is going on today. We didn't have cellphones back in 1990 that could take pictures and video of what was happening and post them right away. I wish we'd had that technology to show people what we were experiencing. It could've changed the trajectory of the outcome.

But that's the formula: placate the public by telling them what they want to hear, that their government is doing their ultimate best to protect their safety. Whereas the message about Indigenous Peoples is that we do not deserve equality when it comes to our human rights. But they aren't in control and so they hide the fact that they had always intended to use force all along. Training of the policing authorities in Canada is to have their soldiers and policing authorities, overtly and covertly, hate Indigenous people—causing racism to be embedded in their training. Again, the "Indian problem" is invoked in a way that must be dealt with swiftly. Serving and protecting Canada means going on the offensive to criminalize and demoralize Indigenous Land Defenders— to discourage others from standing up for their human rights and self-determination. Indigenous people are viewed as public enemy number one, and while there may be Indigenous people in these forces, they're assimilated into the training program nonetheless.

All of this is a continuation of the centuries-long war against Indigenous Peoples of Turtle Island. The conflict that began centuries ago and is evident in uprisings like Wounded Knee in 1973, or here in Kanehsatà:ke and Kahnawà:ke in 1990, or Ipperwash and Gustafsen Lake in 1995, or Elsipogtog in 2013. More recently there is the Wet'suwet'en resistance since 2019, and they're suffering from the ignorance of the government authorities. Canada bought a pipeline protected under the careful watch of a special elite team of RCMP. It's all about economic profit before the environment and people, especially when it comes to Indigenous Peoples.

SEAN: Canada's divide and conquer tactics continue, too. You see this in the news, with some pitting Hereditary Chiefs against band council Chiefs. You hear Canadians say, in the case of the Wet'suwet'en, "well, the elected band council Chiefs are on side with the pipeline, it is just a few fringe, guerilla Hereditary Chiefs that are opposed to the project." I don't want to ask you to comment on another Nation's governance, but I wonder if you have any reflections on that kind of divisive discourse as it has been used against Kanien'kehá:ka people in 1990 and for the past three hundred years? What role do you see divide and conquer politics playing in supporting ongoing colonization today?

ELLEN: Divide and conquer is one of the oldest and most common tactics in the colonizer's playbook. Creating divisions is necessary for the colonizer to succeed and it has worked for centuries.

Dangling money in front of oppressed peoples who have no control over their lives and have lived in poverty for many generations is an effective strategy, otherwise they wouldn't still be using it today. You just have to take the example of the Two Row Wampum, a treaty often referenced by the Haudenosaunee: one path is our laws, our customs and languages, our governance; the other path is the colonizer's laws, language, and customs, and each side does not interfere with the other side.

The Two Row Wampum symbolizes a nation-to-nation relationship. We're travelling in the same direction, but we're in different boats, as it were, and we won't interfere in each other's journey. This is what was supposed be guiding Indigenous-settler relations so that we can live in peace. Peace and dignity are part of international human rights laws, but Canada refuses to acknowledge and respect the Two Row Wampum.

After centuries of attacking our identity and, in brutal ways including starving communities, assimilation has progressed. So there are some in our community, mainly those who support the colonial-imposed creations like the band council system, who turn their backs on their own traditional teachings. It's one of the impacts of colonial assimilation, helped by the churches, resulting in cultural self-hatred. It's not evident to settlers, because it's a societal norm—deferring always to the band council for any decisions. But the Indian Act, a settler government creation, has imposed a hierarchy created and approved by the Minister of Indian Affairs. The imposed band council system is more authoritarian than democratic, and its authority rests upon the approval of the colonizer.

The Canadian government, under the Indian Act and Minister of Indian Affairs (and though the ministry has changed its name, we're still "Indians" under the law),[3] they're the ones who rubber stamp everything as long as it falls in line with their assimilationist agenda. They will continue to push until Canada gets what it wants, which is control over Indigenous Peoples and our lands and resources.

There are communities who are resisting, of course, but Canada keeps coming, pushing until they get some kind of acceptance, on their terms and with their conditions, to press on with these extractive industries which are detrimental to everyone's health. They spend a lot of money and dangle many carrots to sway people into believing that their way is the best way: this is coercion.

There is also a lot of propaganda, and certain media are complicit in this. If we try to show our perspective, it's just opinion, they dismiss it. But you cannot dismiss people who are rights holders. It's our inherent right to protect our lands and waters for present and future generations. However, the band council must obey the Minister of Crown and Indigenous Relations (CIRNAC) and the Indian Act if they expect to sign their funding agreements.

Settler governments have left the path of the Two Row Wampum and have jumped from their canoe into ours—and have been rocking our canoe to throw us off balance for centuries. According to the Two Row Wampum teaching, it's the inherent rights holders who are the ones who have authority over the lands and resources. The colonial way of thinking is a process that does not respect the rights of the environment and all our relations. Under most Indigenous Traditional Laws and governments, you must have respect for the land and all the other creatures that are living with us—including yourself and others.

So if we examine the band council system, they're essentially service providers, and that's the deception that CIRNAC is working on with their "Rights Recognition" strategy. It's not really a governance system at all but the maintenance of the colonial status quo, creating Indigenous municipalities with little power and which, in the end, benefits Canada more than Indigenous Peoples.

SEAN: Many Canadians dismiss Hereditary Chiefs and Traditional Laws and governance because they don't understand, or don't want to understand. They haven't been taught about these ways, how to recognize and acknowledge them, let alone understand and respect them. That's another way in which colonialism continues. Do you notice those same tensions?

ELLEN: In our communities that tension has been there since the time of the missionaries. Band councils are not representative; they're voted into office based on a popularity contest and it's usually a minority of the community that participates to actually elect them—if they have a large enough family to vote them in. There are no criteria to become a band councillor. While I don't have anything personal against those who choose the band council system, it's not an Indigenous system of governance, but one that has been colonially imposed. Many elected council members don't understand their customary laws and governance. There are many community members, including me, who don't recognize the imposed colonial system of governance.

The government has been forcibly imposing this system on us for over one hundred years, but many people are unaware of the history and don't understand all that. They simply accept this system because Canada refused to recognize traditional governments as legitimate, only their colonial-created entities.

To put it into context, it's like if we were to have the president of the United States come into Canada and say that he does not recognize the Prime Minister and impose a new kind of governance structure that will now speak on your behalf. People would see that as a coup, as an invasion. Well, that is what happened to Indigenous Nations with the imposition of the Indian Act—that's how I see it. Some people in our community sadly just accept this dysfunctional state of affairs because of the impacts of colonization and genocide.

SEAN: Another thing we're witnessing is the lack of leadership by the BC NDP leader, who seems intent on trying to ignore the Hereditary Chiefs and their continued demands to sit down and negotiate—even though the government is in the process of implementing UNDRIP, which we talked about earlier. What do you make of this?

ELLEN: It's just the colonial status quo, again. The racial hatred that was demonstrated by taking down the red dresses on the bridge in the 2019 Wet'suwet'en raids is evidence of how little has changed in regard to the level of racism that is the accepted norm. Whether it's the use of extreme force or whether it's through the rhetoric of government, their persistent stalling in addressing issues or refusing to sit down with us to talk about solutions, systemic racism is there.

The government isn't really interested in resolving long-standing historical land issues through diplomacy. Instead, they stall and force our backs against the wall where there are few if any options and criminalize us when we righteously defend our self-determination. All these games of feigning to make the effort are to justify their own violent nature and racism. There is no reconciliation unless there is respect for our human rights and our right to self-determination. There is nothing that is even remotely close to reconciliation in their words and their actions.

For that reason, I don't believe anything they say. It's the same old stuff, it's just more slick talk and no action. They're using social media as a tool, too. If Duncan Campbell Scott had access to social media, his agenda of getting rid of the "Indian problem" would still be the same today.[4] We just need to look at the growing number of Indian Residential School denialists. So, it's just the status quo, just pushing forward to justify the economic prosperity without thinking of the bigger picture and our long-term survival on this earth.

SEAN: While all of that must be dispiriting to see unfold, there are encouraging signs. As Leanne Betasamosake Simpson has noted, "blockades are both a refusal and an affirmation. An affirmation of a different political economy. A world built on a different set of relations and ethics. An affirmation of life." She also argues that this "is about the kinds of worlds we collectively want to live in. . . . We can have the same old arguments we've been having for centuries about inconvenience and the extra-legal nature of blockades. We can pit jobs and the economy versus the environment. We can perform superficial dances of reconciliation and dialogue and negotiate for the cheap gifts of economic and political inclusion. Or we can imagine other worlds."[5]

In thinking about blockades today and imagining other, better worlds, what do you make of the Shut Down Canada movement (2020)? There have been many protests across the country to try to choke that "economy" in solidarity, to demand justice for Indigenous Peoples. We have ongoing blockades of major rail lines, occupations of the BC legislature by Indigenous youth, which is being supported by hundreds of people, among other actions. Non-Indigenous people blocking the ports in Vancouver, stopping shipping in Halifax—with more actions popping up every day as this conflict continues. Would you have envisioned something like that thirty years ago?

ELLEN: It's inspiring to see the unity amongst people. This was the kind of solidarity that happened in 1990. This kind of organizing is very cyclical because it's hard to remain constant. We all have lives and need to work so blockades aren't our first choice. But this kind of solidarity isn't new either. People held big rallies and marches and demonstrations in 1990, in solidarity with Mohawks. People from all over what we call Turtle Island travelled to be with us, in solidarity, and internationally as well. There were UN sanctioned international observers in both Kanehsatà:ke and Kahnawà:ke. Our allies created a peace camp at Oka Park to be witnesses to any police action that might happen and to observe what was

going on in order to protect us, and to tell us, behind the
barricades, that we were not alone.

SEAN: Yeah. I've seen some cool photos from the peace
camp of people like Dionne Brand taking up space in solidarity, showing those interconnections between Black and
Indigenous struggles.

I've been doing some research on the peace camp and
solidarity actions across the country in 1990. I didn't realize
that Stó:lō writer Lee Maracle was at the peace camp, and in
an author's note to a new edition of her famous novel, *Bobbi
Lee: Indian Rebel*, she lays out her thoughts about what was
at stake that summer. Let me read some of what she wrote:

> Creation is not passive. The birth, rebirth process of the
> earth, her storms, eruptions, tidal waves, floods, droughts
> and the coming of periodic ice ages attest to a total lack of
> passivity. The birth process of the plant and animal king-
> dom is not passive. Individually, every living thing on earth
> must labour to recreate itself. Seeds burst from the shell to
> regenerate, and the process of birth for mammals is accom-
> plished only with much bloodshed.
>
> The rebirth of any social order is not passive. We can-
> not live in this world the way it is. What is it when the
> mayor of a foreign town can come into your backyard and
> propose to play golf on the graves of your dead? What is
> it when that foreign country forms its own internal laws to
> make this despicable act legal? At no time in history have
> Europeans ever suggested playing golf on their own graves.
> Yet gravesite after gravesite of our dead are considered
> accessible for the most ridiculous of pasttimes.
>
> The train of rape and defilement stops here. When we
> stand up to say enough, every single Canadian benefits. . . .
>
> Peace. There is no peace in this country. We are abso-
> lutely opposed to a bunch of cowboys in a D-9 cat running

hi-diddle-diddle over the hill playing Texas chainsaw massacre with our trees. Peace: freedom from conditions which
annoy the mind. It annoys our minds to sleep under the
dome of imperialist lust which is constantly looking for
newer and more effective means of attacking our homelands, clawing and digging at them, extracting the insides,
covering our graves with roadways, golf grounds, housing
projects, offices or what-have-you.

We are absolutely opposed to anyone organized with
machine guns, assault rifles and tanks invading another
people's territory to play shoot-'em-up cowboy. It takes
great effort on our part not to leave the barricades and
run all over the town of Oka playing shoot-'em-up cowboy. Despite the abuse, the cheapening of our lives and our
homelands, we don't do it. We still believe life is sacred.

Peaceful struggle is all about expending great, strenu-
ous effort to live free from strife, free from war, free from
conditions which annoy the mind. It annoys our minds to
imagine golfers tramping on the grave of Mohawk grand-
mothers. It annoys our minds to think, to feel, that we are
less than sovereign people in our homelands. And it annoys
a good many Canadians now too.

This summer, if anything, the State convinced a good
many Canadian white people that it does not give a shit
about any of us. These opinions mean nothing when it
comes to us. Money is the only speech the state is prepared to hear. We don't have any money and Canadians in
general have less and less each day. [Brian] Mulroney and
Co. heard not a word from the thousands upon thousands
of us who walked, marched, blocked roads, picketed,
bought ads in newspapers, wrote, spoke on television
and telephoned.

The state is aware that should our laws prevail anywhere in this country, the heyday of corporate imperialism
is over. The difference is that now we care enough about

our sacred being to get up and say no, and the echo of that no continues across the country.

If we are all dead we cannot have peace. If we are allowed to die this country will be left with their violence. They will be left with the memory of inactivity in the face of our genocide. Many of the citizens of this country are not prepared to accept the violence of the State against our people any longer. They know we have done all the unjust dying a people should have to do.

More than that. Apathy is a kind of admission of insignificance, a form of self-erasure. Some of the citizens of this land wish to be significant. They refuse to be erased. They want peace and solidarity, with each other, with all people and with the earth. And they are prepared to actively search out this peace, be resolute and caring about the promise of solidarity.

We/they are refusing to be obedient. From July 11th onward we will listen to one instruction only—love our own. We have been busy over the past summer deciding who "our own" are. They are a range of colours: black, red, brown, yellow and white. And we can recognize them by their loyalty to justice, peace and solidarity. Oka, the people of Kanesatake, brought that home to us.

We did not shed our blood on the streets of Oka. No surrender was negotiated. The men and women tried to make a run for it. We all know that we must talk. Really talk—from a position of wholeness, completeness—about building a sustainable movement in the country that will lead all of us to justice and peace. We know that the country is capable of sending in the troops. This is not Vietnam— we cannot call the boys home if they are in our backyard.[6]

ELLEN: I appreciate these strong words and we felt that solidarity behind the lines, and 1990 was an awakening for many

Indigenous people, but organizing and rallying behind Land and Water Defenders has been there for decades, even if the news cameras didn't focus on it.

The scale of this new movement is impressive, for sure. Meetings for Indigenous solidarity rarely make news; blocking a railway gets more mainstream media attention than a small group staging a protest in their community. I think it's just a natural progression when there are situations like what we're seeing in BC. Society today is more educated on Indigenous issues than thirty years ago. The scale and widespread involvement, especially of youth and non-Indigenous people, is heartening.

But the average Canadian still needs more education to become involved in the solution and justice for Indigenous Peoples. There are some exceptions, of course, good people like yourself or certain people who are in the generations learning about climate change and then realizing that Indigenous people have always been at the forefront of fighting for the environment. So they become aware but, on the whole, there is still a lot of racism, ignorance, and indifference about our struggles. Take for example logging battles in BC in the 1990s. There was the "loggers versus Indigenous people" and calls to protect jobs over respecting the rights of Indigenous Nations to their own resources—even though there were some loggers and supporters who got it. But economic reasons are always used to justify trampling on our rights—like with the European monarchs sending their representatives over here to claim Indigenous land and take our resources to build wealth for themselves and their home nations.

It's like we don't have a collective vision for the future. We're not leaving a great legacy for the small ones, our youth, and the future generations to come. We have a lot of very short-sighted leaders, because people are always in survival mode and there's so much stress in our lives because we have to persistently defend our rights. But this helps maintain the unsustainable status quo way of thinking, that colonized free market economy way of thinking, which threatens the survival of our species and all of our relations. The indifference to things like Indigenous rights and climate change just compounds the threat to our species and our chance to survive the next fifty years, or even just ten years. There are more and more climate emergencies and disasters, and we're not acting fast enough. Our reliance on flawed systems leaves us vulnerable to corrupt systems of government that often have conflicts of interest. The solutions must come from consultations with the people, not solely from what government thinks is best for us.

We need to make changes right away because it's getting seriously worse, and there isn't any time left. We must prepare ourselves to survive what is coming. The fact that we are still fighting the centuries-old battle for respect and basic human rights, that's very frustrating. We keep having to repeat the mistakes of history because there is no political will to make the changes we need. We keep doing this over and over again for each new generation, as if it's something new when it really isn't. Colonization and capitalist development persist, with Canada continuing to refuse to respect our inherent rights. As people indigenous to these lands, our Traditional Knowledge teaches us how to take care of the earth. Indigenous Peoples have been doing this since time immemorial.

SEAN: Given this colonial conundrum, how do you find the strength to continue to navigate this scenario and push for Indigenous laws and governance structures to be respected— and press Canada to follow its own laws without, as Glen Sean Coulthard has pointed out, reinforcing or legitimizing those colonial laws?[7] How did you negotiate this frustrating reality?

ELLEN: It's very challenging and Indigenous Peoples are always the ones staring down the barrel of a gun from the state authorities. We always get doublespeak: we hear a lot about doing research and finding creative ways to help balance Canada's economic prosperity versus Indigenous Peoples' human rights, but the result is always the same. We lose more land, and our rights are insignificant, and that is colonization.

Canada, its provinces and corporations, manipulate the "rule of law" to get what they want, which is more beneficial for them and comes at our expense. That is how it has always been. Diplomacy takes a lot of energy, and we've always tried to negotiate with the colonizers. We have tried. Our ancestors tried diplomacy and were deceived. Even when we're diplomatic, we're dismissed, because Canada and its provinces set the standards and rules of negotiations, which are based upon colonial laws, not Indigenous laws. It remains an imbalanced playing field. They just keep pushing their agenda until they find Indigenous people who will say yes and then the rest of us are demonized.

If you look at the Wet'suwet'en, Chief Namoks (John Ridsdale) is one of the gentlest and most softspoken people I know. He and others in his Nation have tried diplomacy with Canada. They've tried to protect their rights using diplomacy, and they've jumped through all of the hoops, and yet they're still fighting. They haven't gotten anywhere, except more coercion and brute force from the special unit of the RCMP who are happy to do the dirty work to protect Canada and corporate interests.

Indigenous Peoples haven't gotten anywhere by being nice. Canada always pushes us into a corner, gives us no other options to protect ourselves and our Nations, and then they're surprised when blockades go up. It's maddening, but it's how colonialism continues today. I wish it could be better, for all of our sakes, to find peace and justice. This hurts everyone including Canadians, too. I don't want to pass this horrible legacy on to future generations. We want to make change now, for everyone. But it's so difficult under the current colonial laws which ignore all the recommendations of RCAP and the TRC. We haven't succeeded yet, but we will continue for the sake of future generations.

I draw a lot of inspiration from the brave people standing up in recent years, like those involved in Shut Down Canada and Black Lives Matter. There are people who haven't given up and given in and are still fighting for justice. There are people who understand the real issues and are willing to take action to make things better. The people who are on the frontlines are very courageous.

When there are demonstrations with people from all walks of life, that is an indication—at least for me—that there is still hope for the future. If we were alone in this fight, then we would not see any justice. But, because there are ordinary Canadian citizens supporting Indigenous people at demonstrations, because there are still people willing to defend our rights, then there is hope. The inspiration to keep doing what I'm doing stems in part from my Elders and family, who taught me our values of love for the land, and seeing our youth—who still have lots to learn, mind you—being willing to take a stand and learn how to fight for the land and the future generations.

Having been behind the barricades during the siege in 1990 and hearing about the different kinds of solidarity actions that were taking place in support of us, I know it makes a big difference and lifts the spirits of those on the frontlines. It's uplifting, you can feel the positive energy from solidarity. It's very difficult when you're in the thick of things to see the light, when everything feels daunting. Everything is very intense, and you're fearful for everyone's lives when the police show up with weapons to try to remove you from your own land. It's scary, so what ends up happening is you're just existing, trying to survive, hoping no one gets hurt. When things calm down, that's when there is time to think (that's when we learned about the solidarity protests), and it helps keep you going. It gives you the courage to continue the struggle. You know it's a righteous cause, when you realize that other people support you and that there's a wave of support that's huge and powerful. It's very uplifting.

SEAN: In thinking about these events, Leanne Betasamosake Simpson argues in *A Short History of the Blockade*, "Our current world is one fire, warming and melting at an unprecedented rate. The whole world should be standing behind the Wet'suwet'en Hereditary Chiefs and their Clans, paying attention to the world they are refusing, observing how life behind the blockades renews a different vision" of the world and what is possible.[8] Now, a lot of Canadians will approve of "solidarity" campaigns like writing their Member of Parliament, but they're sometimes less willing to support direct-action tactics like blockades. What's your perspective on how people can support Land Defenders?

ELLEN: It all helps, honestly. A diversity of actions—from letter writing to joining in protests or occupations—from a diversity of people can show solidarity, that's extremely important. Every action can make a difference, we need them all so that settler governments know that we are not alone.

We may not have an army, or it might be more correct to say our army looks a bit different, I guess. We don't have the weapons like the Canadian Army or paramilitary police forces, but we have different kinds of tools we can use to fight for truth and our inherent rights. Though not all of these tactics get the same attention. When you have large groups of people taking action together, government cannot ignore and pretend it's not happening. When people are marching in the streets, it's harder to ignore. There are people who recognize the injustices and are helping to raise more awareness and apply pressure to corporations and government. So, we need to keep making our voices heard. We need to keep organizing!

If there is ever going to be trust in the nation-to-nation relationship, then Canada is going to have to work for it and meet us on our terms. Canada must prove its good intentions, its good faith and good will. No more words and empty promises. We need change and to see the results. Reconciliation so far has been false promises and no follow-through. The vast majority of the TRC's Calls to Action haven't been completed. Education to learn about Canada's colonial history is still not going on in a way that depicts the truth about the genocidal project. Apathy and leaving it up to politicians and the police is the norm. This puts future generations in peril. In that sense, the work of reconciliation has barely begun. That's why I'm grateful for historians such as yourself who are interested in helping to teach people about not just 1990 but the whole land struggle and what we've been fighting for.

We can't properly envision a better future without first fully understanding the colonial past and present and its impacts upon Indigenous Peoples. Without that knowledge we won't be able to solve our important problems rooted in the historical genocidal laws and policies of settler colonial governments. There has to be more peaceful and productive ways that hold those who are part of the problem accountable for perpetuating systemic racism. I remain hopeful for the future. I'm encouraged by incremental changes in awareness and the solidarity of supportive Canadian citizens and the youth who are actively involved in supporting the Indigenous resistance movement.

9

LIVING FOR THE LAND

SEAN: I really cherish our conversations, Ellen. I learn so much from you and always feel more inspired after we talk, even though we've been talking about some heavy stuff. Your commitment to a ruthless critique of everything colonial, past and present, is insightful and vigilant. And somehow you still remain hopeful for the future, which is a gift. I hope this project can help share that gift with future generations so they can learn from you as well.

ELLEN: Well, thank you Sean. It has been such a pleasure for me as well. I hope new generations can pick up on our conversations and use them as a guide to help them in their fight for the land and waters, for a sustainable future for all.

SEAN: In that spirit, let's talk more about the role that thinking and dreaming of the future plays in the work of building a better world. In one of our first conversations, I talked about Sioux historian Nick Estes's book, *Our History Is the Future*. In the book, he argues that for Indigenous Nations, "There is no separation between past and present, meaning that an alternative future is also determined by our understanding of our past."[1]

Similarly, in *Rehearsals for Living*, Robyn Maynard and Leanne Betasamosake Simpson make clear that looking backwards, and understanding the devastating effects of genocide

/ slavery / settler colonialism / capitalism, is key to looking forward to a better world. Specifically, Maynard argues: "it is necessary to have the courage to envision the end of *this* world, that is, the world that white supremacy built, to move toward futures that are premised on life rather than (human, ecological, animal, microbial) waste. . . . I believe that world-ending and world-making can occur, are occurring, have always occurred, simultaneously."[2] As Maynard points out, the "future feels daunting," but dreaming of what might be is the only way forward.

ELLEN: We have a teaching that the land is sacred and that we need to also protect it for present and future generations, and for all our relations. When we understand and try to follow our traditional teachings, then we must think about the future and what kind of legacy we're leaving those not yet born. This includes the deer, fish, birds, waters, plants, and even insects. As an Indigenous person, this is what we're supposed to be thinking about as well, but because of colonial assimilation, there are many Indigenous people who don't follow that philosophy or belief nor even respect it. They're focused only on the present and not thinking about their broader responsibilities. It's one of the impacts from the Indian Residential School system and its cultural shaming, with the messaging that we were inferior; it's a sort of survival instinct whereby they're coerced into assimilating this messaging. And so, there are some who turn their backs on their culture and their language, our ways.

But there are lot of young people who are continuing the resistance movement, like Eriel Tchekwie Deranger and Indigenous Climate Action, who are picking up their duties to protect Mother Earth. They're fighting against the tar sands and destructive pipelines out in Alberta and British Columbia. They're on the frontlines of trying to make a better world. They're aware of how destructive fossil fuels are and how human activities are jeopardizing our collective existence on this planet.

For multiple generations Indigenous people have been forced into living in colonial-rooted poverty but after centuries of facing oppression and racism, want better opportunities for themselves, for their children to escape the impacts of the centuries-long genocidal project. We all want to have a better quality of life. But some Indigenous people, because of the impacts of the Indian Residential School system, approve unsustainable resource extraction on their Homelands without realizing the consequence it has—the destruction of the environment and the threat it creates to the quality of life for their families, future generations, and all our relations.

For example, there is a toxic waste dump here in Kanehsatà:ke, created behind closed doors between the band council and the owners of the dump. All done without any consultation with the community; no free, prior, and informed consent. It'll be thousands of years before any generation can enjoy these lands again. It's frustrating because Canada supports this form of dysfunction: it's so sad for the community, the land, and for future generations. But all this waste, most of it toxic, comes from the old infrastructure from the island of Montreal. We're getting their garbage and waste, including raw sewage. People have turned their backs on our traditional teachings and commodified our Mother Earth for personal economic gain. It's lawless and heartless. I think it's part of the punishment that Canada and Quebec have had against the Kanien'kehá:ka of Kanehsatà:ke since 1990. They have abandoned their duty to uphold the highest standards of human rights, and so we in the community are left to protect our own security.

It's important for the general population to understand that Indigenous Peoples have a diversity of languages, cultures, and beliefs. There is a diversity of Indigenous people too, some who want to protect and practise the teachings of our ancestors, the ceremonies, our governance system. But there are also ones who promote the economic agenda of the colonizer, assimilating capitalism into their daily life, which creates havoc in our communities, and they are rewarded and can do what they want without any consequences. They're rewarded by settler society's government, while the rest of us are just labelled radicals, troublemakers, or criminals.

I remember being insulted by an Indigenous representative of a corporation who came to advocate for a mining company (that mines niobium and uranium) in Kanehsatà:ke. He knew I was against that kind of development here and he said I was being unreasonable in my opposition because people in the community should want to reap the economic benefits of development. I told him bluntly: I'm not against sustainable development, to be clear, I'm against unsustainable development that destroys the environment and will contribute to the climate crisis.

But, you know, we see the importance of the land and the health of the land and waters. It's about the health of our people and the natural world. Remember our words of thanks to all our relations, Ohén:ton Karihwatéhkwen. You start by mentioning all of Creation, the Creator, Mother Earth, the water, the fish, the trees, the birds, the medicine. And you go right to the sky, and it reminds you that when we talk and make decisions that they're also affected and that we have to remember them in all our deliberations and speak for their rights too. We bring them into the conversation to remind us of what's important and that we're just a small part of creation—and not the most important part of creation.

When people talk about saving the planet, it's really backwards. We're trying to save our species on this planet because, you know, Mother Earth's been here for billions of years. We're just a tiny blip in her existence. It's an important teaching that people need to be reminded of when they make statements like "mining is progress," or "development is progress," because the focus is on how these projects provide jobs and economic benefit, and we hear the rhetoric that Canada must be competitive in the world market. I think people have a skewed view of what progress is, that it means more money for certain families, but poverty still exists. Progress seems to mean ruining lands that can provide food and medicine for us, lands where we find peace in this frustrating world of ours.

For me, progress refers to how we sustain ourselves on this planet into the future, how we find ways to survive the climate crisis, how we have a peaceful coexistence free from war and violence. But some people in power don't think this way; they're not concerned with finding ways to be economically prosperous while still taking care of the planet for future generations.

I think it's really important that people understand that when we're talking about "environmental activism," we're really talking about having respect for Mother Earth and loving all our relations enough to put our lives on the line to protect the future. When we do these kind of actions, when we put our bodies on the land to protect it, we're often discredited and our reputations attacked, either within our communities or by outside forces that incentivize the divide and conquer approach. But we're only doing what is our responsibility under our own Indigenous laws and obligations. History will show that what we're doing is the only choice we have if we're to be true to ourselves and to honour Mother Earth, giving the future generations a fighting chance to survive the cataclysmic environmental changes from the climate crisis.

SEAN: Maynard and Simpson argue this exact point in *Rehearsals for Living*. Maynard explains, "I believe that I am able, that we are able, to commit together to demanding the impossible because we are steeped in old-new, future-oriented political traditions that show us that there is nothing inevitable about the present, that it need not be permanent." She clarifies by saying, "Abolition is imagination work, anticolonial struggle is imagination work, conjure work, science fiction in real time. It is daring to see that the world now did not need to be as it was, does not need to be as it is, and certainly, most importantly, need not—will not—remain this way. It is *too much justice*, re-imagining and refashioning governance as abundance rather than enclosure."[3]

Thinking about the "imaginative work" of looking to the future, what do you think the next generations will need to contend with? How can we rebuild the world in better ways in the coming decades, especially with the ongoing consequences of the COVID-19 pandemic and as climate change becomes a dominant issue in our lives?[4]

ELLEN: I always try to remain optimistic. So, I'm hopeful we won't just go back to the old normal and that we fight to make the "new normal" more sustainable and inclusive, in many respects.

I want youth to remember those Indigenous Elders and people who fought hard in the resistance movement to try to make changes before they were born; to build on the strategies of the past and learn from the strengths and weaknesses of resistance to make their efforts stronger and more effective. I hope for the youth and those not yet born to be able to live on a planet that has the capability to provide them with clean water, good food that's not contaminated by pesticides. It would be beneficial to use the framework of an Indigenous democratic society, to feel included, to want to become involved in their community.

I want the new generation to be kind and compassionate in their relationship with others and Mother Earth, and to be able to remember their ancestors and how hard they had to fight for what we have today. And so, that's the circle of life. It's not that Eurocentric linear view, it's the circle of understanding where you're from and your responsibility to all of creation, knowing your history and vision for the future. Hopefully people, especially the Indigenous youth, can reconnect with those ancestral teachings and use them to help lead this lost society out of this crisis, and to heal from the genocidal laws that brought our Nations to this point—with all its colonial-rooted social problems, the disruption to our identity, land dispossession, and this kind of codependency on colonialism and the free market economy and extractive capitalism.

We need change, a kind of radical change. We have some serious work to do in restructuring our societies, and we have reconciliation work to do with Mother Earth and all of our relations. There are too many leaders, on all sides of the colonial spectrum, promoting the status quo of oppression, ignoring human rights and environmental rights. They've been ruining the land and waters for centuries, and that's the "normal" we need to move away from. We need to find ways to be kinder to each other and to be more respectful of all life on this beautiful planet.

In the economic world they say there are two things that make the world turn: fear and greed. I see a lot of people afraid of losing money. Greed is such a powerful force in our capitalist world. As an example, the developer who is knowingly selling Kanien'kehá:ka lands to build luxury homes, claims to understand the Kanien'kehá:ka of Kanehsatà:ke, our history and our struggle. However, it's evident from the fact that he never stopped selling lands which don't belong to him, that all he cares about is the bottom line. His goal isn't "reconciliation" but to make money, and it would affect his profit margins if he were to respect our rights. It's all about greed. You know, we, as Indigenous Peoples, try to follow the process we're forced into by colonial laws. We sent him a lawyer's letter to stop selling Kanien'kehá:ka land, yet he still continues to sell land because colonial law protects rich people like him and he knows that.

We must continue the struggle and challenge the colonial laws and policies that are used to contain and constrain Indigenous Peoples. We need to dream and imagine what a better future can look like and work hard to bring it about. But there are so many rich and powerful people with seemingly limitless resources who work hard to maintain the status quo. Those of us demanding justice, our lands returned, are labelled radicals, threats to the economy, dangerous. But in truth, the current "economy," as it functions now, is the real threat to our collective survival on this earth. That's the issue. People who benefit the most from extraction and exploitation want all of that profit to continue, they're okay with the destruction of the earth for their own gain. They have no problem trampling the human and environmental rights of Indigenous Peoples and all people and all our relations.

While Indigenous people are not against "development," many of us want to ensure that development is sustainable and done in ways that benefit and protect future generations—not just a billionaire's profits. We need to really start thinking about this and the best way forward. I hear people say they care so much about children and youth. Well then, the future generations' rights to inherit a healthy environment needs to be prioritized.

Indigenous communities need to have access to clean drinking water, we need to restore the ways of survival we've been given by previous generations. We have to persistently protect our rights, our identity, and our lands. It's because of the Canadian bureaucracy and apathy that the issue of Indigenous Peoples' human rights and our long-standing historical concerns have dragged on for this long. We must be able to protect our languages and cultures, which are the foundations of our relationship with the land and the key to our survival. But it's always the rich—the 1 percent[5] who are calling the shots (businessmen and politicians and corporate lobbyists)—whose motivation is based upon fear and greed but never a human rights-based approach.

Climate change is wrapped up in the consequences of genocide, slavery, colonialism, and capitalism, and we need to fight to change the whole system that is threatening our survival here on earth. That is our shared responsibility as human beings, and I'm not just talking about Indigenous people. Everyone has an obligation to create a better future that allows the faces not yet born a chance for survival and the enjoyment of their human rights and the land. A future in which there is peace and security whereby Indigenous Peoples who are following their Traditional Laws can leave behind a good, peaceful, and prosperous way of life for future generations.

SEAN: Art Manuel talks a lot about how colonialism brought capitalism, and capitalism is about extraction for profit for very few people. And he always says he's not against development, but that Indigenous Nations need to be able to control and benefit from development in ways that take care of future generations—and that will benefit everyone. Nevertheless, many Indigenous Land and Water Defenders are perceived to be against development when, as you're saying, it's about creating a future that can sustain the next seven generations. Do you think there are any positive signs that things are changing?

ELLEN: In some ways, with Indigenous people working with environmental NGOs and other allies, there is growing momentum to work together to protect Mother Earth. The TRC has an important Call to Action[6] that advocates for all members of society, from teachers and social workers to judges, lawyers, and politicians, to learn about Canada's genocidal project and speak the truth about Indigenous Peoples' experiences and realities in the Americas. This includes naming all the religious ideologies and European countries who benefited from Canada's genocidal project. It also calls for people working in government to use a human rights lens and Indigenous rights perspective in their work.

But, you know, Canada has placed most of the burden of reconciliation on the shoulders of Indigenous people. It is, as the TRC said, the responsibility of Canadians to change society and strengthen relations with Indigenous Peoples. Whether we're talking about Indigenous Peoples' right to self-determination or other issues, it all centres on taking care of the people of the land, the environment, ensuring water security, and helping all our relations to survive the climate crisis. But we need to do better because UN climate targets are unrealistic, and many UN members refuse to take the necessary action to combat our impacts upon Mother Earth. No one can afford to be complacent.

Over the five hundred years since Contact, Indigenous people have gone from a collective mindset to an individualistic mindset, and that shift is hurting the people, our cultures and languages, and most importantly, the land. It's really an overwhelming situation. We don't have the opportunity that time can provide because we have passed the tipping point. And as the world struggles with all its problems, Indigenous Peoples' human rights are marginalized, making it harder to decolonize, and so justice in these lands and for its peoples is not equitable. Justice is slow, costly, and not easily accessible—it's only for the rich few. Most Indigenous people cannot afford it. The costly, biased, and racist colonial court system is too expensive, has been ineffective, and sets dangerous precedents for Indigenous people if there are any bad judgments against us.

Lawyers, judges, and colonial laws contribute to all the red tape and bureaucracy that only drags out the process further. They say, "justice delayed is justice denied," and

Indigenous people know this all too well. This is where the colonial-imposed poverty is coming from, so we can never seem to get ahead. We're always being pushed into a corner where there is very little opportunity to move forward.

It has been evident for too long now that the moment to act was decades ago. Indigenous Peoples need to be the ones setting the timelines, the parameters of negotiations, so that we can implement the intergenerational knowledge of how to survive an apocalypse. That's what we've been doing for five hundred years.

At the end of the day, I think all of us, no matter what your belief system is, want to feel safe and be able to feed our families and be able to speak our minds without fear of any kind of reprisals. In many Indigenous communities,

Ellen with Eriel Tchekwie Deranger and Melina Loubican-Massimo at the Montreal Global Climate Strike march, September 2019.

and because of social media bullies and racists, that freedom purportedly attributed to a democracy does not exist. I don't think people really understand what democracy is, that everyone must contribute to society to evolve and create positive change.

How many people are actively involved in the decision-making processes in their communities? Voting every few years isn't enough. A democracy requires that people get involved and take action to protect themselves and the land. When people are passive about their rights and leave the decisions to so-called leaders it opens the doors to corruption. Today it's lobbyists who influence governments so they can justify, through economic prosperity, the violation of everyone's human rights. More attention and vigilance are required from us all.

SEAN: That kind of representative democracy—voting, elections, etc.—is simultaneously important but also defers direct responsibility. As well, as Indigenous scholars such as Audra Simpson and Glen Sean Coulthard point out, engaging with the colonial state and its politics of recognition is a flawed strategy.[7]

ELLEN: Colonial laws have always involved the influence of corporations within governance processes. This has caused the commodification of Indigenous people's human rights and has led people to think that it's all about "tax free" purchases. Governments use fear to support their economic agenda; they are ruled by greed and protecting corporate interests, fuelling the settler colonial machine. And they rely on this strategy of fear to promote their agenda's priorities, their economy, rather than using a human and environmental rights-based approach—showing little care for the future existence of our species or our survival on this beautiful planet. Colonial governance purports to use a democratic framework, but in the end people and the environment are sacrificed for corporate gain.

But hope is very important. I try to be positive simply because I need to be. In spite of my flaws and idiosyncrasies, I still see the beauty in life and the world around me. A lot of that hope comes from Mother Earth—immersing myself in her beauty and gifts—and my relations with good people, like yourself. Drawing on all of that keeps me resilient and inspired to continue this journey of living for the land and all our relations. Staying hopeful for the future is certainly challenging, but we must persevere to protect the legacy we leave behind for the next generations. I can't deny that I struggle, because it's hard work trying to remain hopeful.

I've had really good teachers, especially Indigenous Elders who have helped teach me. There have been a lot of wonderful people who have inspired me on my journey. I have a supportive family (which is part of our cultural values that teach the importance of family). So, I know the importance of the love of family and friends. I also had humble and kind teachers along the way that have made a real difference in my life and that I am thankful for. It's really important to have that love and support, especially as a child growing up in a society that sees you as inferior, or "the other."

So, I have to thank them, my family and mentors, for allowing me to be able to do the things that I do today. And there's so many young, strong Indigenous women leaders out there who really are inspiring me to continue what I'm doing. They inspire me each and every day, and I hope I can inspire them too with my work. Hope and inspiration are cyclical like that.

We are stronger when we pull together and support one another in solidarity. We really have a lot of power as individuals to believe in ourselves and dream of a sustainable and healthy future where our dignity and rights are respected. There's a lot of things wrong with this world, to be sure, but there's a lot of good people out there, too.

We fight for a better world, a better future, together. And in this work, we must learn from the past so we can be more effective in our struggles to defend the land today and give future generations a fighting chance to survive the massive changes that are coming and the natural disasters happening already. What I've learned in my life so far has strengthened my resolve to continue, and whether I'm around to see these positive changes is irrelevant because our rights and issues don't belong to one person. Changing the world and bringing about a better future is our collective responsibility.

I feel privileged and honoured to be able to talk with you about all of this, and I hope others will find bits of wisdom that will help them carry on the struggle for the land and for the betterment of the coming generations.

AFTERWORD[1]

In this conversation between Katsi'tsakwas Ellen Gabriel and Sean Carleton we are offered profound insight into the long game of surviving and resisting settler colonialism.[2] This stark process of taking land and of moving those on the land away is a hallmark of the United States and Canada, two nation-states where settlers stayed. The Kanehsatà:ke and Kahnawà:ke Siege of 1990, or the so-called Oka Crisis,[3] the 78-day armed standoff between Mohawks and several forces of the state, remains one of the clearest manifestations of this process in North America to date. Mohawks were not only "in the way," they put themselves in the way of the extension of a nine-hole golf course that was to not only destroy sacred Pines for white leisure but was also to extend through a Mohawk burial ground.

When the Pine Needles Fall: Indigenous Acts of Resistance teaches us, however, that beneath this clear manifestation was a slow, three-hundred-year buildup to this so-called Crisis. And so, by the end of the book one might wonder, was that even a crisis at all, or rather a logical manifestation of how things were going—they take, we resist. But even more elaborate than just taking is the arsenal of ideological and legal machinations that have worked upon Indigenous Peoples to convert their land into property for sale on an open market alongside of the work to convert their distinct systems of thought and language—their nationhood, their cultures, into de-cultured "populations" that require "racial" management (rather than diplomatic protocols) while also taking that land to sell. So, if they not only take, but do all sorts of other things in addition to taking, we have to do other things as well. Like so many other Indigenous people, Ellen Gabriel's life is testament to those other things.

Readers in Canada will be familiar with one method of that conversion—residential schools—and their work upon Indigenous minds, bodies, and polities to transform them into whitened versions of themselves. This was couched ideologically in the late nineteenth and twentieth century as "benevolence" and a kind of racial uplift that was to ready Indigenous Peoples for lives of property ownership and citizenship, but it had a sinister side, working upon Indigenous Peoples' sense of themselves as members of their own polities, as territorial stewards, as distinct Peoples with relationships and rights to land and to waters. While reworking Indigenous Peoples in these institutions, they were also being alienated from their land and with that, their cultures, their languages, their food sources, their knowledge of how to prepare those foods, their diets, and their health.[4] The irony of gaining literacy here will not be lost on some, as it is alphabetic forms of communication, and the imposition of shared languages (English/French) across distinct Nations that produced a shared capacity to organize across national/cultural lines.

In the history of land theft in Kanehsatà:ke, it is because Onahsakén:rat (Joseph Swan)[5] read documents in the Sulpician archives that he saw Kanehsatà:ke's original title to land and the Sulpicians' subsequent records of sale to farmers. He then started organizing people and petitioning the federal government and the Governor General about wrongful sales by the Sulpicians. Without his knowledge of the original title and the subsequent sales, the community may not have had actionable proof. There's an "upside" to being able to be on top of what is said and done in your name through letters! But these civilizational processes of education, often implemented with violence, were also attacks upon Indigenous people's very sense of being themselves. Onahsakén:rat is instructional in every way. What if residential and boarding schools and the longue durée of settler colonial techniques of control failed? And if people remembered themselves, if they remembered agreements and treaties and were ready to defend them?

When the Pine Needles Fall offers a window into all those ways that Haudenosaunee people have remembered who they are, where they are, and what they have to do to protect their relations. But this is something more even than that—this book offers an account of how taking land has necessitated pushback on that taking. We learn about the flip side of the so-called Indian problem: a "settler problem"—a problem of managing the agonies of settlement. Kanehsatà:ke is the oldest existing Kanien'kehá:ka community which predates European arrival as is evident in the condolence ceremony of Chiefs and Clan Mothers. Its present status is as a place that's held for the "band" (of Indians) and their "use and bene-fit"[6] and a traditional territory that receives this legal, rights-bearing cast with the formation of settler states and their laws. Yet it is this complicated status of reserve that makes Kanehsatà:ke a site of deep contestation, as so much of this land that was supposed to be "held" for those there through a seigneurial land grant was then sold out from under them, and by the Sulpicians, a religious order. Even the category of reserve eludes them.

"Reserves" may seem a grand extension of benevolence, "held" as in reserved for later use—or for present use, with conditions. This parceling of land is part of the settler colonial toolkit of dispossession—converting territories into property-like formations with racialized requirements for ownership.[7] Nowhere does this deeply paternalistic notion of holding or reserving territories say explicitly, "this is such because this place is no longer yours," but the arbitrariness of this startling power move to take and to name and to then claim (but "hold" for another) is implied. Nor are the deeply skewed assumptions about ownership and capability to care for land and thus "own" land made explicit. Like law, these assumptions announce themselves through contestation, as do the assumptions that guide the authority and the power to define who gets what and why. As it is reserved, it can, it is implied, also become unreserved, or alienated, or taken. The relationship of private property—were it even to be desirable—eludes those who live on and belong to and have rights to "reserves." The arbitrariness of the legal status of "reserve"—interpreted by "Indians" as sovereign spaces and to settler law in the states as "Trust Lands"—may appear to be a twentieth or twenty-first century issue, but is in fact a problem of settler governance through time and as such is a very present issue. Kanehsatà:ke has been even more vulnerable to expropriation because of its shaky status legally. It is now defined as an "interim land base."[8]

When the Pine Needles Fall makes clear that Kanehsatà:ke land has been taken from the Kanien'kehá:ka for over three centuries, and that all of their effort from the moment that the Sulpicians arrived there in 1717 has been directed towards retaining or reclaiming the original seigneurial grant. What we have then is a story of this mode of taking land or trying to take land through time, as much as a history of pushback retold through Ellen Gabriel's life, through her involvement with the blockade in 1990 and her life before and beyond the Mohawk Crisis. This book is much more than "one woman's life," or an "as told to" story, with Gabriel's life standing in for all women, or all Mohawks. When the Pine Needles Fall is a vital piece of the history of pushback to settler capitalism; it is a concise analysis of an economic system that's predicated upon plunder and the dehumanization of Black and Indigenous Peoples.

This system of distribution for the most part denies Indigenous sovereignty, even where a seigneurial land grant, agreements, treaties may seem to secure that sovereignty. Were we to periodize this, part of what Gabriel's experiences speak to is the "later phase" in settler colonialism, when lands are thought to be justly taken, when settler nation-states declare their independence from a "mother country" and Indigenous Peoples are either decimated by brute force or sequestered into what is left of their original territories as quasi-citizen subjects that require a kind of governmental management. We find through these conflicts over land that this is in no way finished work, that settler colonialism isn't successful, and Indigenous Peoples are not getting out of the way.

Ellen Gabriel speaks from the experience of Kanien'kehá:ka and Haudenosaunee people who have steadfastly refused these processes in varied forms, who maintain an obligation to hold tightly to their land, to their languages, to their philosophical and governmental systems, even when they appear to have "lost" it via plunder, or citizenship, or any other liberal democratic forms of dispossession at work. They hold on to land not as property, but as relations. Carleton and Gabriel's conversations help us to contextualize movements of care and protection and the stakes of ethics and philosophies driven by land and water, which have much deeper histories than the present. Often represented as a decontextualized grievance with bad governance, or reactive politics, these land defense "movements" are rooted in political traditions and governance systems that pre-date the arrival of others to North America. As such they are mischaracterized even as "movements"—they don't *suddenly* arise.

When the Pine Needles Fall gives us insight into how to live according to that responsibility, care, and action—or, in Haudenosaunee terms, peace, power, and righteousness, living according to the Kaianera'kó:wa or Great Law of Peace.[9] What is the process and what are the stakes of living an otherwise, or insisting upon the life of that otherwise? We might ask if this is even the right phrasing of the question?

"The Otherwise" is the wise, is *the way*, for those who live according to the Kaianera'kó:wa. But we may ask, what is that law an "otherwise" to? This is an alternative to an economic and political system predicated upon inequality, upon accumulation and the murder of lands and waters, if not people. As such, what we have here is more than an autobiographical story recorded in the episodic compendium of personal events. What we have is Gabriel's account and critique and analysis of those processes of accumulation, of the economics and politics of settler society. Hers is a life lived in other ways and other registers to create a world in which we should live, to live in a way that takes care of all living things, that imagines interrelated futures for all.

OHÉN:TON KARIHWATÉHKWEN

Gabriel starts this book with a discussion of the Ohén:ton Karihwatéhkwen, an opening Protocol before Haudenosaunee gatherings that grounds each person in thanks, for the earth (our mother), animals, waters, fish, plants, medicines, animals, trees, the moon—all whom are more than acknowledged, they are offered thanks.[10] This, Gabriel reminds us, is to index our relation: we are "part of the natural world, not separate from it," and most certainly we are not above anything else. This practice of collectively thanking all of these elements of the living world reminds us that what we do affects them as well. What we do has consequences beyond the self, the immediate, the present. This is a different way of thinking about oneself and one's actions.

For Haudenosaunee people, words matter deeply and carry the power to remind us of these relationships and to align minds that then determine action. So this practice of collective, philosophical communication, which takes time, which is done in Kanien'kéha, requires contemplation, sometimes translation, and the deep will to listen, to signal agreement, to reflect. This book is an extension of this Protocol and an extended reflection upon making that under-standing and those commitments actionable. What does it mean to take the words, "With one mind, we greet and thank the tree life?" and then live a life next to trees? Would these trees not be worth standing up for?

The teachings of Ellen Gabriel's life lay not in the excep-tionalism of caring for trees and what gets glossed over as the natural world. Gabriel refuses that exceptionalism at every turn.[11] She was thirty-one years old at the time of the Mohawk Crisis in 1990. Her first language is in Kanien'kéha, and she speaks French and English. She was part of a slow quiet refusal by the women to have a nine-hole golf course extended nine more holes into sacred Pines and a burial ground in Kanehsatà:ke.[12] This quiet, deliberate blockade then turned into an armed encampment and militarized resis-tance that lasted 78 days and inspired solidarity actions from Kahnawà:ke that blocked access points to the south shore of Montreal and others.[13]

There was much to demand and to negotiate—one being a stop to the extension of the golf course; another, the faulty titles to land and centuries of dispossession courtesy of the Sulpicians; and then, the decriminalization of those who defended those lands. She was living those arrangements and the commitment to land that was unjustly in someone else's hands. But what she was translating, however, were not only "demands." She was translating philosophy, the principles and tenets of The Great Law. She was a conduit for the peo-ple, she was not above anyone else—she is the first to say this. And yet, to settler optics, she was.

Ellen Gabriel stood up, with other women, for the Pines because, as she says in the book, "the land belongs to the women. Women are the title holders" who "live for the land." This was not an exceptional thing to do. The record, as we will see, is replete with women doing not only for land but for their communities, for their families, for those that need and deserve care. Gabriel places this within an ambit of responsibility and roles that are assumed when one takes an oath in the Longhouse to live according to the Kaianera'kó:wa. So this is deeply gendered but also not exceptional, and like so many actions that would precede and follow the Mohawk Crisis, whether they be militarized or not, women have been on the frontlines.[14]

When the Pine Needles Fall not only de-exceptionalizes the Mohawk Crisis, removing it from a place of "episode" and placing it within a context of *ongoing* dispossession. It also recentres women within their organizational and political role as caretakers of the land. So much of the coverage that summer focused upon the figure of masked and militarized Mohawk men; what we get here is a very different story in addition to a more expansive account of this resistance in the context of dispossession. This is an event that moves backwards and forwards, as what is done will affect the Rotikonhsatá:tie (the faces not yet born). And her life is of a piece with all that, before, during, and after the Mohawk Crisis.

Like Arthur Manuel, Lee Maracle, and so many before her, she was living her life driven by the priorities of principle, and like Manuel she is ceaselessly pragmatic.[15] She was (and still is) trying at every point and every angle to advance those principles: through her studies, through her art, through the defense of territory, through translation, through her advocacy for women,[16] her advocacy and involvement in Indigenous rights and human rights—even at one point running for the office of National Chief.[17] Like Manuel's strategy, these parts form part of a much greater whole, of living for the land—of squeezing out of every opportunity that opens to her the possibility of advancing these principles and the care and relational freedoms they entail.

The significance of *When the Pine Needles Fall* is as much its revision to the record as its critical analysis of settler politics and economies. Building upon community history that's both written and unwritten, this book contextualizes 1990 into Sulpician aggrandizement, explaining how they were "an elite religious community" that didn't take a vow of poverty and "retained ownership of their individual property and. . . . disposed freely of their wealth. Many members of the Seminary in Montreal came from well-off families, they were sons of judges, surgeons, and small landowners."[18] In 1959, Kanehsata'kehró:non were confronted with a private golf course built on their lands in their territory, the community resisted this and filed an official land claim with Canada in 1970, but it was rejected, setting the stage for what would follow in 1990. By 1989, the then-Mayor of Oka was able to end a moratorium on the proposed extension of the golf course into sacred Pines.

In the book, Gabriel reminds us of the sacredness of pines to Haudenosaunee people, but also how important the Pines were to women, as it was the women of Kanehsatà:ke who, in order to escape the bullies of the Sulpicians from disturbing them during the night, took their families to hide from them, and slept in the Pines for protection from the violence. Gabriel says,

> The Sulpicians were bullies and would forcibly enter people's homes to intimidate Kanehsata'kehró:non—to try to force us off the land so that they could sell it to make more money. During these attacks, men were forced to hide in order to escape the brutality, often leaving the women behind because it was thought that they wouldn't be harmed. That assumption was wrong. The women were harassed late in the evening, by the priests and their bullies. To have protection they would leave their homes and sleep in the Pines at night. So, the Pines are a place of refuge.

In Gabriel's award-winning film *Kanàtenhs: When the Pine Needles Fall* (2022) that foregrounds the voices of women who were there, Arlette Van den Hende offered: "Our bodies have nurtured the land, the trees are part of our . . . great-grandparents, or they are part of those trees. It's an intimacy with the land that I think a lot of people don't have."[19] Furthermore, Gabriel tells us it was mostly women who were at the peaceful barricades that predated the July 11 raid, and paramilitary forces, but "that's not what the media focused on."

These historical and gendered valences revise the record as it is known. But, also, this is a reworking of time itself, of its play upon what matters, the upending of the "event" in its approach and its refusal of the category of an "exceptional historical actor." The 1990 Kanehsatà:ke Siege has been imagined and represented as a discrete and isolatable problem of governance, an exceptional event produced by faulty land title and jurisdictional issues—perhaps this "crisis" was due to an overstepping municipal mayor, perhaps some other bad actors, lack of good faith by Canada, corruption, violence and greed, over time.

When conceptualized as a "crisis" it appears as a "one-off" that's contained to the latter part of the twentieth century.[20] But like the sustained resistances of every form that punctuate Native and settler histories in the US and Canada, this "event" follows other events that are as shattering and receive little to no attention. Yet, when they are considered within their own contexts of articulation, within their own timeframes, we start to see the pattern that Nick Estes has called "histories of resistance."[21] These traditions don't register as histories in and of themselves when the crisis point or the event is focused upon. And like the event, we have the individual historical actor that also, when focused upon, takes away from the longer struggle they are part of.

So often, Indigenous men have stood in for the politics of these resistances as well, as outside optics favors representations of Indigenous men.[22] But those men are part of larger imperatives that have been and are driven by land ethics, ethics that then get obscured by an attention to masculinized militancy.[23] Gabriel insists that her life be put into these layers of context so that her actions are of a larger philosophical, ceremonial, political, and territorial whole and collective of people. In this insistence she is uncontainable by the moment of crisis and her actions, her reflections and her analysis offer us a window into the long game of pushback in the short game of settler occupation. The Mohawk Crisis isn't a one-off. It's a piece with a much larger and much longer process of taking and occupying land. Similarly, Ellen Gabriel's life exceeds and isn't bracketed by that as an event.

FUTURES

In *Our History Is the Future*, Nick Estes argues for an approach to time and to politics in sites of occupation, and privileges this long game, "our histories" of resistance, of defiance, the long arcs of refusal that push upon the conceit that these places are settled, that they were taken, or taken successfully, that Indigenous Peoples have gone away and/or are done with.[24] It is common to hear Haudenosaunee speak of the aforementioned "faces yet to come/not yet born." Those who we act for now, whose future lives are what we work towards, or the animals who work with us to help all to live. This is all in the Ohén:ton Karihwatéhkwen, who we give thanks for. But these thanks, too, are not "one-offs." These are forms of relation, through time, through place. Life lived in anticipation of a future drives this analysis and Ellen Gabriel's life forward.

This is more than a story of a remarkable, noteworthy person (and she is very much a remarkable, noteworthy person).

This is a life lived in a particular way, in an active engagement with knowledge, with history, with what gets glossed over as "tradition" but is a set of principles, a governing system, language, and philosophy predicated on good relations, on having a good mind. It is this expansive and active framework that places Gabriel into a constant emergence and sustained critique, responsibility, and relationship with the world. Of this she says,

> we don't know how many generations have heard the Iroquois Creation Story or all the other legendary stories that have been passed down to us as Indigenous Peoples. But it's those storytellers that have given us that creative ability to imagine our history, our worldview, our cultural values, and there is even more of an impact from these stories through the words of our Onkwehón:we languages. Our languages describe in a visual way which colonial languages cannot.

Her relationship to land, to people, and to a past, present, and future translates those ethics into analysis and action. Gabriel also teaches us how corporatization of government is part of this long game of settler capitalism and governance, and thus has made the work of resistance, the effort of Native people, the labour also of our non-Native allies. If we are to survive this world, we have to not only live in defiance of colonialism and capitalism. We have to live in a posture of active care for each other.

The legacy of Gabriel's work and analysis is its life-sustaining properties. Here we have a model of how to go about things if wanted. We have another road map of how to navigate the world, but also we have an account of the world. This life and analysis sits beside that of Secwépemc writer Arthur Manuel, Stó:lō writer Lee Maracle, and Haudenosaunee writers and poets and organizers as varied as Pauline Johnson,[25] Laura Cornelius Kellogg,[26] and Beth Brant.[27]

Nineteenth and twentieth century Six Nations Mohawk Pauline Johnson used her position and her poetry to smuggle in another story of law, another justice system, while she had command of a non-Native audience.[28] Her piece "A Red Girl's Reasoning"[29] presents the conflict between a settler husband and Indigenous wife over the legitimacy of her parents' "savage"/traditional/unsanctioned marriage—not as "culture clash" but instead as a clash of systems with explosive consequences for intimate and legal arrangements.[30]

More than interpersonal disagreement, this was a deep contestation over the integrity and legitimacy of Indigenous political orders, an "otherwise" to the presumed sanctity of Victorian, Canadian Christian unions. Their conflict and her refusal to back down on the validity of her parents' unsanctioned union opened into the vitality and validity of an entirely different legal, and thus political, framework for relatedness. She smuggled that covert message about Indigenous sovereignty into what seemed to be a trite story about the pitfalls of "interracial" marriage, or a spirited and gendered defense of "culture," or, simply, a "plucky Native woman who returns to buckskin after her time in the big city."[31] No, this is something entirely different. This is a defense of Indigenous laws and a total pushback on the perception of Indigenous Peoples as lawless, as savage, as in need of white, patriarchal salvation.

Haudenosaunee have pushed these ethics of land and the integrity of our cultural and political orders and languages as unvanquished systems of life through the past two centuries. Gabriel's analysis belongs alongside that of those who have acted within the world and presented a position rooted in Haudenosaunee principles. Here she joins twentieth century Oneida organizer Laura Cornelius Kellogg,[32] Chief Deskaheh Levi General who valiantly tried to bring the Haudenosaunee case for sovereign status and freedom from Canadian malfeasance to the League of Nations for international recognition in the 1920s,[33] Chief Clinton Rickard of Tuscarora who pressed for cross border rights,[34] Paul K. Diabo from Kahnawà:ke who refused to pay taxes as an ironworker in Philadelphia and forced interpretation of the Jay Treaty in an American court in the 1920s,[35] as well as Six Nations Mohawk teacher Emily General who took the case of chronic underfunding of education to England in the 1930s and refused to take an oath to the Crown,[36] and the late Cayuga Chief and chronicler of Haudenosaunee politics and culture, Jake Thomas.[37] As well, Gabriel's analysis may find context within the writings of the late Kahnawà:ke Mohawk Louis Hall, who wrote in critical relationship to the Gawi'io, or Code of Handsome Lake, and was so important to the warrior societies in the Northeast.[38]

When the Pine Needles Fall joins the work of writers like the late Tyendinaga poet Beth Brant, Six Nations legal scholar Patricia Monture Angus, and the late Tyendinaga historian Deborah Doxtator.[39] This book also belongs within a body of more contemporary Haudenosaunee thought, literary history, and ethnography written by Theresa McCarthy, Susan Hill, Mishuana Goeman, Rick Monture, Doug Metoxen Kiel, Louellyn White, and Kristina Ackley[40]—a generation of scholars who have documented, interpreted, and theorized lives and territories. Gabriel's analysis manifests Tuscarora visual studies scholar and theorist Jolene Rickard's foundational concept of "visual sovereignty"[41]—the optics of seeing and caring for place—as well as the visual practice of the Six Nations artist Shelley Niro[42] and Kahnawà:ke Mohawk artist Skawennati's futurisms.[43] This is not to forget the work of Haudenosaunee poets January Rogers,[44] Eric Gansworth,[45] and the memoirist Alicia Elliott.[46]

All of these thinkers, writers, artists, and analysts have turned the present on its head, have manifested a different relationship to territory, continuously casting into question the justness of occupation and settler law, and pointed to or manifested those other laws, those other jurisdictions, the alternative and imperative to care for the faces yet to come. In as much as this isn't an episodic account of one's life, it is a story rendered through those relationships.

This book is its own manifestation of a relationship, and expressed through a conversational form, what is called a "communion" in the Preface, that sits like a cousin to Staughton Lynd and Andrej Grubacic's *Wobblies and Zapatistas* and Robyn Maynard and Leanne Betasamosake Simpson's epistolary exchanges in *Rehearsals for Living*.[47] This was prompted by Ellen Gabriel's desire to write a book about her experiences, but a desire thwarted by "things [that] got in the way." So many of those "things" are in this book. They are the stuff of life, interrupted and fought for, cared for, with others. We are immensely better for the efforts of Sean Carleton and Ellen Gabriel to express this form of inter-generational communion for us all now, and for the faces yet to come.

AUDRA SIMPSON

ACKNOWLEDGEMENTS

This collection of conversations is the product of a friendship, a partnership, between us, but getting it out into the world in book form required help and support of many other people along the way. We started the book with Ellen's explanation of Ohén:ton Karihwatéhkwen, as an expression of gratitude, and so we'd like to conclude by returning to that deeply rooted sense of appreciation and thankfulness.

SEAN: First and foremost, I thank Ellen. Learning with her has been a true privilege. I'm honoured to be able to call her a friend and a collaborator and to have played a small role in helping others connect to her important insights and teachings with this book. I'll always cherish this set of conversations, especially those we had during the first spring/summer of COVID-19 isolation. Listening to Ellen speak about her life lived for the land, often as the birds sang in her background, filled my heart with hope for the future. Though this project is now over, our relationship is ongoing. Thank you, Ellen.

I also thank Pamela Palmater and Audra Simpson for their generous contributions, Nancy Kimberley Phillips for transcription help, the University of Manitoba for financial support, and the Between the Lines team, especially Amanda Crocker and Devin Clancy, and our editor, Nadine Ryan for making this book a reality. Finally, I thank my family and friends for their love and continued support, especially Julia.

ELLEN: There have been many teachers in my life who have guided me, taught me, supported me, and for whom I am grateful to being part of my life journey.

Amongst them first and foremost are my family: my sisters Bridget and Mamie, my late brother Archie "Billy" who passed away March 3, 2023, with whom I shared so much of my early life. As we grew older, meeting life's challenges, their love and support helped me through some difficult times post-1990. We have such precious memories of growing up together: playing outside, working on the farm, baling hay, riding horses, playing hockey with my brother Billy, and holiday Christmas pageants. They were lots of fun, and I'm proud to be their sister.

I'm also grateful for my parents, Annie Montour and Archie Gabriel Sr., who gave me my language Kanien'kéha and my Turtle Clan. They taught me love, compassion, my values, and they supported my efforts as an artist at an early age. They taught me that living on a farm with horses was the most wonderful time for a child, and like most kids of my generation, gave us the teaching of the importance of the land, and a love for the land and its bounties. As kids, we played outside no matter the weather. Spending all those hours exploring the fields and hills of the land helped teach us how to read the signs of Mother Earth, to watch Her changes, and gave us precious memories which have enriched our lives to this day. My parents worked hard all their lives, and they gave us strong work ethics and encouraged us to be proud to be Onkwehón:we. I still miss their smiles and hugs.

Thank you to my aunties, the matriarchs of our family, the late Eleanor Montour Van den Hende, the late Phyllis Montour Benson, Christina Montour, and Charlotte Montour-Beaver, my mother's sisters who became our surrogate mothers when my mother passed away on January 1, 1985. They supported my mother when we lost my father in December 1980—just two days after John Lennon was killed. They taught me kindness, laughter, the language, and unconditional love which is important when one becomes an orphan—even as a young adult.

To my niece, Jennifer, and nephews, Daniel and Keith, being your auntie has been one of the greatest honours of my life. Children are a good medicine away from the politics and dysfunction of community, and they certainly gave me great joy spending time with them, taking them to movies or bike rides, or just spending time with them at home. They were good medicine for the stress in my life as an activist / Land Defender. They have all become beautiful adults with good minds and hearts and I'm so proud of them. Niá:wen for still wanting to spend time with your old auntie.

I have two very special cousins who have listened to my woes and shared some laughter together, Arlette Van den Hende and Wanda Gabriel. Their kindness, compassion, and wisdom has given me the strength to continue the work that I do, and pulled me out of some dark places.

I want to acknowledge my dad Archie's horses, who worked so hard for us to have food on the table and clothing on our backs. They frightened me when I was young, but they taught me that one must respect all creatures. While they are strong and beautiful animals, they also have characters like us humans who are free thinking and have their own ways of doing things. Their strength and beauty still touch my heart.

To my precious Elder, the late Walter David Sr., who supported me throughout the 1990 siege of Kanehsatà:ke. Thank you. He encouraged me to continue when I wanted to give up. He taught me about Kaianera'kó:wa and the history he knew of the Iroquois Confederacy. He taught me our definition of what Onkwehón:we sovereignty is and to be steadfast in knowing that we have the right to defend ourselves from the colonial powers that be. He was a marine veteran and was injured on the shores of Iwo Jima in 1945, and saw the soldiers raise the iconic flag on that hill in Japan. I'm honoured that he shared his war stories, and I still think of him fondly and all the adventures we shared, including our trip to The Hague in 1990.

To my friends, Samir Shaheen-Hussain and Nazila Bettache, who constantly inspire me to be a better person. Their dedication to social justice and their compassion for their fellow human beings is inspirational. Their love and care have brought me much joy, happiness, and inspiration.

To my good friend Clifton Nicholas whose brilliance and vast knowledge always inspires me to learn more. He has been a good friend and support throughout all we've been experiencing in the community.

To my good friends Tom Liacas and Louis Ramirez, whose enthusiasm, determination, and sense of humour have brought me inspiration, love, and helped me during some difficult times both in this work and personally. And to Jennifer Preston, Paul Joffe, and Craig Benjamin who have been good friends and allies in the struggles of Indigenous Peoples. Their solidarity has lifted me up when this advocacy work becomes frustrating. I've learned so much from them and continue to.

Finally, niawen'kó:wa to Sean Carleton, whose determination and keeping me on track has given me the opportunity to write this book. I'm so honoured for his kind support, respectful manner, his brilliance and his compassion and advocacy for Indigenous Peoples. Without him, this book would not be possible.

There have been many people along this journey of discovery who have taught me, laughed with me, and given me hope along the way. Those who inspire are often never known, but these important people keep my moccasins on the ground to continue this path of justice for Indigenous Peoples. Thank you.

APPENDICES

SPEECH TO STATUS OF WOMEN COMMITTEE, 2013

On May 7, 2013, Ellen Gabriel gave a speech in the House of Commons in Ottawa, Ontario, in relation to Bill S-2: An Act respecting family homes situated on First Nations reserves and matrimonial interest or rights to structures and lands situated on those reserves.[1]

Greetings to the chair, honourable members of Parliament, and my esteemed colleagues from the Quebec native women's association. This is at least the fourth or fifth time I'm presenting on this issue, in previous times as the president of the Quebec native women's association, so it is a great honour indeed.

As in the previous forms of this bill, several persistent omissions must be taken into consideration if there are to be real and long-lasting solutions to this problem. They first must be placed in context to understand the root causes of this injustice, which originates in the Indian Act and the impositions of colonial and patriarchal values.

I am compelled to note that the goal of this bill is the fair and equitable distribution of matrimonial real property for Indian women on reserves upon the dissolution of a relationship.

This bill should not profess to address the chronic issue of violence against aboriginal women. The issue of violence is best addressed through a national plan of action by Canada, its provinces and territories, and through cultural sensitivity classes on Canada's colonial history for judges, lawyers, members of Parliament, and politicians. It should include a genuine process of reconciliation that recognizes the negative impact of colonialism, the Indian Act, and the Indian residential schools system on indigenous peoples' identity, culture, language, traditional forms of governance, and how they have affected the roles and authority of indigenous women in their nations and communities.

A holistic view is essential if the issue of MRP is to be properly addressed by all levels of government, but in particular within aboriginal forms of governance.

High unemployment rates, lack of sufficient housing, a growing population, dispossession of our lands and resources, the imposition of paternalistic values and processes, outdated funding formulas, poverty, and social ills rooted in colonialism have for generations affected indigenous women's ability to enjoy their fundamental human rights.

There are several areas of concern regarding this bill, which include, one, the incorrect assumption that this bill was accompanied by a consultation process; two, the lack of inclusion of the Constitution Act of 1982, which protects and affirms the inherent and treaty rights of aboriginal peoples; three, the lack of resources for communities in implementation of this bill, and potential court orders supported by a weak implementation process, considering the situation of policing on reserves; and four, the non-legislative measures and lack of access to justice, in particular for those women living in remote communities, and the financial burdens placed upon these women, where homemakers rely on spouses for their incomes.

On the matter of consultation, I must state sincerely that there was none. While engagement sessions were given by Wendy Grant-John—her report came out in March 2007—and an explanation of the issue of matrimonial property was provided, with some discussion on suggesting solutions, even the ministerial representative's report noted that there has not been sufficient time to reach consensus.

While the government firmly believes that there were consultations, I must remind them that the ultimate duty to consult rests with the Government of Canada and its duty to uphold the honour of the crown. It is important to state that there were no consultations on the specific details and nature of Bill S-2 on matrimonial real property.

It is of significant importance to note that during any consultation process, the process of reconciliation must be included and is always ongoing in Canada's relationship with aboriginal peoples. As per the policy of the Government of Canada in its duty to consult, the crown also consults because it is legally obliged to do so. It must give effect to reconciliation and uphold the honour of the crown—the government's ability to adversely affect aboriginal treaty rights is restricted in this reality—and crown conduct must demonstrate respect for aboriginal and treaty rights.

In remote communities women rely on travelling courts. Women must often travel in the same vehicle as their ex-partner to attend court. Remote communities do not have easy access to legal aid. The financial burden placed upon women is cumbersome in their quest for a fair and just settlement.

Access to justice is challenging. With regard to financial compensation to their ex-spouse, should they try to negotiate a fair and just settlement, their measure of worth, of contribution made as homemakers, is not considered. This causes aboriginal women to experience more vulnerability and discrimination, as low-income women would not be able to pay their ex-spouses for the value of their part of matrimonial real property.

The issue of policing on reserves is also an extremely serious question. Provincial courts would only be able to provide temporary occupation orders for the home, and a lot of times police who are reserve police might have trouble implementing them if they're related to the persons involved. In Quebec common law, as Ms. Michel has stated, relationships are not recognized.

If harmonization with provincial and territorial laws was the goal in this bill, then a consultation process that also included the customary laws of indigenous peoples, along with their free, prior, and informed consent, should also have been considered. The trend for over 100 years is to go to Canada's courts if we disagree with Canada's decisions. Aboriginal peoples should not have to go to Canada's courts to protect their inherent and treaty rights.

Another important issue is that of membership codes, the criteria created by the Indian Act, and many times it uses blood quantum. Should a woman not be a member of the community, the woman will never have the right to own the home and its implements, thereby creating another gap.

Lastly, a centre of excellence should not be included since this was never a topic of discussion during talks with Ms. Grant-John. A centre of excellence is another example of the paternalistic attitude of government. It ignores the customary laws of Indigenous Nations and ignores the inherent rights and treaty rights. It seems to be another part of the aboriginal industry where badly needed funding for communities will be directed toward an organization isolated from the communities, instead of going to institutions damaged by the Indian Act such as our languages and cultures and traditional customs and governance, as well as more emergency shelters in the communities, which are essential to this process of reconciliation.

If the centre of excellence is to be created, it should not be headed or controlled by any aboriginal organization. Instead, it should have indigenous women academics, elders with traditional knowledge, and front line workers with experience in domestic and institutionalized racism and abuse.

Like many laws before it, Bill S-2 fails to consider the realities of first peoples and their communities who lack the much-needed financial and human resources for its implementation. Bands are already pushed to their limits by outdated funding formulas, as stated by former Auditor General Sheila Fraser in her 2011 June Status Report, in chapter 4, "Programs for First Nations on Reserves." She states, "Structural impediments explain the lack of progress on reserves." Ms. Fraser goes on to say substandard construction practices or materials, lack of proper maintenance, and overcrowding also contribute. Bill S-2 also does not accommodate the need for more land, nor the fact that in order to develop their own MRP codes, a band must already have been in or be in negotiations on their land.

Legislation that fails to consider [how] the effects of colonialism and assimilation policies, like the Indian residential school system and the Indian Act, creates deficiencies in the promotion and protection of indigenous women's rights. In recent years, great accomplishments in the area of human rights, most notably regarding the collective and individual rights of indigenous peoples through comprehensive human rights instruments like the UN Declaration on the Rights of Indigenous Peoples, must be included in any remedies to injustices faced by indigenous women and their families.

Various human rights agencies, like the UNPFII, have been created to reconcile past injustices experienced by indigenous peoples due to doctrines of superiority and colonialism, which regrettably still exist today in Canada. There is a movement forward to end the discriminatory practices perpetuated under Canada's Indian Act laws and policies. It behooves the Government of Canada to implicate itself wholeheartedly within the processes of reconciliation in all its dealings with aboriginal peoples. Canada must amend Bill S-2, listen to the voices of Indigenous women and their communities, embrace human rights instruments, and repeal Bill S-2. Thank you very much for your consideration.

SPEECH AT THE UNITED NATIONS PERMANENT FORUM ON INDIGENOUS ISSUES, 2009

On May 19, 2009 Ellen Gabriel gave a speech as President of Quebec Native Women at the United Nations Permanent Forum on Indigenous Issues.[2]

Mme Chair, PF delegates, elders, and all my relations. It is with great honor that we are participating today on behalf of the many Indigenous women who could not be here today. While we are encouraged by the various reports of the UNPFII, there remains much work to be done for the world's Indigenous Peoples. Canada and other states that continue to oppose the UNDRIP have demonstrated a lack of respect and understanding of this important instrument that would truly address the discrimination of Indigenous people in particular, Indigenous women.

Due to the impacts of colonization Indigenous women suffer multiple discriminations based on race, gender and economic status. Indigenous women's roles and authority continue to be targeted and undermined through legislation under Canada's Indian Act. Decolonization should include traditional governance structures whereby Indigenous women are partners in decision-making processes. In Canada, forced assimilation practices are evident in policies and programs which threaten the nationality and identity of Indigenous peoples. Therefore it is important that we create our own governance structures that reflect women's roles in order to prevent further assimilation of Indigenous peoples.

The UN Declaration on the Rights of Indigenous Peoples is an international instrument that addresses the situation of multiple discriminations faced by Indigenous women, even though the Canadian government has yet to endorse the Declaration.

It is therefore disappointing to note that the Government of Canada continues to oppose the UNDRIP that recognizes the equal rights of Indigenous peoples. While some attempts have been made by Canada to provide Indigenous women and their communities access to human rights instruments, the Indian Act continues to undermine the equality of Indigenous women's rights.

Without the reinforcement of Indigenous women's role in nation building, there is no assurance that our traditional customs, languages and forms of governance will be perpetuated. Consequently, our identity as Indigenous peoples could be reduced to artifacts in museums.

Therefore it is imperative that all states practice in good faith, the process of free, prior and informed consent.

And while the international community congratulates the Government of Canada for its June 11th, 2008 apology to the Indian Residential School survivors, there has been no change in the status quo. Poverty, inadequate housing, sexual discrimination amongst the Aboriginal population remains unchanged.

Quebec Native Women recommends to the PFII that all member states including Canada do the following:

> Create a national strategy on promoting and preventing violence against Indigenous Women and Children; which incorporates customary Indigenous initiatives of child care and family support.

> Provide public services, consulted with and adapted to Indigenous culture and traditions.

> That all states implement the Convention on the Rights of the Child; as well as implementing the UNDRIP Articles 21, 22, 23, 24 inter alia, to adequately help Indigenous peoples overcome the effects of colonization.

> That all states implement the norm of free, prior and informed consent, including the rights pertaining to the equality of Indigenous women.

> A gender based analysis be implemented in all state policies and programs especially those that affect the collective rights of Indigenous peoples.

> That access to safe water be recognized as a basic human right and that Indigenous people have a meaningful role in the watershed protection.

> Ensure that states ensure that Indigenous women and their organizations will be equitably represented in the decision making processes regarding land management and water rights.

> Prevent the exploitation of Indigenous lands before the settlement of the land claims.

> Urge the few remaining states opposed to the UNDRIP, in particular Canada [to] fully support and implement the UNDRIP.

GLOSSARY

MOHAWK WORDS

Ahkwesásne A Mohawk community near Cornwall, Ontario, with five jurisdictions running through it: Canada, US, Quebec, Ontario, and New York State.

Haudenosaunee Also known as the Iroquois Confederacy, the Haudenosaunee Confederacy consists of the Mohawk, Oneida, Onondaga, Cayuga, Seneca, and Tuscarora Nations.

Kahnawà:ke Kanien'kehá:ka community near Montreal across the St. Lawrence River using the Mercier Bridge.

Kaianera'kó:wa The Great Law of Peace.

Kaianera'shera'kó:wa The Great Shining Peace.

Kanàtakon The village of Kanehsatà:ke where Kanien'kehá:ka lived for centuries, it is now known as the colonial imposed name of Oka.

Kanehsatà:ke Means "the place where the crusty sand dunes lie."

Kanehsata'kehró:non People from Kanehsatà:ke.

Kanien'kéha Refers to the language of the Kanien'kehá:ka people.

Kanien'kehá:ka People of the Flint (Mohawk is a name given to the people by the colonizers).

Kanién:ke Kanien'kehá:ka community in New York state.

Kanonhsésne The Longhouse—refers to the building.

Niá:wen Thank you.

Niawenkó:wa A big thank you.

Ohén:ton Karihwatéhkwen The Words That Come Before All Else.

Onkwehón:we Indigenous people/person.

Rotikonhsatá:tie The faces not yet born.

Rotinonhseshá:ka The People of the Longhouse.

Rotinonshón:ni The Haudenosaunee (Iroquois Confederacy).

Skén:nen Wishing you peace.

OTHER RELEVANT TERMS AND PHRASES

Akwesasne Notes: A newspaper published by the Mohawk Nation at Ahkwesásne between 1968 and the 1990s.

American Indian Movement (AIM): An influential Indigenous-led grassroots social movement founded in Minneapolis, Minnesota in 1968.

Bourassa, Robert: Quebec's premier during the summer of 1990. In August 1990, he ended negotiations with the Mohawks and invoked the National Defence Act, resulting in the federal government sending in the Canadian Armed Forces.

Ciaccia, John: Quebec's Minister of Indian Affairs during the summer of 1990.

Collège d'enseignement general et professionnel (CEGEP): A general and professional teaching college in the province of Quebec.

Deer, Kenneth Atsenhaienton: A Mohawk political activist from Kahnawà:ke, newspaper publisher, and editor of *The Eastern Door*. He has done extensive work at the United Nations, including being part of the Working Group on Indigenous Populations since 1987 and the UN Working Group on the Draft Declaration on the Rights of Indigenous Peoples since 1995.

Department of Indian Affairs: The department of the federal government responsible for managing Indian Affairs in Canada. Today there are two departments, the Department of Indigenous Services and Crown-Indigenous Relations and Northern Affairs Canada.

Deskaheh Levi General: A Haudenosaunee Traditional Chief who, in the 1920s, tried to bring concerns before the League of Nations. Deskaheh was refused the opportunity of addressing delegates but his efforts have inspired others to seek international justice for Indigenous peoples in Canada and the United States.

Dibaajimowinan: In Anishinaabemowin, teachings that roughly translate in English as echoes, linking past, present, and future.

Doctrine of Discovery: A legal and religious concept that has been used for centuries to justify Christian colonial conquest and land theft.

École Polytechnique massacre: A misogynist mass shooting that took place at the engineering school affiliated with the Université de Montréal on December 6, 1989. Fourteen women were murdered, and ten women and four men were injured when they were shot by an antifeminist terrorist.

Elsipogtog Protest: In 2013, the RCMP raided a protest camp set up by members of Elsipogtog Nation to prevent fracking on their unceded territory in New Brunswick, leading to an excessive use of force and arrests of Indigenous Land Defenders.

Expert Mechanism on the Rights of Indigenous Peoples (EMRIP): The Expert Mechanism provides the UN's Human Rights Council with expertise and advice on the rights of Indigenous Peoples as set out in the UN Declaration on the Rights of Indigenous Peoples.

Gustafsen Lake Standoff: A month-long conflict (August 18–September 17, 1995) between Secwépemc Land Defenders and the RCMP in central British Columbia. Similar to the Siege of Kanehsatà:ke in 1990 and the Ipperwash Standoff (also happening in summer of 1995), the police operation in Secwépemc territory was a large-scale paramilitary show of force to intimidate Indigenous Land Defenders and protect the settler capitalist rule of law.

Honoré Mercier Bridge: A bridge connecting the Montreal borough of LaSalle on the Island of Montreal with the Mohawk community of Kahnawà:ke and the suburb of Châteauguay on the south shore of the Saint Lawrence River. On the morning of July 11, 1990, Mohawks from Kahnawà:ke blocked the bridge in solidarity with the Mohawks of Kanehsatà:ke. This resulted in racist backlash, with settlers from Châteauguay attacking Mohawks and even lighting a Mohawk effigy on fire during a demonstration.

Idle No More: A grassroots movement started in 2012 to oppose Bill C-35 which threatened reserve lands, removed protections of many waterways, and weakened Canada's environmental laws. Indigenous-led protests spread internationally and garnered non-Indigenous solidarity to strengthen the movement.

Indian Act: Canadian legislation enacted in 1876 that defines the relationship between registered status Indians and the federal government.

Indian Residential Schools: A national system of church-run and state-funded boarding schools for Indigenous Peoples in Canada. For more than a century (1883–1997), the system undercut Indigenous lifeways through coercive assimilation to facilitate settler colonialism, capitalism, and Canadian nation-building.

Ipperwash Standoff: In 1995, members of the Stony Point First Nation re-occupied part of Ipperwash Provincial Park that had been appropriated by the federal government for use as a military camp in 1942 but not returned to the Nation. The Ontario Provincial Police raided a protest camp, resulting in the killing of Ojibwa Land Defender Dudley George by a police sniper.

Kanesatake Interim Land Base Governance Act: A contested 2001 agreement with respect to the governance of the land base between the Mohawk Council of Kanesatake and the federal government.

Lemay, Francine: Corporal Marcel Lemay's sister. Since 1990, Francine has become an important ally, helping Quebecers understand the history and perspectives of Indigenous Peoples. She translated *At the Woods' Edge: An Anthology of the History of the People of Kanehsatà:ke* into French.

Lemay, Marcel: A police officer killed during the SQ's Siege of Kanehsatà:ke on July 11, 1990.

Missing and Murdered Indigenous Women and Girls (MMIWG): A human rights crisis wherein Indigenous women, girls, and Two Spirited people (sometimes rendered MMIWG2S) face disproportionate rates of discrimination, violence, and murders. In the 2019 report of the National Inquiry into Missing and Murdered Indigenous Women and Girls, the commissioners identified the crisis as genocide.

Mohawk Council of Kanesatake (MCK): The band council elected to represent Kanehsatà:ke according to the electoral system imposed on First Nations by the federal government through the Indian Act.

Mohawk Warrior Flag, or Unity Flag: Created in the 1970s by Kahnawà:ke artist, writer, and activist Karoniaktajeh Louis Hall.

Mulroney, Brian: Canada's prime minister during the summer of 1990.

Onahsakén:rat Joseph Swan: An important Mohawk leader from Kanehsatà:ke (1845–1881). He studied at the Petit Séminaire de Montréal alongside Métis leader Louis Riel, becoming educated and realizing that the Sulpicians were lying to steal Mohawk lands. He was criminalized by the Sulpicians for organizing against their land theft and fraud. He died mysteriously in 1881.

One Dish, One Spoon: A philosophy used by the Haudenosaunee and Anishinaabeg to describe how land can be shared to the mutual benefit of all its inhabitants.

Ouellette, Jean: Mayor of Oka in the late 1980s and early 1990s.

Permanent Forum on Indigenous Issues (PFII): The Permanent Forum is an advisory body to the UN's Economic and Social Council and has the mandate to discuss Indigenous issues related to economic and social development, culture, the environment, education, health, and human rights.

Quebec Native Women (QNW): Founded in 1974, Quebec Native Women represents women from the Indigenous Peoples in Quebec and Indigenous women living in urban areas.

Royal 22nd Regiment: Commonly known as the Van Doos, the infantry regiment of the Canadian Army deployed to Kanehsatà:ke and Kahnawà:ke in 1990.

Royal Canadian Mounted Police (RCMP): Commonly known as the Mounties, the RCMP was established in 1920 as an amalgamation of the Royal North-West Mounted Police and the Dominion Police. The North-West Mounted Police were created as a paramilitary force in 1873 to serve and protect Canada's colonial interests in what is now known as Western Canada.

Royal Commission on Aboriginal Peoples (RCAP): A royal commission (1991–1996) set up by the federal government in response to the Mohawk Resistance and chaired by Georges Erasmus, a former National Chief of the Assembly of First Nations, and René Dussault, a judge of the Quebec Appeals Court. RCAP's five-volume report was released in 1996 and contained 440 recommendations to transform Canada's institutions to improve Indigenous-settler relations. Despite offering a blueprint for better relations, subsequent governments ignored RCAP's recommendations.

Siddon, Tom: Canada's Minister of Indian Affairs during the summer of 1990.

Special Weapons and Tactical Team (SWAT): The Sûreté du Québec's Groupe tactique d'intervention, used during the Siege of Kanehsatà:ke on July 11, 1990.

Sulpicians: Missionaries and members of the Seminary of St. Sulpice who oversaw land theft and fraud in Mohawk territory for over two centuries.

Sûreté du Québec (SQ): The provincial police force for the province of Quebec, established in 1870, responsible for the Siege of Kanehsatà:ke on July 11, 1990.

Truth and Reconciliation Commission (TRC): Established in June of 2008, the TRC's mandate was to document the truth about the history and ongoing legacy of Canada's Indian Residential School system. The TRC's Final Report (consisting of six volumes and 94 Calls to Action for reconciliation) was released in 2015.

Two-Axe Earley, Mary: A Mohawk and Oneida women's activist (1911–1996) from Kahnawà:ke. She helped establish the Equal Rights for Indian Women organization and co-founded Quebec Native Women.

Unist'ot'en: A protest camp and Indigenous healing centre in the traditional territory of the Unist'ot'en clan of the Wet'suwet'en Nation. In 2019 and 2020, the camp was raided by the RCMP to dismantle blockades and checkpoints set up to prevent the construction of the Coastal Gaslink Pipeline through the unceded territory. The resistance continues today.

United Nations Declaration on the Rights of Indigenous Peoples (UNDRIP): A resolution passed by the United Nations in 2007 outlining the individual and collective rights of Indigenous peoples globally. Notably, powerful settler capitalist nations such as Canada, Australia, New Zealand, and the United States initially voted against the declaration. These countries have since reversed their position, with UNDRIP receiving royal assent in Canada on June 21, 2021. It remains unclear how the laws of Canada will be made consistent with UNDRIP.

Wel'alin: Thank you (Mi'gmaq)

NOTES

FOREWORD BY PAMELA PALMATER

1. For more on the Great Law of Peace, as a "recognition of and respect for all life forms and the basic human rights of all people," see Brenda Katlatont Gabriel-Doxtater and Arlette Kawanatatie Van den Hende, *At the Woods' Edge: An Anthology of the History of the People of Kanehsatà:ke* (Kanehsatà:ke: Kanehsatà:ke Education Centre, 1995), 8–14.

PREFACE BY SEAN CARLETON

1. Ellen Gabriel, "Epilogue: Fraudulent Theft of Mohawk Land by the Municipality of Oka," *This Is an Honour Song: Twenty Years Since the Blockades*, eds. Leanne Simpson and Kiera L. Ladner (Winnipeg: ARP, 2010), 346.
2. Kim Tallbear, "Standing With and Speaking as Faith: A Feminist-Indigenous Approach to Inquiry," *Sources and Methods in Indigenous Studies*, eds. Chris Andersen and Jean M. O'Brien (New York: Routledge, 2016), 78–85.
3. Linda Tuhiwai Smith, *Decolonizing Methodologies: Research and Indigenous Peoples* (London: Zed 2021).
4. Leanne Betasamosake Simpson, *As We Have Always Done: Indigenous Freedom Through Radical Resistance* (Minneapolis: University of Minnesota Press, 2017), 15.
5. Staughton Lynd and Andrej Grubacic, *Wobblies and Zapatistas: Conversations on Anarchism, Marxism and Radical History* (Oakland: PM Press, 2008).

1. THE LAND IS OUR TEACHER

1. Leanne Betasamosake Simpson, *A Short History of the Blockade: Giant Beavers, Diplomacy, and Regeneration in Nishnaabewin* (Edmonton: University of Alberta Press, 2021), 3.
2. Arthur Manuel and Grand Chief Ronald Derrickson, *The Reconciliation Manifesto: Recovering the Land, Rebuilding the Economy* (Toronto: Lorimer, 2017), 76.
3. For more on the Shingwauk school and Canada's Indian Residential School system generally, see J. R. Miller, *Shingwauk's*

Vision: A History of Native Residential Schools (Toronto: University of Toronto Press, 1996). See also Truth and Reconciliation Commission of Canada, "Honouring the Truth, Reconciling for the Future: Summary of the Final Report of the Truth and Reconciliation Commission," *Final Report of the Truth and Reconciliation Commission of Canada, Volume One: Summary* (Toronto: Lorimer, 2015).

4. For more about Indian Day Schools, see indiandayschools.com.

5. On Indian Day School experiences and the shift to integrated schooling see, for example, Helen Raptis with Members of the Tsimshian Nation, *What We Learned: Two Generations Reflect on Tsimshian Education and the Day Schools* (Vancouver: UBC Press, 2016).

6. Jeannette Armstrong, *Slash* (Penticton: Theytus Books, 1985).

7. See, for example, Lee Maracle, *Bobbi Lee: Indian Rebel* (Toronto: Women's Press, 2017); Armstrong, *Slash*; and Thomas King, *The Inconvenient Indian: A Curious Account of Native People in North America* (Toronto: Anchor Canada, 2013), 127–158.

8. Armstrong, *Slash*, xiii.

9. See Simpson, *This Is an Honour Song*; and Isabelle St-Amand, *Stories of Oka: Land, Film, and Literature* (Winnipeg: University of Manitoba Press, 2018). See also Brenda Katlatont Gabriel-Doxtater and Arlette Kawanatatie Van den Hende, *At the Woods' Edge: An Anthology of the History of the People of Kanehsatà:ke* (Kanehsatà:ke, Quebec: Kanehsatà:ke Education Centre, 1995). Note: Ellen's original art appears on the front cover of *At the Woods' Edge* and is also featured throughout.

10. For more, see *The Spirit of Annie Mae*, directed by Catherine Anne Martin (National Film Board of Canada, 2002), nfb.ca.

11. For more on the mass shooting, see Peter Elgin and Stephen Hester, *The Montreal Massacre: A Story of Membership Categorization Analysis* (Waterloo: Wilfrid Laurier University Press, 2003).

2. PROTECTING THE PINES

1. Frantz Fanon, *The Wretched of the Earth* (New York: Grove Press, 1963), 2, 15.

2. See Brenda Katlatont Gabriel-Doxtater and Arlette Kawanatatie Van den Hende, *At the Woods' Edge: An Anthology of the*

History of the People of Kanehsatà:ke (Kanehsatà:ke: Kanehsatà:ke Education Centre, 1995).

3. Audra Simpson, *Mohawk Interruptus: Political Life Across the Border of Settler States* (Durham, NC: Duke University Press, 2014), 11. See also Glen Sean Coulthard, *Red Skin, White Masks: Rejecting the Colonial Politics of Recognition* (Minneapolis: University of Minnesota Press, 2014).

4. Leanne Betasamosake Simpson, *A Short History of the Blockade: Giant Beavers, Diplomacy, and Regeneration in Nishnaabewin* (Edmonton: University of Alberta Press, 2021), 11.

5. See Nick Estes, *Our History Is the Future: Standing Rock versus the Dakota Access Pipeline, and the Long Tradition of Indigenous Resistance* (London: Verso, 2019), 14, 18.

6. For more on Onahsakén:rat, see Gabriel-Doxtater and Van den Hende, *At the Woods' Edge*, 103–115.

7. John Ciaccia quoted in Vincent Schilling, "Remembering Oka: Canadian Forces vs. Mohawks over a Golf Course and a Burial Ground," *Indian Country Today*, July 11, 2019, ictnews.org.

3. THE SIEGE OF KANEHSATÀ:KE AND KAHNAWÀ:KE

1. For more on Ciaccia's views on the summer of 1990 and his role in trying to mediate the conflict, see John Ciaccia, *The Oka Crisis: A Mirror of the Soul* (Dorval, Quebec: Maren Publications Inc., 2000).

4. ECHOES

1. Leanne Simpson and Kiera L. Ladner, eds., *This Is an Honour Song: Twenty Years Since the Blockades* (Winnipeg: ARP, 2010). We note that Ellen wrote an epilogue for the book entitled "Fraudulent Theft of Mohawk Land by the Municipality of Oka."

2. Damien Lee, "Echoes of Impermanence: Kanehsatà:ke, Bimaadiziiwin and the Idea of Canada," *This Is an Honour Song*, 236–237.

3. Lee, "Echoes of Impermanence," 236–237.

4. The Canadian Security Intelligence Service is Canada's main national intelligence agency. It is responsible for collecting, analyzing, reporting, and disseminating intelligence on threats

to Canada's national security, and conducting operations, covert and overt, within Canada and abroad.

5. Fifteenth-century Papal Bulls gave Christian explorers the right to claim title to the lands they "discovered" for their Christian Monarchs. Any land that was not inhabited by Christians was available to be claimed in the name of European monarchs. If the "pagan" inhabitants could be converted, they might be spared. If not, they were to be enslaved or killed. It is the basis for the acts of genocide committed against Indigenous Peoples in the Americas.

6. Glen Sean Coulthard, "For Our Nations to Live, Capitalism Must Die," NationsRising.org, November 5, 2013, nationsrising.org.

7. See *The Oka Legacy*, directed by Sonia Bonspille Boileau (Quebec, Canada; Resolution Pictures, 2015), cbc.ca.

8. Truth and Reconciliation Commission, "Truth and Reconciliation Commission of Canada: Calls to Action" (Winnipeg: Truth and Reconciliation Commission of Canada, 2012), nctr.ca.

9. See Government of Canada, Kanesatake Interim Land Base Governance Act (S.C. 2001, c. 8), last amended July 15, 2019, laws-lois.justice.gc.ca.

10. Section 29 of the Indian Act states: "Reserve lands are not subject to seizure under legal process." The underlying title to the land remains vested with the Crown. See the Indian Act, R.S.C., 1985, c. I–5, last amended August 15, 2019, laws-lois. justice.gc.ca.

11. For more on the history of Mohawk struggles over trees and wood, see Daniel Rück, *The Laws and the Land: The Settler Colonial Invasion of Kahnawà:ke in Nineteenth-Century Canada* (Vancouver: UBC Press, 2021), 123–160.

12. Tsilhqot'in Nation v. British Columbia, [2014] 2 S.C.R. 257 (CanLII), canlii.ca.

13. June 21, 2021, the United Nations Declaration on the Rights of Indigenous Peoples Act received Royal Assent and came into force immediately. See the United Nations Declaration on the Rights of Indigenous Peoples Act, S.C., 2021, c. 14, current to January 14, 2024, laws-lois.justice.gc.ca.

14. Leanne Betasamosake Simpson in Robyn Maynard and Leanne Betasamosake Simpson, *Rehearsals for Living* (Toronto: Knopf Canada, 2022), 82.

5. THE ART OF RESISTANCE

1. My father Archie Gabriel passed away on December 11, 1980; my mother Annie Montour-Gabriel passed away on January 1, 1985. Both were born in Kanehsatà:ke.
2. For more on Hall and the Unity flag, see Louis Karoniaktajeh Hall, eds. Philippe Blouin, Matt Peterson, Malek Rasamny, and Kahentinetha Rotiskarewake, *The Mohawk Warrior Society: A Handbook on Sovereignty and Survival* (Toronto: Between the Lines, 2023).
3. For more about film, see Simona Rosenfield, "Gabriel Directs Award-Winning Film on the Pines," *The Eastern Door*, August 8, 2022, easterndoor.com.

6. WOMEN'S RIGHTS

1. Michael Orsini, "The Journalist and the Angry White Mob: Reflections from the Field," *This Is an Honour Song*, 249 and 252.
2. Amnesty International, "Canada: Stolen Sisters: A Human Rights Response to Discrimination and Violence against Indigenous Women in Canada" (Stolen Sisters Report, Index Number AMR 10/003/2003, October 3, 2004), amnesty.org.
3. Convention on Biological Diversity, "Nagoya Protocol on Access to Genetic Resources and the Fair and Equitable Sharing of Benefits Arising from their Utilization to the Convention on Biological Diversity: Text and Annex" (United Nations Environmental Programme, 2011), cbd.int.
4. The United Nations Declaration on the Rights of Indigenous Peoples, preamble, para. 4, was adopted by the General Assembly on Thursday, September 13, 2007, by a majority of 144 states in favour, 4 votes against (Australia, Canada, New Zealand, and the United States) and 11 abstentions. See "United Nations Declaration on the Rights of Indigenous Peoples" (Report, United Nations, 2007), un.org. Today the UNDRIP is a consensus document with no state opposing it.
5. Human Rights Watch, "Those Who Take Us Away: Abusive Policing and Failures in Protection of Indigenous Women and Girls in Northern British Columbia, Canada" (Report, Feb 13, 2013), hrw.org.
6. Without prior notice to the Chiefs, they were removed from office by an order-in-council on the morning of October 7,

1924. The Royal Canadian Mounted Police seized the wampum used to sanction council proceedings, and posted a proclamation on the doors of the council house announcing the date and procedures for an elected government on the Six Nations reserve. See Jeremy Patzer, "The Indian Act: Disempowering, Assimilatory and Exclusionary" (Circles for Reconciliation Gathering, 2021), circlesforreconciliation.ca.

7. For an intervention by Green Party leader Elizabeth May, see "Elizabeth May: Kanesatake Needs Solutions to Toxic Waste Dumping on their Territory," *The Green Party of Canada— Parti vert du Canada*, February 16, 2022, youtube.com.

8. Glen Sean Coulthard, *Red Skin, White Masks: Rejecting the Colonial Politics of Recognition* (Minneapolis: University of Minnesota Press, 2014), 160.

9. Sean Carleton, "Idle No More and the Lessons of History," *Rabble*, January 10, 2013, rabble.ca.

10. Sean Carleton, "Challenging Canadian Colonialism in London, England: #J11 Solidarity Actions," *Rabble*, January 11, 2013, rabble.ca.

11. The Kino-nda-niimi Collective, *The Winter We Danced: Voices from the Past, the Future, and the Idle No More Movement* (Winnipeg: ARP, 2014).

12. For more on Bill C-45, see "Idle No More Sees Bigger Issues Than C-45," *Idle No More* (website), idlenomore.ca.

13. Kelly Boutsalis, "Why the Wet'suwet'en Matriarchs are *Chatelaine* Women of the Year," *Chatelaine*, November 23, 2020, chatelaine.com.

7. INDIGENOUS INTERNATIONALISM

1. See Nick Estes, *Our History Is the Future: Standing Rock Versus the Dakota Access Pipeline, and the Long Tradition of Indigenous Resistance* (London: Verso, 2019), 203. See also Leanne Betasamosake Simpson, *As We Have Always Done: Indigenous Freedom Through Radical Resistance* (Minneapolis: University of Minnesota Press, 2017), 55–70.

2. Estes, *Our History Is the Future*, 248.

3. Stephen Harper quoted in "Really Harper, Canada Has No History of Colonialism?," *Vancouver Sun*, September 27, 2009, vancouversun.com.

4. See Peter McFarlane with Doreen Manuel, *Brotherhood to Nationhood: George Manuel and the Making of the Modern Indian Movement* (Toronto: Between the Lines, 2020), 158–59.
5. See Chief Deskaheh Levi General, "The Redman's Appeal for Justice," *Indigenous Peoples' Centre for Documentation, Research and Information*, August 6, 1923, cendoc.docip.org.
6. "United Nations Declaration," preamble, para. 9, laws-lois. justice.gc.ca.
7. Ellen Gabriel, "Bill C-15 Is Chance 'to Actually Break with the Colonial Status Quo,'" *Ricochet*, April 12, 2021, ricochet.media.
8. Gabriel, "Bill C-15 Is Chance."

8. RESURGENCE

1. Sean Carleton, "Putting the RCMP Raid on the Wet'suwet'en in Historical Perspective," *Toronto Star*, February 11, 2020, thestar.com.
2. See Delgamuukw v. British Columbia, [1997] 3 S.C.R. 1010 (Supreme Court Judgments), scc-csc.lexum.com. For more on the complicated nature of colonial law and "rights," as a double-edge sword for Indigenous Peoples see, for example, Michael Asch, *On Being Here to Stay: Treaties and Aboriginal Rights in Canada* (Toronto: University of Toronto Press, 2014) and Shiri Pasternak, *Grounded Authority: The Algonquins of Barriere Lake Against the State* (Minneapolis: University of Minnesota Press, 2017).
3. Indian and Northern Affairs is now called Crown-Indigenous Relations and Northern Affairs Canada (CIRNAC).
4. Duncan Campbell Scott was the Deputy-Superintendent General of Indian Affairs in the early 1900s. For more on his legacy, see Brian E. Titley, *A Narrow Vision: Duncan Campbell Scott and the Administration of Indian Affairs in Canada* (Vancouver: UBC Press, 1986). In 1883, Scott's father, Rev. William Scott, wrote an in-depth report on the Kanehsatà:ke land struggle, siding with the Sulpicians and recommending that the Mohawks relocate to Muskoka in Ontario. See Willam Scott, *Report Relating to the Affairs of the Oka Indians made to the Superintendent General of Indian Affairs* (Ottawa: Printed by Maclean, Roger & Co., 1883).

5. Leanne Betasamosake Simpson, *A Short History of the Blockade: Giant Beavers, Diplomacy, and Regeneration in Nishnaabewin* (Edmonton: University of Alberta Press, 2021), 56–57.
6. Lee Maracle, *Bobbi Lee: Indian Rebel* (Toronto: Women's Press, 2017), xvi–xviii.
7. Glen Sean Coulthard, *Red Skin, White Masks: Rejecting the Colonial Politics of Recognition* (Minneapolis: University of Minnesota Press, 2014).
8. Simpson, *A Short History of the Blockade*, 58.

9. LIVING FOR THE LAND

1. See Nick Estes, *Our History Is the Future: Standing Rock versus the Dakota Access Pipeline, and the Long Tradition of Indigenous Resistance* (London: Verso, 2019), 14.
2. Maynard and Simpson, *Rehearsals for Living* (Toronto: Knopf Canada, 2022), 25–26.
3. Robyn Maynard and Leanne Betasamosake Simpson, *Rehearsals for Living* (Toronto: Knopf Canada, 2022), 176.
4. See David Camfield, *Future on Fire: Capitalism and the Politics of Climate Change* (Oakland: PM Press, 2022).
5. "An Economy for the 99 Percent," Oxfam Canada, January 15, 2017, oxfam.ca.
6. See: Eva Jewell and Ian Mosby, "Calls to Action Accountability: 2023 Status Update on Reconciliation" (Yellowhead Institute, 2023), yellowheadinstitute.org.
7. See Audra Simpson, *Mohawk Interruptus: Political Life Across the Border of Settler States* (Durham, NC: Duke University Press, 2014) and Glen Sean Coulthard, *Red Skin, White Masks: Rejecting the Colonial Politics of Recognition* (Minneapolis: University of Minnesota Press, 2014).

AFTERWORD BY AUDRA SIMPSON

1. This was written while a Distinguished Visiting Professor in the Department of Race, Diaspora, and Indigeneity at the University of Chicago. Thanks to Cathy Cohen and colleagues there for providing the space and support to think, research, and write unencumbered by the demands of service and teaching. So much gratitude to Sheehan Moore for research and editorial assistance, Doug Metoxen Kiel and Joanne Barker

for conversation and sources. Niawenkó:wa Ellen Gabriel and Sean Carleton for the honour of the invitation to reflect on this book.

2. Jessica R. Cattelino and Audra Simpson, "Rethinking Indigeneity: Scholarship at the Intersection of Native American Studies and Anthropology," *Annual Review of Anthropology* 51, no. 1 (October 2022): 365–81; Haunani-Kay Trask, *From a Native Daughter: Colonialism and Sovereignty in Hawaii* (Honolulu: University of Hawaii Press, 1999); Gerald Vizenor, ed., *Survivance: Narratives of Native Presence* (Lincoln: University of Nebraska Press, 2008); Patrick Wolfe, "Settler Colonialism and the Elimination of the Native," *Journal of Genocide Research*, 8, no. 4 (December 2006): 387–409; Kyle Powys Whyte, "Is It Colonial Déjà Vu? Indigenous Peoples and Climate Injustice," *Humanities for the Environment* (Routledge, 2016), 102–19.

3. Please see the interview with Ellen Gabriel in *The Eastern Door*: "'People still call it "Oka Crisis,"' Gabriel explained, 'I prefer the Mohawk Crisis if anything because Kanehsatake is not Oka. Oka is the colonial-imposed name for the community of Kanehsatake. There's so many inaccuracies.'" Simona Rosenfield, "Gabriel Directs Award-Winning Film on the Pines," *The Eastern Door*, August 8, 2022, easterndoor.com.

4. For specific attention to the effects of residential schools in the U.S. on (Wisconsin) Oneida corn cultivation and diet, see Rebecca M. Webster, "The Wisconsin Oneida and the WPA: Stories of Corn, Colonialism, and Revitalization," *Ethnohistory* 68, no. 3 (2021): 407–27. See also Louellyn White, "Who Gets to Tell the Stories? Carlisle Indian School: Imagining a Place of Memory Through Descendant Voices," *Journal of American Indian Education* 57, no. 1 (2018): 122–44, for an account of the legacy of Carlisle boarding school in White's family. Haudenosaunee north of the border were either sent to the Mohawk Institute in Brantford, Ontario, or St. Peter Claver School for Boys or St. Joseph's School for Girls in Spanish, Ontario. These two schools are also referred to in everyday speech as "Spanish."

5. Onahsakén:rat was trained in the Séminaire de Montréal (with Louis Riel!), returned to Kanehsatà:ke, and worked temporarily with the Sulpicians. His literacy uncovered their malfeasance. He ran for Chief in 1868 and died under suspicious circumstances at the age of thirty-five.

6. See the Indian Act, R.S.C., 1985, c. I–5, laws-lois.justice.gc.ca. In reference to a "band": "*band* means a body of Indians (a) for whose use and benefit in common, lands, the legal title to which is vested in Her Majesty, have been set apart before, on or after September 4, 1951."

7. Note that this "ownership" is effectively a right to reside within a place. For an extraordinarily nuanced account and analysis of the race/property nexus in the surveying of Indians' lands and their aftereffects in what is now Western New York, please see Meredith Alberta Palmer, "Rendering Settler Sovereign Landscapes: Race and Property in the Empire State," *Environment and Planning D: Society and Space* 38, no. 5 (2020): 793–810. For a book-length study of these twentieth century land transfers at Kahnawà:ke, see Gerald F. Reid, *Kahnawà:ke: Factionalism, Traditionalism, and Nationalism in a Mohawk Community* (Lincoln: University of Nebraska Press, 2004) and Daniel Rück, *The Laws and the Land: The Settler Colonial Invasion of Kahnawà:ke in Nineteenth-Century Canada* (Vancouver: UBC Press, 2021). For a gendered analysis of the careful ways in governance at Six Nations and the management of lands outside of racial regimes of property transfer see Susan M. Hill, *The Clay We Are Made Of: Haudenosaunee Land Tenure on the Grand River* (Winnipeg: University of Manitoba Press, 2017); an attendant discussion of this book's focus upon land ethics may be found in Audra Simpson, "Reading for Land: Susan Hill's *The Clay We Are Made Of: Haudenosaunee Land Tenure on the Grand River*," *Native American and Indigenous Studies* 6, no. 1 (2019): 149–56.

8. Eleven years after the "Crisis," the Kanesatake Interim Land Base Governance Act (Bill S-24) was devised to "harmonize relations" between Kanehsatà:ke and surrounding areas, and defines the community as not yet a reserve, requiring the creation of a land policy in order to move towards that legal ("protected," wardship) status. See Mary C. Hurley, "Bill S-24: The Kanesatake Interim Land Base Governance Act" (Law and Government Division, 2001), publications.gc.ca.

9. See Kevin White's article in *Indian Country Today* for an explication of these core concepts of the Great Law. Kevin J. White, "Economic Peace, Power and Righteousness," *ICT News*, September 12, 2018 (originally published October 31, 2008), ictnews.org. For an excellent discussion of the encoding

of these principles in representational form, the Peacemaker's belt, please consult Darren Bonaparte, "The Remembrance Belt: Conflicting Traditions of an Onondaga Wampum," *The Wampum Chronicles* (blog), n.d., wampumchronicles.com. Kaianera'kó:wa unites the formerly divided Five Nations into a Peace. It lays out the responsibilities of each Nation, methods for achieving clear-mindedness, governance, and relations across time and territory. Wampum belts encode the law but also treaties and ethics and are recited or read into the present day. Bonaparte's blog contextualizes and interprets these belts with recourse to contemporary readings, such as that done by the late, condoled Cayuga Chief Jake Thomas and the contemporary linguist Ieieia'taiéri Logan.

10. A copy can be found on the Smithsonian's website, taken from John Stokes, David Kanawahienton Benedict, and Dan Rokwaho Thompson, *Haudenosaunee Thanksgiving Address: Greetings to the Natural World* (The Tracking Project, 1993), americanindian.si.edu.

11. Please see her film for accounts of the significance of these trees to Kanehsata'kehró:non: *Kanàtenhs: When the Pine Needles Fall*, written, directed, and produced by Ellen Gabriel, released November 15, 2022.

12. Gabriel notes these are "the last vestiges of the common land in this community." For a deep history of Kanehsatà:ke, please see Brenda Katlatont Gabriel-Doxtater and Arlette Kawanatatie Van den Hende, *At the Woods' Edge: An Anthology of the History of the People of Kanehsatà:ke* (Kanehsatà:ke: Kanesatake Education Center, 1995).

13. Please see Shiri Pasternak, "Blockade: A Meeting Place of Law," *Whose Land Is It Anyway? A Manual for Decolonization*, ed. Peter McFarlane and Nicole Schabus (Federation of Post-Secondary Educators of BC, 2017), 32–35, on the significance of blockades for making Indigenous law clear.

14. See also Kim TallBear, "Badass (Indigenous) Women Caretake Relations: #NoDAPL, #IdleNoMore, #BlackLivesMatter," *Hot Spots*, Society for Cultural Anthropology, December 22, 2016, culanth.org. For Hawaii, see Moanike'ala Akaka, Maxine Kahaulelio, Terrilee Keko'olani-Raymond, and Loretta Ritte, eds., *Nā Wāhine Koa: Hawaiian Women for Sovereignty and Demilitarization* (Honolulu: University of Hawaii Press, 2018). For an urban example, see Susan Applegate Crouse's history

of the Milwaukee Indian schools in the 1970s—in which three Oneida mothers, Marge Funmaker, Darlene Funmaker Neconish, and Marj Stevens, started teaching children in their living rooms because of their frustration with the Milwaukee public schools: Susan Applegate Krouse, "What Came out of the Takeovers: Women's Activism and the Indian Community School of Milwaukee," *American Indian Quarterly* 27, no. 3/4 (2003): 533–47. An important Haudenosaunee ethnography of political action that foregrounds the voices and motivations of women is Theresa McCarthy, *In Divided Unity: Haudenosaunee Reclamation at Grand River* (Tucson: University of Arizona Press, 2016).

15. See Arthur Manuel and Grand Chief Ronald Derrickson, *The Reconciliation Manifesto: Recovering the Land, Rebuilding the Economy* (Toronto: James Lorimer & Company, 2017); and Arthur Manuel and Grand Chief Ronald M. Derrickson, *Unsettling Canada: A National Wake-up Call* (Toronto: Between the Lines, 2021).

16. Please see Kim Anderson, "An Interview with Kasti'tsawkwas Ellen Gabriel, of the Kanien'kehàka Nation, Turtle Clan," *First Voices: An Aboriginal Women's Reader*, ed. Patricia Anne Monture and Patricia Danielle McGuire (Toronto: Inanna, 2009).

17. From her statement on her blog, announcing her intent to run, "Today as I put my name forward as the next advocate for First Nations peoples, the role of national Chief of the Assembly of First Nations I do so with trepidation, but as well, with the hope that like the 1990 Oka Crisis when Indigenous peoples in Canada woke up and started taking direct action to defend their lands, that Indigenous peoples on Turtle Island will wake up and defend their rights. Indigenous Peoples in Canada and throughout the world need strong leaders with the courage of conviction not to waver from upholding our self-determining rights. A leader that must stay the course in spite of government's tactics to maintain the status quo relationship or in spite of funding cuts; that has been our 'Achilles heel.' Indigenous peoples' rights are Human Rights. We can no longer tolerate a moderate voice as we are facing a huge bureaucratic machine that has an endless amount of resources to dispossess us of our lands and our rights." From Ellen Gabriel, "Ellen Gabriel, Turtle Clan, Kanien'kehá:ka Nation, Kanehsatà:ke

Mohawk Territory," *Sovereign Voices* (blog), June 26, 2012, sovereignvoices1.wordpress.com.

18. Brenda Katlatont Gabriel-Doxtater and Arlette Kawanatatie Van den Hende, *At the Woods' Edge: An Anthology of the History of the People of Kanehsatà:ke* (Kanehsatà:ke: Kanehsatà:ke Education Centre, 1995), 57.

19. Best Short Documentary from the LA Independent Women Film Awards, eighth edition, 2022.

20. Audra Simpson, *Mohawk Interruptus: Political Life Across the Borders of Settler States* (Durham, NC: Duke University Press, 2014), 153.

21. See Nick Estes, *Our History Is the Future: Standing Rock Versus the Dakota Access Pipeline, and the Long Tradition of Indigenous Resistance* (New York: Verso, 2019); and Nick Estes, Melanie K. Yazzie, Jennifer Nez Denetdale, and David Correia, *Red Nation Rising: From Bordertown Violence to Native Liberation* (Chicago: PM Press, 2021).

22. I'm grateful to Joanne Barker for putting this so clearly and succinctly in conversation about this piece.

23. From Gabriel's film *Kanàtenhs: When the Pine Needles Fall*: "The police . . . didn't want to talk to us. They didn't think the women were the proper people to be discussing things with, because we were women."

24. Estes, *Our History Is the Future*.

25. See Rick Monture, *We Share Our Matters: Two Centuries of Writing and Resistance at Six Nations of the Grand River* (Winnipeg: University of Manitoba Press, 2014); and Mishuana Goeman, *Mark My Words: Native Women Mapping Our Nations* (Minneapolis: University of Minnesota Press, 2013).

26. See Kristina Ackley and Cristina Stanciu, eds., *Laura Cornelius Kellogg: Our Democracy and the American Indian and Other Works* (Syracuse: Syracuse University Press, 2015); and Doug Kiel, *Unsettling Territory: Oneida Nation Resurgence and Anti-Sovereignty Backlash* (New Haven: Yale University Press, Forthcoming).

27. For a reading of Brant that places her correspondences within a tradition and practice of reading and condolence, see Gage Karahkwí:io Diabo, "'I Didn't Hear the Birds Singing': Beth Brant's Echoes of Condolence," *Canadian Literature*, no. 250 (2022): 12–31.

28. Born in 1851 at Six Nations, Mohawk poet and performer E. Pauline Johnson is sometimes referred to as a poet laureate of sorts, but these formal titles were not awarded to poets federally until 2002. She toured all over Canada and Europe. Her complicated position as the daughter of a hereditary Chief and a British mother is explored by Margery Fee and Dory Nason in their introduction to *Tekahionwake: E. Pauline Johnson's Writings on Native North America* (Broadview Press, 2015), an excellent collection of her writings. Johnson's failure to defend the Confederacy and her position within Six Nations is examined by Rick Monture in *We Share Our Matters: Two Centuries of Writing and Resistance at Six Nations of the Grand River* (Winnipeg: University of Manitoba Press, 2015), 63–65.

29. E. Pauline Johnson, *The Moccasin Maker* (Norman, OK: University of Oklahoma Press, 1998).

30. See Mishuana Goeman's reading in *Mark My Words*, 41–85.

31. I'm indebted to Mishuana Goeman's reading in *Mark My Words* for my own analysis here.

32. See Doug Kiel's forthcoming *Unsettling Territory*; and David Myer Temin, "Our Democracy: Laura Cornelius Kellogg's Decolonial-Democracy," *Perspectives on Politics* 19, no. 4 (December 2021): 1082–97.

33. Rick Monture, "'An Enemy's Foot Is on Our Country': Conflict, Diplomacy, and Land Rights," in *We Share Our Matters: Two Centuries of Writing and Resistance at Six Nations of the Grand River* (Winnipeg: University of Manitoba Press, 2014), 107–40.

34. "Jolene Rickard, Diversifying Sovereignty and the Reception of Indigenous Art," *Art Journal* 76, no. 2 (Summer 2017), 81–84.

35. Gerald F. Reid, "Illegal Alien? The Immigration Case of Mohawk Ironworker Paul K. Diabo," *Proceedings of the American Philosophical Society* 151, no. 1 (2007): 61–78.

36. Alison Norman, "'True to My Own Noble Race': Six Nations Women Teachers at Grand River in the Early Twentieth Century," *Ontario History* 107, no. 1 (2015): 5–34.

37. Jacob E. Thomas and Terry Boyle, *Teachings from the Longhouse* (Toronto: Stoddart, 1994).

38. Louis Karoniaktajeh Hall, *The Mohawk Warrior Society: A Handbook on Sovereignty and Survival* (Toronto: Between the Lines Press, 2023).

39. See in particular her essay in Woodland Cultural Centre, *Godi'nigoha': The Women's Mind* (Brantford: Woodland Cultural Centre, 1997).

40. Theresa McCarthy, *In Divided Unity: Haudenosaunee Reclamation at Grand River* (Tucson: University of Arizona Press, 2016); Susan M. Hill, *The Clay We Are Made of: Haudenosaunee Land Tenure on the Grand River* (Winnipeg: University of Manitoba Press, 2017); Mishuana Goeman, *Mark My Words: Native Women Mapping Our Nations* (Minneapolis: University of Minnesota Press, 2013); Rick Monture, *We Share Our Matters: Two Centuries of Writing and Resistance at Six Nations of the Grand River* (Winnipeg: University of Manitoba Press, 2015); Doug Kiel, *Unsettling Territory: Oneida Nation Resurgence and Anti-Sovereignty Backlash* (New Haven: Yale University Press, Forthcoming); Louellyn White, *Free to Be Mohawk: Indigenous Education at the Akwesasne Freedom School* (Norman: University of Oklahoma Press, 2015); Kristina Ackley and Cristina Stanciu, eds., *Laura Cornelius Kellogg: Our Democracy and the American Indian and Other Works* (Syracuse: Syracuse University Press, 2015). I would group my own book, *Mohawk Interruptus*, with these other works: Audra Simpson, *Mohawk Interruptus: Political Life Across the Borders of Settler States* (Durham, NC: Duke University Press, 2014).

41. Jolene Rickard, "Sovereignty: A Line in the Sand," *Aperture*, Summer (1995): 50–59.

42. Ryan Rice and Wanda Nanibush, *Shelley Niro: Scotiabank Award 2017* (Steidl Verlag, 2018).

43. See Jason Edward Lewis and Skawennati's Aboriginal Technologies in Cyberspace (AbTeC) (website), abtec.org.

44. Janet Rogers, *As Long as the Sun Shines*, trans. Jeremy Green (Bookland Press, 2019).

45. Eric Gansworth, *Nickel Eclipse: Iroquois Moon* (East Lansing: Michigan State University Press, 2000).

46. Alicia Elliot, *A Mind Spread Out on the Ground* (Melville House, 2020).

47. Staughton Lynd and Andrej Grubacic, *Wobblies and Zapatistas: Conversations on Anarchism, Marxism and Radical History* (Oakland: PM Press, 2008); Robyn Maynard and Leanne Betasamosake Simpson, *Rehearsals for Living* (Chicago: Haymarket Books, 2022).

APPENDICES

1. Ellen Gabriel, "Status of Women Committee Speech," Open Parliament (website), May 7, 2013, openparliament.ca.
2. Ellen Gabriel, "Indigenous Women" (Speech, United Nations Permanent Forum on Indigenous Issues, Eight Session, May 19, 2009), web.archive.org.

ILLUSTRATION CREDITS

INDEX

Page numbers in *italics* represent illustrations. Page numbers in **bold** represent glossary entries.

KATSI'TSAKWAS ELLEN GABRIEL is a Kanien'kehá:ka, Wakeniáhton (Turtle Clan), artist, documentarian, and Indigenous human rights and environmental rights activist living in Kanehsatà:ke Kanien'kehá:ka Homelands.

SEAN CARLETON is a settler historian and professor of history and Indigenous Studies at the University of Manitoba in Winnipeg, Manitoba, Treaty 1 Territory.